MW00743898

The Writer's Library

Women and Men

The HarperCollins Editors

with

Josephine Koster Tarvers

HarperCollins *CollegePublishers*

Acquisitions Editor: Patricia Rossi
Series Editor: David Munger
Cover Design: Stacy Agin
Production Administrator: Linda Murray
Printer and Binder: R. R. Donnelley & Sons Company
Cover Printer: The Lehigh Press, Inc.

For permission to use copyrighted material, grateful acknowledgement is made to the copyright holders on page 238 which is hereby made part of the copyright page.

Women and Men
Copyright © 1992 by HarperCollins College Publishers

All rights reserved. Printed in the United States of America. No part of this book may be used or reproduced in any manner whatsoever without written permission, except in the case of brief quotations embodied in critical articles and reviews. For information address HarperCollins College Publishers, 10 East 53rd Street, New York, NY 10022.

Library of Congress Cataloging-in-Publication Data

Women and men / the HarperCollins editors ; with Josephine Koster Tarvers.
p.   cm. -- (The Writer's library)
ISBN: 0-06-501124-4
1. Readers--Sex role. 2. Sex role--Problems, exercises, etc. 3. English language--Rhetoric. 4. College readers. I. Tarvers, Josephine Koster, 1956-   . II. HarperCollins (firm) III. Series: Writer's library (New York, NY)
PE1127.S4W66 1992
808'.0427--dc20   92-1500
                                                      CIP

95   9 8 7 6 5 4

Contents

✧

✧

✧

1 Interactions

✧ ✧ ✧

2 Stereotypes of Women

❖ ❖ ❖

3 Stereotypes of Men

❖ ❖ ❖

4 Work vs. Women's Work

❖ ❖ ❖

5 Sexual Harassment: The Price of Silence

✧ ✧ ✧

6 Pornography

✧ ✧ ✧

7 A Framework for Feminism

✧ ✧ ✧

Rhetorical Contents

Narrative

Description/Example

Classification

✧ ✧ ✧

Comparison/Contrast

✧ ✧ ✧

Cause/Effect

✧ ✧ ✧

Definition

✦ ✦ ✦

Argument

✦ ✦ ✦

Researched Writing

✧ ✧ ✧

Preface

The Series

As editors, we see dozens of proposals for new readers every year. Each proposal is unique because it represents the thinking of an instructor at a different school, with different ideas about how to teach freshman composition. And every year, we publish several new readers based on those differing ideas, hoping composition programs will be able to adapt their own theories about teaching writing to the strategies advocated in our books. Unfortunately, if the teaching strategy of a given composition program does not closely match the available texts, the inevitable result is compromise.

The Writer's Library represents a revolutionary change from that type of thinking. Rather than choosing a text which forces them to adapt to its style of teaching, programs using *The Writer's Library* adapt *the text* to suit *their needs*. *The Writer's Library* is unique among readers for freshman composition because it is a flexible series of books, rather than a single, restrictive text. By using only the volumes they need, instructors can gain flexibility and save their students money—each volume of *The Writer's Library* is less than one-third the price of the average freshman composition reader.

Each volume of *The Writer's Library* covers a single theme, and is divided into chapters—sub-themes and issues that interest students. Each chapter has an introduction which contextualizes and demonstrates the relationships between readings. Each reading includes an introduction with a brief author biography, and suggestions for discussion and writing. An instructor's manual with suggested teaching strategies and suggested responses to discussion and writing questions is available.

The Writer's Library is flexible enough to be used in almost any composition classroom. Instructors who want to use a rhetoric or a handbook and supplement it with a few readings can choose one volume from the series at minimal additional cost to their students. Instructors who place a strong emphasis on reading can choose the two or three volumes that interest them—saving their students from purchasing lengthy readers and then using less than half of the selections.

This Volume

When we asked writing instructors what subjects we should cover in *The Writer's Library*, the topic which met with the most constant and enthusiastic support was *Women and Men*. Instructors felt it was a topic which attracted student interest and generated good writing. We followed their advice, and found a wealth of good readings on the subject. Those we chose to include here are sure to lead to lively discussions and thoughtful essays.

This volume is organized into chapters which cover many of the issues associated with gender. The final chapter gives a historical context through some of the great works in the history of feminism. Included for the first time in a reader is a chapter on sexual harassment, focusing on the question as it affected the Clarence Thomas confirmation hearings.

Instructors can follow the readings in the order they are presented, skip around in the text, or even alternate the readings in this volume with selections from other volumes in *The Writer's Library*.

Acknowledgements

The production of this series was a team effort, combining the varied talents of publishing professionals and writing instructors. We applied the ideas of dozens of writing instructors to shape the texts, and then worked with Judith Olson-Fallon and Josephine Koster Tarvers, experienced writing instructors both, to create the final product. Along the way, we received assistance from many talented individuals. Mark Gerrard contributed many suggestions while copy editing the final manuscript. Maria Paone was always there with a suggestion or wry remark. Robert Ravas provided advice for obtaining permissions. But by far the most copious and helpful suggestions came from the instructors who helped us shape the original concept or reviewed draft manuscripts: Chris Anson, University of Minnesota; Thomas Blues, University of Kentucky; Mary Buckalew, North Texas State University; Marianne Cooley, University of Houston; George Gadda, UCLA; John Gage, University of Oregon; Anne Greene, Wesleyan University; Elizabeth Hodges, Virginia Commonwealth University; William Ingram, University of Michigan; Jim Killingsworth, Texas A&M University; Carl Klaus, University of Iowa; Barry Kroll, Indiana University; Bruce Leland, Western Illinois University; David Jolliffe, University of Illinois at Chicago; Russell Larson, Eastern Michigan University; Jay Ludwig, Michigan State University; Anne Matthews, Princeton University; George Miller, University of Delaware; Mark Patterson, University of Washington; Robert Perrin, Indiana State University; Paul Ranieri, Ball State University; Ruth Ray, Wayne State University; Tom Recchio, University of Connecticut; Kelly Reed, Northeastern University; Todd Sammons, University of Hawaii at Manoa; Charles I. Schuster, University of Wisconsin—Milwaukee; Joyce Smoot, Virginia Tech; Joyce Stauffer, Indiana University—Purdue; Irwin Weiser, Purdue University; Mark Wiley, California State University—Long Beach; and Richard Zbaracki, Iowa State University.

David Munger
Patricia Rossi
Laurie Likoff
Jane Kinney

To the Student

The essays in *Women and Men* have been chosen for three reasons. First, they illuminate interesting points about the relationships between the sexes. Second, they should provide you with many possibilities for discussion, journal-keeping, and writing. And finally, they demonstrate a wide variety of rhetorical strategies and styles that you can profitably study.

This doesn't mean that these are the only worthy essays about these subjects, or that they're perfect essays: far from it! In fact, as writers, you may learn things from their weaknesses as well as their strengths. Most of these essays appeared in popular periodicals at specific points in history, responding to particular events. As a result, some of them may seem a bit dated to you, and you may have to work harder to appreciate some than others. But all offer worthwhile ideas and rhetorical models for your consideration.

You may find the "feminist" slant of this anthology disturbing. Or you may find it biased toward women at the expense of men. This is largely due to two factors: there are more recent essays about women's issues than there are about men's issues (although that balance is slowly shifting as "men's studies" evolve), and most of the essays about women are written from a feminist viewpoint. We aren't asking you to *become* feminists, or necessarily agree with these essays; we aren't asking you to become anything except better writers. For the five or eight or ten or twelve or fifteen weeks of this course, we are asking you, as writers, to consider the relationships between women and men from a variety of viewpoints. Men will need to appreciate women's points of view, women to appreciate men's points of view, and both sexes to appreciate the complexity of the female-male relationship.

Wherever we could, we've included the author's date of birth (and death, if appropriate), something about her or his background, other works by the author, and the place and date of original publication. This information will help you discuss the possible audiences and purposes for these essays as you consider their rhetorical features. In addition, we hope you will want to explore some of the other works by these authors.

The questions following each essay are intended to promote exploration of these issues, both in content and writing strategies. Your instructor may ask you to use them for class discussion, as journal prompts, or as writing assignments, or combinations of these activities. If your instructor wants you to work in groups, the questions will suit that format as well. Each set of questions asks you to react both as readers and as writers, and to discuss both the ideas in the essays and the authors' rhetorical choices in composing them. For the most part, these are "thought" questions rather than objective ones, and they have many possible answers. We particularly encourage you to set up dialogues between essays and to compare the authors' techniques and points of view, and to discuss the issues and techniques with each other.

At least one question after each selection moves away from the particular essay to consider larger issues, and asks you to connect your writing class to the "real world." You may want to use the library materials and ideas from other courses, interviews, and people around you to answer these questions. They are also designed to offer you ideas for researched writing. We hope that as you explore the complex world of *Women and Men*, you will become more confident of yourself both as a participant in these issues and as a writer about them.

1 Interactions

Is it possible for women and men to really understand each other? When we talk, are we talking about the same things? Do we give words the same meanings? The essays in this section tackle one of the biggest problems between women and men: language. John Pfeiffer explores the differences in masculine and feminine conversational styles, and uses those styles to suggest interpretations of our social roles. James Thurber describes the language and rituals of courtship at different levels of the animal kingdom, with unique results. Claire Safran looks at how the language and behaviors teachers use with young children may influence their school success. Alleen Pace Nilsen looks at the same question from the point of view of adult language use. Lindsy Van Gelder offers a modest proposal for those who think using the generic word "he" for all people is "simpler." And Robin Tolmach Lakoff looks at the power language has on our lives and attitudes, and how men and women use that power differently. As you read and consider these essays, ask, "How much power does language have over my life? Is it true that sticks and stones may break my bones, but words can never hurt me?"

John Pfeiffer
Girl Talk—Boy Talk

JOHN C. PFEIFFER, born in 1915, has long been one of America's most respected science journalists. He has served as science director of CBS, science editor of *Newsweek,* and as a member of the editorial board of *Scientific American.* Some of his books are *The Emergence of Man* (1969), *The Emergence of Society* (1977), and *The Creative Explosion: An Inquiry into the Origins of Art and Religion* (1982), which tried to understand the links between the creation of art and humankind's search for symbols and meaning. The article that follows originally appeared in *Science 86.*

An investigator, pencil in hand, is transcribing two minutes of an "unobtrusively" recorded coffee-shop conversation between two university students, male and female—listening intently, making out words and pronunciations, noting hesitations, timing utterances. The tape whirs in reverse for a replay and then again, eight replays in all. Part of the final transcript:

Andrew: *It's about time uh that my family* really *went on a vacation* (pause) *y'know my father goes places all the time* (prolonged syllable) *but he y'know goes on business like he'll go ta' Tokyo for the afternoon 'n he'll get there at* (stammer) *at ten in the morning 'n catch a nine o'clock flight leaving. . .*

(two-second pause)

Betsy: *That sounds fantastic* (pause) *not everybody can jus' spend a day in someplace*—(interruption)

Andrew: *Well, we've already established the fact that um y'know he's not just* anyone.

(eight-second pause)

Betsy: *Don't you I* (stammer) *well it seems to me you you you probably have such an um interesting background that you must y'know have trouble finding um people uh like to talk to if you—*(interruption)

Andrew: *Most definitely . . .*

2   Candace West and Don Zimmerman, the researchers who analyzed these recordings, were particularly interested in the interruptions. The pattern is typical. According to these University of California sociologists, it held for all two-person, cross-sex conversations recorded mainly in public places: Males accounted for some 96 percent of the interruptions. In same-sex conversations males also cut off males and females cut off females, but in 20 recorded encounters, interruptions were equally distributed between the speakers.

3   This study is part of an active and rapidly expanding field of language research—the role of gender in speech, with the accent primarily on how, under what conditions, and why the sexes talk differently. A 1983 bibliography of relevant publications includes some 800 titles, compared with about 150 titles in a bibliography published eight years before. The boom started little more than a decade ago, inspired by the women's movement. A new generation of investigators began taking hard looks at some of the things that had been written about women's talk by earlier investigators, mainly male. They encountered a number of statements like the following from Otto Jespersen, a Danish linguist who has earned a prominent place in the feminist rogues' gallery: "[W]omen much more often than men break off without finishing their sentences, because they start talking without having thought out what they are going to say."

4   Such belittlement of female conversation may be somewhat less frequent nowadays. But it lives on in everyday contexts, hardly surprising since it involves attitudes imbedded in thinking that get passed on like bad genes from generation to generation. The latest issue of a women-and-language newsletter notes items involving sexism in everything from the *New England Journal of Medicine* and Maidenform bra ads to campaign speeches and government offices in Japan.

5   Work focused on interruption contributes to understanding who controls conversations and how. To check on their original observations in a more casual context, West and Zimmerman conducted an

experiment in which students meeting for the first time were told to "relax and get to know one another," with familiar results. Males again turned out to be the chief culprits, although they made only 75 percent of the interruptions, compared with that 96 percent figure for previously acquainted pairs—perhaps because they were more restrained among new acquaintances.

6   Men not only do the lion's share of the interrupting (and the talking) but often choose what to talk about. This can be seen in a study conducted by public relations consultant Pamela Fishman. Her subjects were three couples, a social worker and five graduate students, who consented to having tape recorders in their apartments, providing some 52 hours of conversation, 25 of which have been transcribed.

7   Fishman's first impression: "At times I felt that all the women did was ask questions. . . I attended to my own speech and discovered the same pattern." In fact, the women asked more than 70 percent of the questions. Dustin Hoffman put this speech pattern to use in the motion picture Tootsie, using the questioning intonation frequently when impersonating a woman and rather less frequently when acting unladylike.

8   In her study, Fishman discovered that a particular question was used with great frequency: "D'ya know what?" Research by other investigators had described how children frequently use this phrase to communicate with their elders. It serves as a conversation opener, calling for an answer like "What?" or "No, tell me," a go-ahead signal that they may speak up and that what they have to say will be heeded.

9   Pursuing this lead, Fishman found out why women need such reassurances when she analyzed the 76 efforts in taped conversations to start conversations or keep them going. Men tried 29 times and succeeded 28 times. That is, in all but a single case the outcome was some discussion of the topic broached. Women tried 47 times, sometimes for as long as five minutes, with dead-end results 30 times, an unimpressive .362 batting average. (It could have been worse. Each of the male subjects in this experiment professed sympathy for the women's movement.)

10   Other actions that control conversation (and often power) are more complicated, less open to statistical analysis. Cheris Kramarae, professor of speech communication at the University of Illinois in Urbana-Champaign, tells what happened when, as the only woman member of an important policy-shaping committee, she tried to

communicate with the chairman before the start of the meeting. She suggested that certain items be added to the agenda, apparently to no effect. "He paid no attention to me, and I gave up." Once the meeting got under way, however, he featured her ideas in a review of the agenda and, turning to a male colleague, commented: "I don't remember who suggested these changes. I think it was Dick here."

11   Kramarae cites such instances of being heard but not listened to, "as if you were speaking behind a glass," as the sort of thing women must cope with every day. Other examples of everyday difficulties include being first-named by people who address males by last names plus "Mr." or "Dr.," hearing men discuss hiring a "qualified" woman, and looking a block ahead to see whether men are around who might make catcalls or pass out unwanted compliments.

12   These sorts of affronts lead women to a guarded way of life that fosters sensitivity to biases in the King's English. There is the intriguing record of efforts to abolish the generic masculine where *man* means not just males but all humans (as in "Man is among the few mammals in which estrus has disappeared entirely," from *Emergence of Man* by John Pfeiffer, 1978). *Woman* is used only in reference to a female, a rule established by male grammarians some 250 years ago.

13   At first the move to a more generalized language was widely opposed, mainly on the grounds of triviality and the inviolability of language. Critics included some feminists, the linguistic faculty at Harvard, and *Time* magazine, the latter exhibiting its usual delicate touch in an essay entitled "Sispeak: A Msguided Attempt to Change Herstory." Then a number of psychologists, among them Donald MacKay and Wendy Martyna of the University of California, ran tests showing that, whatever the speaker or writer intended, most people associate *man* and the matching pronoun *he* with a male image and that the generic masculine could hurt the way *boy* hurts blacks. Today it is common practice to edit such references out of textbook manuscripts and other writings.

14   Meanwhile research continues along a widening front, trying to cope with unconscious attitudes, sexist and otherwise, which distinguish women and men—"two alien cultures, oddly intertwined," in the words of Barrie Thorne of Michigan State University. Recent studies of the American male culture by and large support previous findings. Men spend considerable time playing the dominance game, either at a joking level or for real. The telling of a tall tale, fol-

lowed by a still taller tale in an I-can-top-that atmosphere, seems to be typically male.

15   In this game, keeping cool commands the respect of the other players, with an occasional flash of emotion commended, providing it has to do with politics or sports or shop talk—practically anything but personal feelings. Elizabeth Aries of Amherst College, who has recorded 15 hours of conversation among newly acquainted male students, reports that certain males consistently dominated the conversation. Her subjects addressed the entire group rather than individuals at least a third of the time, nearly five times more often than women interacting under similar conditions.

16   Detailed studies of women's conversations are rare, mainly conducted in the past few years. Aries discovered that leaders in all-female groups tend to assume a low profile and encourage others to speak, while leaders among men tend to resist the contributions of others. Mercilee Jenkins of San Francisco State University studied the conversation of mothers in a discussion group over a five-month period. She was interested in subject matter as well as conversational style. She found that the young mothers discussed a broad range of subjects—much beyond domestic problems.

17   Storytelling makes up a large proportion of conversational encounters, with narrative styles that reflect other gender differences. "The universe is made of stories, not atoms," said poet Muriel Rukeyser, and linguistic analysis confirms her insight. As a rule, the women in the Jenkins study avoided first-person narratives. In 26 out of 57 transcribed stories, the narrator played no role at all, while men frequently shine in their own stories. The women listening became heavily involved in the incidents recounted and chimed in with stories supporting the narrator, challenging the preceding story in only about five percent of the cases.

18   Mixing sexes conversationally produces some interesting reactions, at least among newly acquainted Harvard students in the Aries study. The men softened, competing less among themselves and talking more about their personal lives. (This may be a kind of instinctive mating or courting display, an attracting mechanism, discarded upon closer acquaintance when the male usually reassumes his impersonal ways.) Women students responded with a pattern of their own, becoming more competitive. Aries notes that "the social significance of women for one another in a mixed groups was low." They maintained

a supportive style in talking with men, but it was every woman for herself as they spoke disproportionately more to the men than to each other.

19   The "music" of conversation may be as meaningful as the words. Women not only have higher voices, but the pitch is notably higher than can be explained solely by the anatomy of the female vocal apparatus. Moreover, Sally McConnell-Ginet of Cornell University finds that women's voices are more colorful—they vary more in pitch and change pitch more frequently than do men's voices. In one experiment, women immediately assumed a monotone style when asked to imitate men's speech. McConnell-Ginet regards speaking tunefully as an effective strategy for getting and holding attention, a strategy used more often by women than men, perhaps because they are more often ignored.

20   No one has a workable theory that accounts for all these differences. Even the longest running, most thorough searches for the root causes of differences between the sexes raise more questions than they answer. Carol Nagy Jacklin of the University of Southern California and Eleanor Maccoby of Stanford University have been tracking the development of 100 children from birth to age six. These children have been observed at several stages, in various settings. When this group reached 45 months of age, the researchers focused on how 58 of them interacted with their parents during playtime.

21   A surprising conclusion emerged: Discrimination by gender originates mainly outside the home. "Mothers do little behavior stereotyping," Jacklin summarizes. "They appear to treat [their own] little boys and girls much the same." (While fathers tend to treat their children in more gender-stereotyped ways during playtimes, they ordinarily have less influence on childrearing and on actually creating the home environment.)

22   The implication is intriguing. If it is true that outsiders are largely responsible, and since most outsiders are also parents, it follows that parents have gender-based preconceptions more often about other people's children than about their own. In any event, school is one place where highly significant changes take place. In the beginning, teacher is "home base," a surrogate parent to whom children come for reassurance and support, and that holds for all children—until second grade.

23   At that point boys but not girls begin increasingly to turn away

from teacher and toward one another. The stress is more and more on hierarchy, jockeying for position in speech as well as action, in talking as well as playing cowboy, soldier, Star Wars, and so on. All this is part of a constellation of changes. In playgrounds girls tend to go around in pairs, usually near teachers and the school building; boys form groups of half a dozen or so, usually as far away as possible. Boys may get more attention than girls because they are often more disruptive.

24   In discussing such patterns, Thorne cites the classic psycho-analytic theory that boys, being raised mainly by women at home, feel the need at school to assert themselves as "not female." Also, teachers may have biased expectations about boys. But, according to Raphaela Best of the Montgomery County school system in Maryland, a high price may be paid for early male-male competition. She suggests that the resulting tensions may help account for the fact that reading disabilities are at least five times more frequent among boys than among girls.

25   Though the study of gender-based differences is relatively new, significant steps have been taken. Furthermore—a totally unexpected development—gender-related work has helped spark renewed interest in general language use. The ways in which men talk to men and women talk to women have come under scrutiny, as have the speech differences between people of different cultures and professional backgrounds.

26   West, for example, is currently interested in exchanges between doctors and patients. This work demands looking as well as listening, analyzing a kind of choreography of nonverbal as well as verbal behavior. Her raw data consists of videotapes complete with sound tracks. So far she has spent more than 550 hours transcribing seven hours of conversation in 21 patient-physician meetings at a family-practice center in the southern United States. Preliminary analysis indicates that doctors out-interrupt their patients, male and female, by a two-to-one—margin except when the doctor is a woman. In that case, the situation is reversed, with patients—both male and female—out-interrupting by the same margin.

27   Similar studies are tuning in on the finer points of speech and behavior. An outstanding and continuing analysis by Marjorie Harness Goodwin of the University of South Carolina shows that girls as well as boys form social groups, except that the girls tend to

form exclusive "coalitions," whereas boys form all-inclusive hier-archies. With the girls not everyone gets to play, while with the boys everyone, even the nerds, can play as long as they respect rank. Girls also are far less direct in arguing with one another, and their debates may simmer for weeks, in contrast to male arguments, which generally end within a few minutes.

28   These findings are based on taped observations of black children at play in an urban setting. Other observations hint that the same points might apply more widely, a possibility that remains to be probed. What holds true for one culture or society may not for another. Male dominance in speech seems to be a global phenomenon. But the most notable exception cries for analysis: Sexism is probably at a lower level in Bali, where to vote or be otherwise active as a citizen, one must be part of a couple.

29   While most of the recent research has revealed conflict between the sexes, Carole Edelsky of Arizona State University has discovered a trend worth noting. She has studied five "very informal" meetings of a standing faculty committee consisting of seven women and four men—7.5 hours of taped conversation. It started as a "fishing expe-dition" project—a search for sexisms, and there were plenty. As usual, men talked longer and interrupted more, appearing to hold the floor longer.

30   But Edelsky also recognized a second method of holding the floor. She identified short interludes, between the more formal ad-dresses, that featured mutual support and "greater discourse equality." (These episodes were most informal and laughter-filled.) At first Edelsky had the impression that the women were doing most of the talking during these periods. But actual counts of words and time per turn revealed an equal-time situation (thus supporting the observation that a "talkative" woman is one who talks as much as the average man). These episodes made up less than 20 percent of total talk time, but such encounters as these may reflect a change in communication between the sexes.

31   The future may see great change in our current perception of a conversational gap between the sexes. It may also see a correction of imbalance in present-day research—a shift in the gender composition of the researchers. Today in the United States there are about 200 inves-tigators of language and gender, and all but a dozen of them are women. Many of the researchers believe that as more men enter the

field, the "two alien cultures" will draw closer together.

Suggestions for Discussion and Writing

1. What is the thesis of Pfeiffer's article? Does he state it directly or imply it? Why do you think he made that choice?

2. Do you agree with Pfeiffer that women and men have different ways of talking? What arguments and evidence would you use to prove or disprove his contentions?

3. Pfeiffer uses the title and an example from one of his own books to show how authors tangle with sexist language in a text. Can you find examples in other books or magazines where authors avoid sexist language? Where they don't? How do those choices affect you as a reader?

4. If it's true that "discrimination by gender originates mainly outside the home," where else besides school might that discrimination happen? Can you cite instances from your own life and experiences to prove or disprove his point?

5. Try to duplicate the research Pfeiffer describes in his early paragraphs: record and transcribe the speech of women talking to men, women talking to women, and men talking to men. Do your observations support or contradict the research Pfeiffer found? Can you suggest some factors that influence your conclusions?

James Thurber
Courtship Through the Ages

JAMES THURBER (1894-1961), writer, playwright, astigmatic, and cartoonist, is a name most people associate with the *New Yorker*. Thurber wrote for that magazine from 1927 until his death, in his own innocent way lampooning the pretenses of American society. One of his trademark themes is the henpecked male. With E.B. White, Thurber wrote *Is Sex Necessary?* in 1929; this essay, written in 1942, continues his bemused struggles with the battles between men and women.

Surely nothing in the astonishing scheme of life can have nonplussed Nature so much as the fact that none of the females of any of the species she created really cared very much for the male, as such. For the past ten million years Nature has been busily inventing ways to make the male attractive to the female, but the whole business of courtship, from the marine annelids up to man, still lumbers heavily along, like a complicated musical comedy. I have been reading the sad and absorbing story in Volume 6 (Cole to Dama) of the *Encyclopaedia Britannica*. In this volume you can learn all about cricket, cotton, costume designing, crocodiles, crown jewels, and Coleridge, but none of these subjects is so interesting as the Courtship of Animals, which recounts the sorrowful lengths to which all males must go to arouse the interest of a lady.

2   We all know, I think, that Nature gave man whiskers and a mustache with the quaint idea in mind that these would prove attractive to the female. We all know that, far from attracting her, whiskers and mustaches only made her nervous and gloomy, so that man had to go in for somersaults, tilting and lances, and performing feats of parlor magic to win her attention; he also had to bring her candy, flowers, and the furs of animals. It is common knowledge that in spite of all these "love displays" the male is constantly being turned down, insulted, or thrown out of the house. It is rather comforting, then, to discover that the peacock, for all his gorgeous plumage, does not have a particularly easy time in courtship; none of the males in the world do. The first peahen, it turned out, was only faintly stirred by her suitor's beautiful train. She would often go quietly to sleep while he was whisking it around. The *Britannica* tells us that the peacock actually had to learn a certain little trick to wake her up and revive her interest: he had to learn to vibrate his quills so as to make a rustling sound. In ancient times man himself, observing the ways of the peacock, probably tried vibrating his whiskers to make a rustling sound; if so, it didn't get him anywhere. He had to go in for something else; so, among other things, he went in for gifts. It is not unlikely that he got

this idea from certain flies and birds who were making no headway at all with rustling sounds.

3   One of the flies of the family Empidae, who had tried everything, finally hit on something pretty special. He contrived to make a glistening transparent balloon which was even larger than himself. Into this he would put sweetmeats and tidbits and he would carry the whole elaborate envelope through the air to the lady of his choice. This amused her for a time, but she finally got bored with it. She demanded silly little colorful presents, something that you couldn't eat but that would look nice around the house. So the male Empis had to go around gathering flower petals and pieces of bright paper to put into his balloon. On a courtship flight a male Empis cuts quite a figure now, but he can hardly be said to be happy. He never knows how soon the female will demand heavier presents, such as Roman coins and gold collar buttons. It seems probable that one day the courtship of the Empidae will fall down, as man's occasionally does, of its own weight.

4   The bowerbird is another creature that spends so much time courting the female that he never gets any work done. If all the male bowerbirds became nervous wrecks within the next ten or fifteen years, it would not surprise me. The female bowerbird insists that a playground be built for her with a specially constructed bower at the entrance. This bower is much more elaborate than an ordinary nest and is harder to build; it costs a lot more, too. The female will not come to the playground until the male has filled it up with a great many gifts: silvery leaves, red leaves, rose petals, shells, beads, berries, bones, dice, buttons, cigar bands, Christmas seals, and the Lord knows what else. When the female finally condescends to visit the playground, she is in a coy and silly mood and has to be chased in and out of the bower and up and down the playground before she will quit giggling and stand still long enough even to shake hands. The male bird is, of course, pretty well done in before the chase starts, because he has worn himself out hunting for eyeglass lenses and begonia blossoms. I imagine that many a bowerbird, after chasing a female for two or three hours, says the hell with it and goes home to bed. Next day, of course, he telephones someone else and the same trying ritual is gone through with again. A male bowerbird is as exhausted as a night-club habitue before he is out of his twenties.

5   The male fiddler crab has a somewhat easier time, but it can

hardly be said that he is sitting pretty. He has one enormously large and powerful claw, usually brilliantly colored, and you might suppose that all he had to do was reach out and grab some passing cutie. The very earliest fiddler crabs may have tried this, but, if so, they got slapped for their pains. A female fiddler crab will not tolerate any caveman stuff; she never has and she doesn't intend to start now. To attract a female, a fiddler crab has to stand on tiptoe and brandish his claw in the air. If any female in the neighborhood is interested—and you'd be surprised how many are not—she comes over and engages in light badinage, for which he is not in the mood. As many as a hundred females may pass the time of day with him and go on about their business. By night-fall of an average courting day, a fiddler crab who has been standing on tiptoe for eight or ten hours waving a heavy claw in the air is in pretty sad shape. As in the case of the males of all species, however, he gets out of bed next morning, dashes some water on his face, and tries again.

6   The next time you encounter a male web-spinning spider, stop and reflect that he is too busy worrying about his love life to have any desire to bite you. Male web-spinning spiders have a tougher life than any other males in the animal kingdom. This is because the female web-spinning spiders have very poor eyesight. If a male lands on a female's web, she kills him before he has time to lay down his cane and gloves, mistaking him for a fly or a bumblebee who has tumbled into her trap. Before the species figured out what to do about this, millions of males were murdered by ladies they called on. It is the nature of spiders to perform a little dance in front of the female, but before a male spinner could get near enough for the female to see who he was and what he was up to, she would lash out at him with a flat-iron or a pair of garden shears. One night, nobody knows when, a very bright male spinner lay awake worrying about calling on a lady who had been killing suitors right and left. It came to him that this business of dancing as a love display wasn't getting anybody anywhere except the grave. He decided to go in for web-twitching, or strand-vibrating. The next day he tried it on one of the nearsighted girls. Instead of dropping in on her suddenly, he stayed outside the web and began monkeying with one of its strands. He twitched it up and down and in and out with such a lilting rhythm that the female was charmed. The serenade worked beautifully; the female let him live. The *Britannica's* spider-watchers, however, report that this system is not

always successful. Once in a while, even now, a female will fire three bullets into a suitor or run him through with a kitchen knife. She keeps threatening him from the moment he strikes the first low notes on the outside strings, but usually by the time he has got up to the high notes played around the center of the web, he is going to town and she spares his life.

7   Even the butterfly, as handsome a fellow as he is, can't always win a mate merely by fluttering around and showing off. Many butterflies have to have scent scales on their wings. Hepialus carries a powder puff in a perfumed pouch. He throws perfume at the ladies when they pass. The male tree cricket, Oecanthus, goes Hepialus one better by carrying a tiny bottle of wine with him and giving drinks to such doxies as he has designs on. One of the male snails throws darts to entertain the girls. So it goes, through the long list of animals, from the bristle worm and his rudimentary dance steps to man and his gift of diamonds and sapphires. The golden-eye drake raises a jet of water with his feet as he flies over a lake; Hepialus has his powder puff, Oecanthus his wine bottle, man his etchings. It is a bright and melancholy story, the age-old desire of the male for the female, the age-old desire of the female to be amused and entertained. Of all the creatures on earth, the only males who could be figured as putting any irony into their courtship are the grebes and certain other diving birds. Every now and then a courting grebe slips quietly down to the bottom of a lake and then, with a mighty "Whoosh!," pops out suddenly a few feet from his girl friend, splashing water all over her. She seems to be persuaded that this is a purely loving display, but I like to think that the grebe always has a faint hope of drowning her or scaring her to death.

8   I will close this investigation into the mournful burdens of the male with the *Britannica's* story about a certain Argus pheasant. It appears that the Argus displays himself in front of a female who stands perfectly still without moving a feather. . . . The male Argus the *Britannica* tells about was confined in a cage with a female of another species, a female who kept moving around, emptying ashtrays and fussing with lampshades all the time the male was showing off his talents. Finally, in disgust, he stalked away and began displaying in front of his water trough. He reminds me of a certain male (Homo sapiens) of my acquaintance who one night after dinner asked his wife to put down her detective magazine so that he could read a poem of

which he was very fond. She sat quietly enough until he was well into the middle of the thing, intoning with great ardor and intensity. Then suddenly there came a sharp, disconcerting slap! It turned out that all during the male's display, the female had been intent on a circling mosquito and had finally trapped it between the palms of her hands. The male in this case did not stalk away and display in front of a water trough; he went over to Tim's and had a flock of drinks and recited the poem to the fellas. I am sure they all told bitter stories of their own about how their displays had been interrupted by females. I am also sure that they all ended up singing "Honey, Honey, Bless Your Heart."

Suggestions for Discussion and Writing

1. Thurber here uses a very informal style to describe the "facts" of animal courtship. How does he modify that style? What effects does his style have on you as a reader?

2. What attitudes does Thurber project toward women? toward men?

3. Can you think of situations where women court men? How could those encounters be described?

4. Pick a situation from your life where women and men interact. Write a Thurber-like description of that situation. What sorts of details will you need to include?

5. Courtship rituals can be described very differently, depending on the observer's background and interest. What would human courtship look like if it were described by an anthropologist? A sociologist? A psychiatrist? A lawyer? Pick one of these roles and create such a description.

Claire Safran
Hidden Lessons:
Do Little Boys Get a Better
Education Than Little Girls?

CLAIRE SAFRAN is a prolific journalist; she published more than 60 articles in the last decade, on subjects ranging from archaeology to high blood pressure to incest. She is also the author of *Secret Exodus* (1987), an account of the airlift of 10,000 Ethiopian Jews to Israel. In this 1983 article, she reports on the ways teachers treat their male and female students.

Our public school teachers are targets once again of the researchers. This time, they have been charged with sex-biased instructional methods.

2   Drs. David and Myra Sadker of American University in Washington, D.C., sent observers to 100 classrooms in five states to sit in on teaching sessions. The Sadkers' researchers cited instances of boys being taught differently from girls in elementary schools, where women teachers far outnumber men, through secondary schools, where more than half the teachers are male.

3   The bias generally is unintentional and unconscious, says Myra Sadker, dean of the School off Education at American University. She notes: "We've met teachers who call themselves feminists. They show me their nonsexist textbooks and nonsexist bulletin boards. They insist there is equity in their classrooms. Then," she continues, "I videotape them as they're teaching—and they're amazed. If they hadn't seen themselves at work on film, they'd never have believed that they were treating boys and girls so differently."

4   Such videotaping of teachers is among the functions of 12 U.S. Department of Education Centers for Sex Equity in educational districts across the country.

5   From nursery school to beyond graduate school, studies show that teachers call on male students in class far more often than they call on female students. That difference in involvement in the learning process is crucial, say educators, who add that the students who are active in class are the ones who go on to higher achievement and a more positive attitude.

6   Many teachers unwittingly hinder girls from being active in class. Dr. Lisa Serbin of Concordia University in Montreal studied nursery schools in Suffolk County, N.Y. She tells how a teacher poured water into containers of different heights and widths, then told a little boy to try it—to learn for himself how water can change its shape without changing its amount.

7   "Can I do it?" a little girl asked.

8   "You'll have to wait your turn," the teacher replied, giving the pitcher to a second boy. The girl asked again, but it was time to put the materials away.

9   "You can help me do that," the teacher offered.

10   Who gets to pour the water is important. Learning is connected to instruction and direction, and boys get more of that than girls do all through school. Why? Partly because teachers tend to question the students they expect will have the answers. Since girls traditionally don't do so well as boys in such "masculine" subjects as math and science, they're called on least in those classes. But girls are called on most in verbal and reading classes, where boys are expected to have the trouble. The trouble is in our culture, not in our chromosomes. In Gremany, everything academic is considered masculine, most teachers are men, and girls have the reading problems. In Japan, there's no sex bias about reading, and neither sex has special problems with it.

11   In most U.S. schools, there are remedial classes for reading—the "boys' problem"—and boys quickly catch up to the girls. But there are very few remedial classes in math and science—the "girls' problems." Thus boys have the most skill in these subjects, which can lead to better-paying jobs later.

12   According to the National Assessment of Educational Progress, an organization in Denver that surveys both public and private schools nationally, girls get better math grades than boys do at age 9, but their

scores decline as they progress while boys' math scores rise. Researchers say such things happen because boys are taught to take a more active part in learning than girls.

13   This differing of the educational process for the sexes starts at home. For example, in one study, preschool youngsters were shown a drawing of a house and asked, "How far can you go from your own house?" Most girls pointed to an area quite near the house and said that was how far their parents permitted them to go and how far they actually went. Most boys pointed to a much wider perimeter of permission and generally said they exceeded it. In the classroom, unconscious sex bias takes various forms:

- Girls tend to be called on if they sit close to the teacher— irst row—right under his or her nose. Boys tend to be called on wherever they sit. (*Girls' Lesson*: Be dependent—stay close to the teacher, and you'll be rewarded. *Boys' Lesson*: Be independent—sit anywhere; you'll be rewarded.)

- The Sadkers report this interchange. Fourth-grade teacher to a girl: "That's a neat paper. The margins are just right." To a boy: "That's a good analysis of the cause of the Civil War." (*Girl's Lesson*: Form, not content, is all that's expected of you. *Boy's Lesson*: Analytical thinking is what's expected of you.)

- Dr. Carol Dweck, professor of education at Harvard University, cites these comments by a teacher to students who have given incorrect answers. To a girl: "That's wrong." To a boy: "You'd know the right answer if you'd done your homework." (*Girl's Lesson*: The failure may be due to your own lack of ability. *Boy's Lesson*: You can do better if you make the effort.) Told that effort brings success, both sexes try—and succeed. Otherwise, both stop trying. Educators call this concept "attribution to effort."

14   Some teachers are learning to recognize—and then change—their methods. And small changes can make large differences. The Sadkers, for example, found that if teachers wait a few seconds after asking a question before they call on a student, more students will participate and their answers will be more complete.

15   Parents disturbed by sex bias in classrooms might first test themselves for it at home. Those who want to help combat teachers' sex bias might arrange to observe classes in their children's schools, and they might discuss sex bias at PTA meetings. On this issue, awareness is the first step.

Suggestions for Discussion and Writing

1. Safran calls this essay "Hidden Lessons." What are the implications of that title? After you read the essay, can you think of any other hidden lessons than the ones she identifies?

2. Safran seems to make a distinction between "teachers" and "educators" in her argument. What's the difference? Is it important?

3. What kinds of evidence does Safran provide? Is it enough to persuade you to agree with her conclusions? If you would have liked to have seen different kinds of evidence, what kinds would you want, and why?

4. The research Safran presents seems to suggest that teacher behavior is the chief cause of boys' success in math and science, and girls' success in reading and communication skills. Do you agree? Can you think of other factors that might contribute to these outcomes?

5. Safran's conclusion turns the focus from teachers to parents. If you had to expand on this advice to parents, what would you suggest they do to improve their children's education? You might want to look in *The Education Index* or a similar library resource to gather ideas.

Alleen Pace Nilsen
Sexism and Language

ALLEEN PACE NILSEN, who teaches at Arizona State University, is a specialist in children's and adolescent literature. In her doctoral dissertation, she examined the ways in which the language in various children's books encouraged sexism and stereotyping. This essay is taken from a book she edited, *Sexism and Language* (1977), a collection of essays that is still one of the standard reference works on the subject.

With Kenneth L. Donelson, she is also the author of *Literature for Today's Young Adults* (1985), a standard text in education courses.

O ver the last hundred years, American anthropologists have travelled to the corners of the earth to study primitive cultures. They either became linguists themselves or they took linguists with them to help in learning and analyzing languages. Even if the culture was one that no longer existed, they were interested in learning its language because besides being tools of communication, the vocabulary and structure of a language tell much about the values held by its speakers.

2   However, the culture need not be primitive, nor do the people making observations need to be anthropologists and linguists. Anyone living in the United States who listens with a keen ear or reads with a perceptive eye can come up with startling new insights about the way American English reflects our values.

Animal Terms for People—Mirrors of the Double Standard

3   If we look at just one semantic area of English, that of animal terms in relation to people, we can uncover some interesting insights into how our culture views males and females. References to identical animals can have negative connotations when related to a female, but positive or neutral connotations when related to a male. For example, a *shrew* has come to mean "a scolding, nagging, evil-tempered woman," while *shrewd* means "keen-witted, clever, or sharp in practical affairs; astute. . . businessman, etc." (*Webster's New World Dictionary of the American Language*, 1964).

4   A *lucky dog* or a *gay dog* may be a very interesting fellow, but when a woman is a *dog* she is unattractive, and when she's a *bitch* she's the personification of whatever is undesirable in the mind of the speaker. When a man is self-confident, he may be described as *cocksure* or even *cocky*, but in a woman this same self-confidence is likely to result in her being called a *cocky bitch*, which is not only a mixed metaphor, but also probably the most insulting animal metaphor we have. *Bitch* has taken on such negative connotations—children are taught it is a swear word—that in everyday American English, speakers are hesitant to call a female dog a *bitch*. Most of us feel that we would be insulting the dog. When we want to insult a man by comparing him to a dog, we call him a *son of a bitch*, which quite literally is an insult

to his mother rather than to him.

5   If the female is called a *vixen* (a female fox), the dictionary says this means she is "an ill-tempered, shrewish, or malicious woman." The female seems both to attract and to hold on longer to animal metaphors with negative connotations. A *vampire* was originally a corpse that came alive to suck the blood of living persons. The word acquired the general meaning of an unscrupulous person such as a blackmailer and then, the specialized meaning of "a beautiful but unscrupulous woman who seduces men and leads them to their ruin." From this latter meaning we get the word *vamp*. The popularity of this term and of the name *vampire bat* may contribute to the idea that a female being is referred to in a phrase such as *the old bat*.

6   Other animal metaphors do not have definitely derogatory connotations for the female, but they do seem to indicate frivolity or unimportance, as in *social butterfly* and *flapper*. Look at the differences between the connotations of participating in a *hen party* and in a *bull session*. Male metaphors, even when they are negative in connotation, still relate to strength and conquest. Metaphors related to aggressive sex roles, for example, *buck, stag, wolf* and *stud*, will undoubtedly remain attached to males. Perhaps one of the reasons that in the late sixties it was so shocking to hear policemen called *pigs* was that the connotations of *pig* are very different from the other animal metaphors we usually apply to males.

7   When I was living in Afghanistan, I was surprised at the cruelty and unfairness of a proverb that said, "When you see an old man, sit down and take a lesson; when you see an old woman, throw a stone." In looking at Afghan folk literature. I found that young girls were pictured as delightful and enticing, middle-aged women were sometimes interesting but more often just tolerable, while old women were always grotesque and villainous. Probably the reason for the negative connotation of old age in women is that women are valued for their bodies while men are valued for their accomplishments and their wisdom. Bodies deteriorate with age but wisdom and accomplishments grow greater.

8   When we returned home from Afghanistan, I was shocked to discover that we have remnants of this same attitude in America. We see it in our animal metaphors. If both the animal and the woman are young, the connotation is positive, but if the animal and the woman are old, the connotation is negative. Hugh Hefner might never have made it to

the big time if he had called his girls *rabbits* instead of *bunnies*. He probably chose *bunny* because he wanted something close to, but not quite so obvious as *kitten* or *cat*—the all-time winners for connoting female sexuality. Also *bunny*, as in the skiers' *snow bunny*, already had some of the connotations Hefner wanted. Compare the connotations of *filly* to *old nag*; *bird* to *old crow* or *old bat*; and *lamb* to *crone* (apparently related to the early modern Dutch *kronje*, *old ewe* but now *withered old woman*).

9   Probably the most striking examples of the contrast between young and old women are animal metaphors relating to cats and chickens. A young girl is encouraged to be *kittenish*, but not *catty*. And though most of us wouldn't mind living next door to a *sex kitten*, we wouldn't want to live next door to a *cat house*. Parents might name their daughter *Kitty* but not *Puss* or *Pussy*, which used to be a fairly common nickname for girls. It has now developed such sexual connotations that it is used mostly for humor, as in the James Bond movie featuring Pussy Galore and her flying felines.

10   In the chicken metaphors, a young girl is a *chick*. When she gets old enough she marries and soon begins feeling *cooped up*. To relieve the boredom she goes to *hen parties* and *cackles* with her friends. Eventually she has her *brood*, begins to *henpeck* her husband, and finally turns into an *old biddy*.

How English Glorifies Maleness

11   Throughout the ages physical strength has been very important, and because men are physically stronger than women, they have been valued more. Only now in the machine age, when the difference in strength between males and females pales into insignificance in comparison to the strength of earth-moving machinery, airplanes, and guns, males no longer have such an inherent advantage. Today a man of intellect is more valued than a physical laborer, and since women can compete intellectually with men, their value is on the rise. But language lags far behind cultural changes, so the language still reflects this emphasis on the importance of being male. For example, when we want to compliment a male, all we need to do is stress the fact that he is male by saying he is a *he-man*, or he is *manly*, or he is *virile*. Both *virile* and *virtuous* come from the Latin *vir*, meaning *man*.

12   The command or encouragement that males receive in sentences like "Be a man!" implies that *to be a man* is to be honorable, strong,

righteous, and whatever else the speaker thinks desirable. But in contrast to this, a girl is never told to be a *woman*. And when she is told to be a *lady*, she is simply being encouraged to "act feminine," which means sitting with her knees together, walking gracefully, and talking softly.

13   The armed forces, particularly the Marines, use the positive masculine connotation as part of their recruitment psychology. They promote the idea that to join the Marines (or the Army, Navy, or Air Force) guarantees that you will become a man. But this brings up a problem, because much of the work that is necessary to keep a large organization running is what is traditionally thought of as *women's work*. Now, how can the Marines ask someone who has signed up for a *man-sized job* to do *women's work*? Since they can't, they euphemize and give the jobs titles that either are more prestigious or, at least, don't make people think of females. Waitresses are called *orderlies*, secretaries are called *clerk-typists*, nurses are called *medics*, assistants are called *adjutants*, and cleaning up an area is called *policing* the area. The same kind of word glorification is used in civilian life to bolster a man's ego when he is doing such tasks as cooking and sewing. For example, a *chef* has higher prestige than a *cook* and a *tailor* has higher prestige than a *seamstress*.

14   Little girls learn early in life that the boy's role is one to be envied and emulated. Child psychologists have pointed out that experimenting with the role of the opposite sex is much more acceptable for little girls than it is for little boys. For example, girls are free to dress in boys' clothes, but certainly not the other way around. Most parents are amused if they have a daughter who is a *tomboy*, but they are genuinely distressed if they have a son who is a *sissy*. The names we give to young children reflect this same attitude. It is all right for girls to have boys' names, but pity the boy who has a girl's name! Because parents keep giving boys' names to girls, the number of acceptable boys' names keeps shrinking. Currently popular names for girls include *Jo, Kelly, Teri, Chris, Pat, Shawn, Toni, and Sam* (short for *Samantha*). *Evelyn, Carroll, Gayle, Hazel, Lynn, Beverley, Marion, Francis,* and *Shirley* once were acceptable names for males. But as they were given to females, they became less and less acceptable. Today, men who are stuck with them self-consciously go by their initials or by abbreviated forms such as *Haze, Shirl, Frank,* or *Ev*. And they seldom pass these names on to their sons.

15   Many common words have come into the language from people's names. These lexical items again show the importance of   maleness compared to the triviality of the feminine activities being described. Words derived from the names of women include *Melba* toast, named for the Australian singer Dame Nellie Melba; *Sally Lunn* cakes, named after an eighteenth-century woman who first made them; *pompadour*, a hair style named after Madame Pompadour; and the word *maudlin*, as in *maudlin sentiment*, from Mary Magdalene, who was often portrayed by artists as displaying exaggerated sorrow.

16   There are trivial items named after men—*teddy bear* after Theodore Roosevelt and *sideburns* after General Burnside—but most words that come from men's names relate to significant inventions or developments. These include *pasteurization* after Louis Pasteur, *sousaphone* after John Philip Sousa, *mason jar* after John L. Mason, *boysenberry* after Rudolph Boysen, *pullman car* after George M. Pullman, *braille* after Louis Braille, *franklin stove* after Benjamin Franklin, *diesel engine* after Rudolf Diesel, *ferris wheel* after George W. G. Ferris, and the verb *to lynch* after William Lynch, who was a vigilante captain in Virginia in 1780.

17   The latter is an example of a whole set of English words dealing with violence. These words have strongly negative connotations. From research using free association and semantic differentials, with university students as subjects, James Ney concluded that English reflects both an anti-male and an anti-female bias because these biases exist in the culture (*Etc.: A Review of General Semantics*, March 1976, pp. 67-76). The students consistently marked as masculine such words as *killer, murderer, robber, attacker, fighter, stabber, rapist, assassin, gang, hood, arsonist, criminal, hijacker, villain,* and *bully*, even though most of these words contain nothing to specify that they are masculine. An example of bias against males, Ney observed, is the absence in English of a pejorative term for women equivalent to *rapist*. Outcomes of his free association test indicated that if "English speakers want to call a man something bad, there seems to be a large vocabulary available to them but if they want to use a term which is good to describe a male, there is a small vocabulary available. The reverse is true for women."

18   Certainly we do not always think positively about males; witness such words as *jerk, creep, crumb, slob, fink,* and *jackass*. But much of what determines our positive and negative feelings relates to the roles

people play. We have very negative feelings toward someone who is hurting us or threatening us or in some way making our lives miserable. To be able to do this, the person has to have power over us and this power usually belongs to males.

19   On the other hand, when someone helps us or makes our life more pleasant, we have positive feelings toward that person or that role. *Mother* is one of the positive female terms in English, and we see such extensions of it as *Mother Nature, Mother Earth, mother lode, mother superior,* etc. But even though a word like *mother* is positive it is still not a word of power. In the minds of English speakers being female and being powerless or passive are so closely related that we use the terms *feminine* and *lady* either to mean female or to describe a certain kind of quiet and unobtrusive behavior.

Words Labelling Women as Things

20   Because of our expectations of passivity, we like to compare females to items that people acquire for their pleasure. For example, in a recent commercial for the television show "Happy Days," one of the characters announced that in the coming season they were going to have not only "cars, motorcycles, and girls," but also a band. Another example of this kind of thinking is the comparison of females to food since food is something we all enjoy, even though it is extremely passive. We describe females as such delectable morsels as a *dish,* a *cookie,* a *tart, cheesecake, sugar and spice,* a *cute tomato, honey,* a *sharp cookie,* and *sweetie pie.* We say a particular girl has a *peaches and cream complexion* or "she looks good enough to eat." And parents give their daughters such names as *Candy* and *Cherry.*

21   Other pleasurable items that we compare females to are toys. Young girls are called *little dolls* or *China dolls,* while older girls—if they are attractive—are simply called *dolls.* We might say about a woman, "She's pretty as a picture," or "She's a fashion plate." And we might compare a girl to a plant by saying she is a *clinging vine,* a *shrinking violet,* or a *wallflower.* And we might name our daughters after plants such as *Rose, Lily, Ivy, Daisy, Iris,* and *Petunia.* Compare these names to boys' names such as *Martin* which means warlike, *Ernest* which means resolute fighter, *Nicholas* which means victory, *Val* which means strong or valiant, and *Leo* which means lion. We would be very hesitant to give a boy the name of something as passive as a flower although we might say about a man that he is a *late-*

bloomer. This is making a comparison between a man and the most active thing a plant can do, which is to bloom. The only other familiar plant metaphor used for a man is the insulting *pansy*, implying that he is like a woman.

Suggestions for Discussion and Writing

1. This essay seems to jump around and touch on a number of subjects relating to sexism in language. What do you think its overall thesis is? Does Nilsen express it explicitly? Why do you think she chose that strategy?

2. As a reader, how do you react to the long lists of examples Nilsen uses to support her points? Why do you think she chose to use these lists? Does it give her an advantage?

3. Do you agree with Nilsen that "American English reflects our values"? Why? If you disagree, how would you modify her statement to make it more agreeable?

4. Nilsen points out pairs of words such as *tailor/seamstress* that seem to have value judgments as well as gender clues built into them. Brainstorm a list of other job titles (for instance, *nurse, pilot, repairman, beautician*) that seem to suggest a particular gender. Can you see any patterns emerging as to what gender has the prestige jobs? Do you find sets of job titles (for instance *barber/stylist/beautician*) that distinguish between genders, or seem to be gender-free? What conclusions can you draw about sexism and language from the terms you collect?

5. Once you have compiled a list of about 25 job titles, survey some of your friends and relations, asking them to tell you if the job name suggests a female or male worker to them. What results do you get? Do you see any differences in response among people of different age groups? backgrounds? level of education? What does this tell you about American values?

Lindsy Van Gelder

The Great Person-Hole Cover Debate
A Modest Proposal for Anyone Who Thinks the Word "He" Is Just Plain Easier...

LINDSY VAN GELDER, born in New Jersey in 1944, has at one time or another been a columnist, journalism professor, and television commentator as well as a writer. She received her B.A. from Sarah Lawrence College in 1966. Among her best-known works are exposés on the massage parlors surrounding New York City's Times Square and her coverage of Anita Bryant's campaign against homosexuals in Dade County, Florida. This essay, which originally appeared in *Ms.* in 1980, demonstrates one of the main concerns of her writing: "how to convey seemingly radical ideas to an unconvinced audience."

I wasn't looking for trouble. What I was looking for, actually, was a little tourist information to help me plan a camping trip to New England.

2   But there it was, on the first page of the 1979 edition of the State of Vermont *Digest of Fish and Game Laws and Regulations:* a special message of welcome from one Edward F. Kehoe, commissioner of the Vermont Fish and Game Department, to the reader and would-be camper, *i.e.,* me.

3   This person (i.e., me) is called "the sportsman."

4   "We have no 'sportswomen, sportspersons, sportsboys, or sportsgirls,'" Commissioner Kehoe hastened to explain, obviously antici-

pating that some of us sportsfeminists might feel a bit overlooked. "But," he added, "we are pleased to report that we do have many great sportsmen who are women, as well as young people of both sexes."

5   It's just that the Fish and Game Department is trying to keep things "simple and forthright" and to respect "long-standing tradition." And anyway, we really ought to be flattered, "sportsman" being "a meaningful title being earned by a special kind of dedicated man, woman, or young person, as opposed to just any hunter, fisherman, or trapper."

6   I have heard this particular line of reasoning before. In fact, I've heard it so often that I've come to think of it as The Great Person-Hole Cover Debate, since gender-neutral manholes are invariably brought into the argument as evidence of the lengths to which humorless, Newspeak-spouting feminists will go to destroy their mother tongue.

7   Consternation about woman-handling the language comes from all sides. Sexual conservatives who see the feminist movement as a unisex plot and who long for the good olde days of *vive la différence,* when men were men and women were women, nonetheless do not rally behind the notion that the term "mankind" excludes women.

8   But most of the people who choke on expressions like "spokesperson" aren't right-wing misogynists, and this is what troubles me. Like the undoubtedly well-meaning folks at the Vermont Fish and Game Department, they tend to reassure you right up front that they're only trying to keep things "simple" and to follow "tradition," and that some of their best men are women, anyway.

9   Usually they wind up warning you, with great sincerity, that you're jeopardizing the worthy cause of women's rights by focusing on "trivial" side issues. I would like to know how anything that gets people so defensive and resistant can possibly be called "trivial," whatever else it might be.

10   The English language is alive and constantly changing. Progress—both scientific and social—is reflected in our language, or should be.

11   Not too long ago, there was a product called "flesh-colored" Band-Aids. The flesh in question was colored Caucasian. Once the civil rights movement pointed out the racism inherent in the name, it was dropped. I cannot imagine reading a thoughtful, well-intentioned company policy statement explaining that while the Band-Aids would

continue to be called "flesh-colored" for old time's sake, black and brown people would now be considered honorary whites and were perfectly welcome to use them.

12   Most sensitive people manage to describe our national religious traditions as "Judeo-Christian," even though it takes a few seconds longer to say than "Christian." So why is it such a hardship to say "he or she" instead of "he"?

13   I have a modest proposal for anyone who maintains that "he" is just plain easier: since "he" has been the style for several centuries now—and since it really includes everybody anyway, right—it seems only fair to give "she" a turn. Instead of having to ponder over the intricacies of, say, "Congressman" versus "Congressperson" versus "Representative," we can simplify things by calling them all "Congresswoman."

14   Other clarifications will follow: "a woman's home is her castle". . . "a giant step for all womankind". . . "all women are created equal". . . "Fisherwoman's Wharf.". . .

15   And don't be upset by the business letter that begins "Dear Madam," fellas. It means you, too.

Suggestions for Discussion and Writing

1. Van Gelder uses a number of pronouns—"I", "they", "you"—in her essay. What points of view does this allow her to use? What are the advantages and disadvantages of writing an essay like this in the personal "I" voice rather than an impersonal "One might say" voice?

2. Van Gelder notes that some people call paying attention to sexism in language a "trivial" issue. Do you think it is? Does it really distract from "the worthy cause of women's rights"?

3. How true is Van Gelder's statement that "Progress—both scientific and social—is reflected in our language—or should be"? Can you think of areas in your life that are not reflected in the language used by you and the people around you?

4. Van Gelder uses a personal anecdote in the first five paragraphs of her essay. How does this affect the response of you, the reader, to the rest of her essay?

5. The essay's subtitle reminds readers of Jonathan Swift's famous essay "A Modest Proposal." Read a copy of that essay, and consider why Van Gelder decided to echo it here. Are there other subjects in your life about which you might offer modest proposals of your own?

Robin Lakoff
You Are What You Say

ROBIN TOLMACH LAKOFF, born in 1942, is one of America's foremost linguists. A long-time professor at the University of California at Berkeley, she has been a leader in exploring how language helps people develop stereotypes and sex roles. Among her books are *Language and Women's Place* (1975), *Face Value: The Politics of Beauty* (1984), and *Talking Power* (1990). This essay appeared in *Ms.* in 1974.

"Women's language" is that pleasant (dainty?), euphemistic, never aggressive way of talking we learned as little girls. Cultural bias was built into the language we were allowed to speak, the subjects we were allowed to speak about, and the ways we were spoken of. Having learned our linguistic lesson well, we go out in the world, only to discover that we are communicative cripples—damned if we do, and damned if we don't.

2   If we refuse to talk "like a lady," we are ridiculed and criticized for being unfeminine. ("She thinks like a man" is, at best, a left-handed compliment.) If we do learn all the fuzzy-headed, unassertive language of our sex, we are ridiculed for being unable to think clearly, unable to take part in a serious discussion, and therefore unfit to hold a position of power.

3   It doesn't take much of this for a woman to begin feeling she deserves such treatment because of inadequacies in her own intel-

ligence and education.

4   "Women's language" shows up in all levels of English. For example, women are encouraged and allowed to make far more precise discriminations in naming colors than men do. Words like *mauve, beige, ecru, aquamarine, lavender,* and so on, are unremarkable in a woman's active vocabulary, but largely absent from that of most men. I know of no evidence suggesting that women actually *see* a wider range of colors than men do. It is simply that fine discriminations of this sort are relevant to women's vocabularies, but not to men's; to men, who control most of the interesting affairs of the world, such distinctions are trivial—irrelevant.

5   In the area of syntax, we find similar gender-related peculiarities of speech. There is one construction, in particular, that women use conversationally far more than men: the tag-question. A tag is midway between an outright statement and a yes-no question; it is less assertive than the former, but more confident than the latter.

6   A *flat statement* indicates confidence in the speaker's knowledge and is fairly certain to be believed; a *question* indicates a lack of knowledge on some point and implies that the gap in the speaker's knowledge can and will be remedied by an answer. For example, if, at a Little League game, I have had my glasses off, I can legitimately ask someone else: "Was the player out at third?" A *tag question*, being intermediate between statement and question, is used when the speaker is stating a claim, but lacks full confidence in the truth of that claim. So if I say, "Is Joan here?" I will probably not be surprised if my respondent answers "no"; but if I say, "Joan is here, isn't she?" instead, chances are I am already biased in favor of a positive answer, wanting only confirmation. I still want a response, but I have enough knowledge (or think I have) to predict that response. A tag question, then, might be thought of as a statement that doesn't demand to be believed by anyone but the speaker, a way of giving leeway, of not forcing the addressee to go along with the views of the speaker.

7   Another common use of the tag-question is in small talk when the speaker is trying to elicit conversation: "Sure is hot here, isn't it?"

8   But in discussing personal feelings or opinions, only the speaker normally has any way of knowing the correct answer. Sentences such as "I have a headache, don't I?" are clearly ridiculous. But there are other examples where it is the speaker's opinions, rather than perceptions, for which corroboration is sought, as in "The situation in Southeast

Asia is terrible, isn't it?"

9   While there are, of course, other possible interpretations of a
sentence like this, one possibility is that the speaker has a particular
answer in mind—"yes" or "no"—but is reluctant to state it baldly.
This sort of tag question is much more apt to be used by women than
by men in conversation. Why is this the case?

10   The tag question allows a speaker to avoid commitment, and
thereby avoid conflict with the addressee. The problem is that, by so
doing, speakers may also give the impression of not really being sure
of themselves, or looking to the addressee for confirmation of their
views. This uncertainty is reinforced in more subliminal ways, too.
There is a peculiar sentence intonation-pattern, used almost exclusively by women, as far as I know, which changes a declarative answer
into a question. The effect of using the rising inflection typical of a
yes-no question is to imply that the speaker is seeking confirmation,
even though the speaker is clearly the only one who has the requisite
information, which is why the question was put to her in the first
place:

> (Q) When will dinner be ready?
> (A) Oh. . . around six o'clock . . . .

It is as though the second speaker were saying, "Six o'clock—if that's
okay with you, if you agree." The person being addressed is put in the
position of having to provide confirmation. One likely consequence
of this sort of speech-pattern in a woman is that, often unbeknownst to
herself, the speaker builds a reputation of tentativeness, and others
will refrain from taking her seriously or trusting her with any real
responsibilities, since she "can't make up her mind," and "isn't sure of
herself."

11   Such idiosyncrasies may explain why women's language sounds
much more "polite" than men's. It is polite to leave a decision open,
not impose your mind, or views, or claims, on anyone else. So a tag
question is a kind of polite statement, in that it does not force agreement or belief on the addressee. In the same way a request is a polite
command, in that it does not force obedience on the addressee, but
rather suggests something be done as a favor to the speaker. A clearly
stated order implies a threat of certain consequences if it is not followed, and—even more impolite—implies that the speaker is in a
superior position and able to enforce the order. By couching wishes in

the form of a request, on the other hand, a speaker implies that if the request is not carried out, only the speaker will suffer; noncompliance cannot harm the addressee. So the decision is really left up to the addressee. The distinction becomes clear in these examples:

12   Close the door.

13   Please close the door.

14   Will you close the door?

15   Will you please close the door?

16   Won't you close the door?

17   In the same ways as words and speech patterns used *by* women undermine her image, those used to *describe* women make matters even worse. Often a word may be used of both men and women (and perhaps of things as well); but when it is applied to women, it assumes a special meaning that, by implication rather than outright assertion, is derogatory to women as a group.

18   The use of euphemisms has this effect. A euphemism is a substitute for a word that has acquired a bad connotation by association with something unpleasant or embarrassing. But almost as soon as the new word comes into common usage, it takes on the same old bad connotations, since feelings about the things or people referred to are not altered by a change of name; thus new euphemisms must be constantly found.

19   There is one euphemism for *woman* still very much alive. The word, of course is *lady*. *Lady* has a masculine counterpart, namely *gentleman*, occasionally shortened to *gent*. But for some reason *lady* is very much commoner than *gent(leman)*.

20   The decision to use *lady* rather than *woman* or vice versa, may considerably alter the sense of a sentence, as the following examples show:

> (a) A woman (lady) I know is a dean at Berkeley.
> (b) A woman (lady) I know makes amazing things out of shoelaces and old boxes.

21   The use of *lady* in (a) imparts a frivolous, or nonserious, tone to the sentence: the matter under discussion is not one of great moment. Similarly, in (b), using *lady* here would suggest that the speaker considered the "amazing things" not to be serious art, but merely a hobby or an aberration. If *woman* is used, she might be a serious sculptor. To say *lady doctor* is very condescending, since no one ever says *gentleman*

doctor or even *man doctor*. For example, mention in the San Francisco *Chronicle* of January 31, 1972, of Madalyn Murray O'Hair as the *lady atheist* reduces her position to that of scatterbrained eccentric. Even *woman atheist* is scarcely defensible: sex is irrelevant to her philosophical position.

22   Many women argue that, on the other hand, *lady* carries with it overtones recalling the age of chivalry: conferring exalted stature on the person so referred to. This makes the term seem polite at first, but we must also remember that these implications are perilous: they suggest that a "lady" is helpless, and cannot do things by herself.

23   *Lady* can also be used to infer frivolousness, as in titles of organizations. Those that have a serious purpose (not merely that of enabling "the ladies" to spend time with one another) cannot use the word *lady* in their titles, but less serious ones may. Compare the *Ladies' Auxiliary* of a men's group, or the *Thursday Evening Ladies' Browning and Garden Society* with *Ladies' Liberation* or *Ladies' Strike for Peace*.

24   What is curious about this split is that *lady* is in origin a euphemism—a substitute that puts a better face on something people find uncomfortable—for *woman*. What kind of euphemism is it that subtly denigrates the people to whom it refers? Perhaps *lady* functions as a euphemism for *woman* because it does not contain the sexual implications present in *woman:* it is not "embarrassing" in that way. If this is so, we may expect that, in the future, *lady* will replace woman as the primary word for the human female, since *woman* will have become too blatantly sexual. That this distinction is already made in some contexts at least is shown in the following examples, where you can try replacing *woman* with *lady:*

> (a) She's only twelve, but she's already a woman.
> (b) After ten years in jail, Harry wanted to find a woman.
> (c) She's my woman, see, so don't mess around with her.

25   Another common substitute for *woman* is *girl*. One seldom hears a man past the age of adolescence referred to as a boy, save in expressions like "going out with the boys," which are meant to suggest an air of adolescent frivolity and irresponsibility. But women of all ages are "girls": one can have a man—not a boy—Friday, but only a girl—never a woman or even a lady—Friday; women have girlfriends, but men do not—in a nonsexual sense—have boyfriends. It may be that this

use of *girl* is euphemistic in the same way the use of *lady* is: in stressing the idea of immaturity, it removes the sexual connotations lurking in *woman*. *Girl* brings to mind irresponsibility: you don't send a girl to do a woman's errand (or even, for that matter, a boy's errand). She is a person who is both too immature and too far from real life to be entrusted with responsibilities or with decisions of any serious or important nature.

26   Now let's take a pair of words which, in terms of the possible relationships in an earlier society, were simple male-female equivalents, analogous to *bull* : *cow*. Suppose we find that, for independent reasons, society has changed in such a way that the original meanings now are irrelevant. Yet the words have not been discarded, but have acquired new meanings, metaphorically related to their original senses. But suppose these new metaphorical uses are no longer parallel to each other. By seeing where the parallelism breaks down, we discover something about the different roles played by men and women in this culture. One good example of such a divergence through time is found in the pair, *master* : *mistress*. Once used with reference to one's power over servants, these words have become unusable today in their original master-servant sense as the relationship has become less prevalent in our society. But the words are still common.

27   Unless used with reference to animals, *master* now generally refers to a man who has acquired consummate ability in some field, normally nonsexual. But its feminine counterpart cannot be used this way. It is practically restricted to its sexual sense of "paramour." We start out with two terms, both roughly paraphrasable as "one who has power over another." But the masculine form, once one person is no longer able to have absolute power over another, becomes usable metaphorically in the sense of "having power over *something*." Master requires as its object only the name of some activity, something inanimate and abstract. But mistress requires a masculine noun in the possessive to precede it. One cannot say: "Rhonda is a mistress." One must be someone's mistress. A man is defined by what he does, a woman by her sexuality, that is, in terms of one particular aspect of her relationship to men. It is one thing to be an *old master* like Hans Holbein, and another to be an *old mistress*.

28   The same is true of the words *spinster* and *bachelor*—gender words for "one who is not married." The resemblance ends with the definition. While *bachelor* is a neuter term, often used as a com-

pliment, *spinster* normally is used pejoratively, with connotations of prissiness, fussiness, and so on. To be a bachelor implies that one has the choice of marrying or not, and this is what makes the idea of a bachelor existence attractive, in the popular literature. He has been pursued and has successfully eluded his pursuers. But a spinster is one who has not been pursued, or at least not seriously. She is old, unwanted goods. The metaphorical connotations of *bachelor* generally suggest sexual freedom; of *spinster,* puritanism or celibacy.

29   These examples could be multiplied. It is generally considered a *faux pas,* in society, to congratulate a woman on her engagement, while it is correct to congratulate her fiance. Why is this? The reason seems to be that it is impolite to remind people of things that may be uncomfortable to them. To congratulate a woman on her engagement is really to say, "Thank goodness! You had a close call!" For the man, on the other hand, there was no such danger. His choosing to marry is viewed as a good thing, but not something essential.

30   The linguistic double standard holds throughout the life of the relationship. After marriage, bachelor and spinster become man and wife, not man and woman. The woman whose husband dies remains "John's widow"; John, however, is never "Mary's widower."

31   Finally, why is it that salesclerks and others are so quick to call women customers "dear," "honey," and other terms of endearment they really have no business using? A male customer would never put up with it. But women, like children, are supposed to enjoy these endearments, rather than be offended by them.

32   In more ways than one, it's time to speak up.

Suggestions for Discussion and Writing

1. Many popular books now focus on the differences between men's and women's perceptions and language. Why do you think this is so? Is one sex more interested in this subject than the other? Why?

2. Is it true that women are more polite in speech than men are? Can you think of some examples that would prove or disprove this theory? Are there circumstances where men imitate women's speaking behaviors, or vice-versa? Why would people want to do this?

3. Is "You Are What You Say" an appropriate title for this

essay? If you had to choose an alternate title, what would you use, and why?

   4. Lakoff spends considerable time on the subject of tag questions. Do you or people you know use these questions? In what situations? Does your use agree with the profile Lakoff suggests?

   5. Lakoff lists colors as one of the areas in which women have a more expansive vocabulary than men. Can you think of other areas that fit this pattern? How about areas where men have a wider vocabulary than women? (You might want to survey friends, family, and classmates to gather material.) Based on your results, what can you say about the kinds of activities and interests our society expects each sex to have?

2 Stereotypes of Women

The picture our culture has painted of women has changed greatly iin the last two generations, and continues to evolve. This chapter presents five examinations of the stereotypes often associated with women. Pat Mainardi looks at the stereotypes of why women are 'better' at housework than men; K.C. Cole looks at the reasons why women may not succeed in math and science. Phyllis Schlafly presents a controversial contrast between Positive Women and feminists, and Anthony Burgess adds his comments on viragoes and women artists. Finally, James Dubik, a career Army officer, looks at how his perceptions of women have changed throughout his lifetime. As you read and consider these essays, ask, "Does my view of women match any of these? What do these views leave out? How is my view different from my parents' view of women? Do I have female heroes as well as male heroes?"

Pat Mainardi
Politics of Housework

PATRICIA MAINARDI, born in 1942, wrote her first
book about American quilts but is best known as an
influential art critic. She is especially interested in how
governments support or interfere with artists, their
works, and art expositions; her book *Art and Politics
of the Second Empire: The Universal Expositions of
1855 and 1867* (1987) is an excellent example of her
critical judgment at work. This essay first appeared in
Ms. Magazine.

> Though women do not complain of the power of husbands, each
> complains of her own husband, or of the husbands of her friends. It is
> the same in all other cases of servitude; at least in the commencement
> of the emancipatory movement. The serfs did not at first complain of
> the power of the lords, but only of their tyranny.
>
> JOHN STUART MILL
> *On the Subjection of Women*

Liberated women—very different from Women's Liberation!
The first signals all kinds of goodies, to warm the hearts (not to men-
tion other parts) of the most radical men. The other signals—
HOUSEWORK. The first brings sex without marriage, sex before
marriage, cozy housekeeping arrangements ("I'm living with this
chick") and the self-content of knowing that you're not the kind of
man who wants a doormat instead of a woman. That will come later.
After all, who wants that old commodity anymore, the Standard
American Housewife, all husband, home and kids? The New
Commodity, the Liberated Woman, has sex a lot and has a Career,
preferably something that can be fitted in with the household

chores—like dancing, pottery, or painting.

2   On the other hand is Women's Liberation—and housework. What? You say this is all trivial? Wonderful! That's what I thought. It seemed perfectly reasonable. We both had careers, both had to work a couple of days a week to earn enough to live on, so why shouldn't we share the housework? So I suggested it to my mate and he agreed—most men are too hip to turn you down flat. You're right, he said. It's only fair.

3   Then an interesting thing happened. I can only explain it by stating that we women have been brainwashed more than even we can imagine. Probably too many years of seeing television women in ecstasy over their shiny waxed floors or breaking down over their dirty shirt collars. Men have no such conditioning. They recognize the essential fact of housework right from the very beginning. Which is that it stinks.

4   Here's my list of dirty chores: buying groceries, carting them home and putting them away; cooking meals and washing dishes and pots; doing the laundry; digging out the place when things get out of control; washing floors. The list could go on but the sheer necessities are bad enough. All of us have to do these things, or get someone else to do them for us. The longer my husband contemplated these chores, the more repulsed he became, and so proceeded the change from the normally sweet, considerate Dr. Jekyll into the crafty Mr. Hyde who would stop at nothing to avoid the horrors of—housework. As he felt himself backed into a corner laden with dirty dishes, brooms, mops and reeking garbage, his front teeth grew longer and pointier, his fingernails haggled and his eyes grew wild. Housework trivial? Not on your life! Just try to share the burden.

5   So ensued a dialogue that's been going on for several years. Here are some of the high points:

6   "I don't mind sharing the housework, but I don't do it very well. We should each do the things we're best at." MEANING: Unfortunately I'm no good at things like washing dishes or cooking. What I do best is a little light carpentry, changing light bulbs, moving furniture (how often do you move furniture?). ALSO MEANING: Historically the lower classes (black men and us) have had hundreds of years experience doing menial jobs. It would be a waste of manpower to train someone else to do them now. ALSO MEANING: I don't like the dull, stupid, boring jobs, so you should do them.

7   "I don't mind sharing the work, but you'll have to show me how
to do it." MEANING: I ask a lot of questions and you'll have to show
me everything every time I do it because I don't remember so good.
Also don't try to sit down and read while I'M doing my jobs because
I'm going to annoy the hell out of you until it's easier to do them
yourself.

8   "We used to be so happy!" (Said whenever it was his turn to do
something.) MEANING: I used to be so happy. MEANING: Life without housework is bliss. No quarrel here. Perfect Agreement.

9   "We have different standards, and why should I have to work to
your standards? That's unfair." MEANING: If I begin to get bugged by
the dirt and crap I will say, "This place sure is a sty" or "How can anyone live like this?" and wait for your reaction. I know that all women
have a sore called "Guilt over a messy house" or "Household work is
ultimately my responsibility." I know that men have caused that sore—
if anyone visits and the place is a sty, they're not going to leave and say,
"He sure is a lousy housekeeper." You'll take the rap in any case. I can
outwait you. ALSO MEANING: I can provoke innumerable scenes over
the housework issue. Eventually doing all the housework yourself
will be less painful to you than trying to get me to do half. Or I'll
suggest we get a maid. She will do my share of the work. You will do
yours. It's women's work.

10   "I've got nothing against sharing the housework, but you can't
make me do it on your schedule." MEANING: Passive resistance. I'll
do it when I damned well please, if at all. If my job is doing dishes,
it's easier to do them once a week. If taking out laundry, once a month.
If washing the floors, once a year. If you don't like it, do it yourself
oftener, and then I won't do it at all.

11   "I hate it more than you. You don't mind it so much."
MEANING: Housework is garbage work. It's the worst crap I've ever
done. It's degrading and humiliating for someone of my intelligence
to do it. But for someone of your intelligence . . .

12   "Housework is too trivial to even talk about." MEANING: It's
even more trivial to do. Housework is beneath my status. My purpose
in life is to deal with matters of significance. Yours is to deal with
matters of insignificance. You should do the housework.

13   "This problem of housework is not a man-woman problem. In
any relationship between two people one is going to have a stronger
personality and dominate." MEANING: That stronger personality had

better be me.

14   "In animal societies, wolves, for example, the top animal is usually a male even where he is not chosen for brute strength but on the basis of cunning and intelligence. Isn't that interesting?" MEANING: I have historical, psychological, anthropological and biological justification for keeping you down. How can you ask the top wolf to be equal?

15   "Women's liberation isn't really a political movement." MEANING: The revolution is coming too close to home. ALSO MEANING: I am only interested in how I am oppressed, not how I oppress others. Therefore the war, the draft and the university are political. Women's liberation is not.

16   "Man's accomplishments have always depended on getting help from other people, mostly women. What great man would have accomplished what he did if he had to do his own housework?" MEANING: Oppression is built into the system and I, as the white American male, receive the benefits of this system. I don't want to give them up.

17   Participatory democracy begins at home. If you are planning to implement your politics, there are certain things to remember:

18   1. He *is* feeling it more than you. He's losing some leisure and you're gaining it. The measure of your oppression is his resistance.

19   2. A great many American men are not accustomed to doing monotonous, repetitive work which never issues in any lasting, let alone important, achievement. This is why they would rather repair a cabinet than wash dishes. If human endeavors are like a pyramid with man's highest achievements at the top, then keeping oneself alive is at the bottom. Men have always had servants (us) to take care of this bottom stratum of life while they have confined their efforts to the rarefied upper regions. It is thus ironic when they ask of women—Where are your great painters, statesmen, etc.? Mme. Matisse ran a millinery shop so he could paint. Mrs. Martin Luther King kept his house and raised his babies.

20   3. It is a traumatizing experience for someone who has always thought of himself as being against any oppression or exploitation of one human being by another to realize that in his daily life he has been accepting and implementing (and benefiting from) this exploitation; that his rationalization is little different from that of the racist who says, "Black people don't feel pain" (women don't mind

doing the shitwork); and that the oldest form of oppression in history has been the oppression of fifty percent of the population by the other fifty percent.

21   4. Arm yourself with some knowledge of the psychology of oppressed peoples everywhere, and a few facts about the animal kingdom. I admit playing top wolf or who runs the gorillas is silly but as a last resort men bring it up all the time. Talk about bees. If you feel really hostile bring up the sex life of spiders. They have sex. She bites off his head.

22   The psychology of oppressed peoples is not silly. Jews, immigrants, black men and all women have employed the same psychological mechanisms to survive: admiring the oppressor, glorifying the oppressor, wanting to be like the oppressor, wanting the oppressor to like them, mostly because the oppressor held all the power.

23   5. In a sense, all men everywhere are slightly schizoid—divorced from the reality of maintaining life. This makes it easier for them to play games with it. It is almost a cliche that women feel greater grief at sending a son off to a war or losing him to that war because they bore him, suckled him, and raised him. The men who foment those wars did none of those things and have a more superficial estimate of the worth of human life. One hour a day is a low estimate of the amount of time one has to spend "keeping" oneself. By foisting this off on others, man has seven hours a week—one working day more to play with his mind and not his human needs. Over the course of generations it is easy to see whence evolved the horrifying abstractions of modern life.

24   6. With the death of each form of oppression, life changes and new forms evolve. English aristocrats at the turn of the century were horrified at the idea of enfranchising working men—were sure that it signaled the death of civilization and a return to barbarism. Some working men were even deceived by this line. Similarly with the minimum wage, abolition of slavery, and female suffrage. Life changes but it goes on. Don't fall for any line about the death of everything if men take a turn at the dishes. They will imply that you are holding back the revolution (their revolution). But you are advancing it (your revolution).

25   7. Keep checking up. Periodically consider who's actually *doing* the jobs. These things have a way of backsliding so that a year later once again the woman is doing everything. After a year make a list of

jobs the man has rarely if ever done. You will find cleaning pots, toilets, refrigerators and ovens high on the list. Use time sheets if necessary. He will accuse you of being petty. He is above that sort of thing (housework). Bear in mind what the worst jobs are, namely the ones that have to be done every day or several times a day. Also the ones that are dirty—it's more pleasant to pick up books, newspapers, etc., than to wash dishes. Alternate the bad jobs. It's the daily grind that gets you down. Also make sure that you don't have the responsibility for the housework with occasional help from him. "I'll cook dinner for you tonight" implies it's really your job and isn't he a nice guy to do some of it for you.

26   8. Most men had a rich and rewarding bachelor life during which they did not starve or become encrusted with crud or buried under the litter. There is a taboo that says women mustn't strain themselves in the presence of men—we haul around 50 pounds of groceries if we have to but aren't allowed to open a jar if there is someone around to do it for us. The reverse side of the coin is that men aren't supposed to be able to take care of themselves without a woman. Both are excuses for making women do the housework.

27   9. Beware of the double whammy. He won't do the little things he always did because you're now a "Liberated Woman," right? Of course he won't do anything else either . . .

28   I was just finishing this when my husband came in and asked what I was doing. Writing a paper on housework. Housework? he said. *Housework?* Oh my god how trivial can you get? A paper on housework.

Suggestions for Discussion and Writing

1. Is it true that men have no conditioning to do housework? If you agree, why do you think that is so?

2. Mainardi gives examples of dialogues between her and her husband about housework, with "subtitles" interpreting the conversation. Do you agree with her interpretations? Can you suggest alternate interpretations for her husband's statements?

3. This essay is full of examples from Mainardi's personal experience. Do they strengthen or weaken her points? Why? Are all men and women like this couple?

4. Mainardi argues that housework is a political activity. Do you think she's right to insist on this definition? What "political" strategies does she use to reinforce her points?

5. Historically, have women always done all the housework? How has housework changed? You might want to interview older friends and relatives, or look in your library's card catalog under "Home Economics," "Home Appliances," and "Housewives."

✧ ✧ ✧

K. C. Cole

Women and Physics

K.C. COLE is a writer and journalist who attempts to make science accessible to lay audiences. She formerly served as an editor for *Saturday Review* and *Newsday*, and wrote a column on philosophy in science for *Discover*. Among her books are *Sympathetic Vibrations: Reflections on Physics as a Way of Life* (1984), a study of women and science; and several collections of essays. This essay was first published in 1981 in the *New York Times*.

I know few other women who do what I do. What I do is write about science, mainly physics. And to do that, I spend a lot of time reading about science, talking to scientists and struggling to understand physics. In fact, most of the women (and men) I know think me quite queer for actually liking physics. "How can you write about that stuff?" they ask, always somewhat askance. "I could never understand that in a million years." Or more simply, "I hate science."

2   I didn't realize what an odd creature a woman interested in physics was until a few years ago when a science magazine sent me to Johns Hopkins University in Baltimore for a conference on an electrical phenomenon known as the Hall effect. We sat in a huge lecture

hall and listened as physicists talked about things engineers didn't understand, and engineers talked about things physicists didn't understand. What I didn't understand was why, out of several hundred young students of physics and engineering in the room, less than a handful were women.

3   Some time later, I found myself at the California Institute of Technology reporting on the search for the origins of the universe. I interviewed physicist after physicist, man after man. I asked one young administrator why none of the physicists were women. And he answered: "I don't know, but I suppose it must be something innate. My 7-year-old daughter doesn't seem to be much interested in science."

4   It was with that experience fresh in my mind that I attended a conference in Cambridge, Massachusetts, on science literacy, or rather the worrisome lack of it in this country today. We three women—a science teacher, a young chemist and myself—sat surrounded by a company of august men. The chemist, I think first tentatively raised the issue of science illiteracy in women. It seemed like an obvious point. After all, everyone had agreed over and over again that scientific knowledge these days was a key factor in economic power. But as soon as she made the point, it became clear that we women had committed a grievous social error. Our genders were suddenly showing; we had interrupted the serious talk with a subject unforgivably silly.

5   For the first time, I stopped being puzzled about why there weren't any women in science and began to be angry. Because if science is a search for answers to fundamental questions then it hardly seems frivolous to find out why women are excluded. Never mind the economic consequences.

6   A lot of the reasons why women are excluded are spelled out by the Massachusetts Institute of Technology experimental physicist Vera Kistiakowsky in a recent article in *Physics Today* called "Women in Physics: Unnecessary, Injurious and Out of Place?" The title was taken from a 19th-century essay written in opposition to the appointment of a female mathematician to a professorship at the University of Stockholm. "As decidedly as two and two make four," a woman in mathematics is a "monstrosity," concluded the writer of the essay.

7   Dr. Kistiakowsky went on to discuss the factors that make women in science today, if not monstrosities, at least oddities. Contrary to much popular opinion, one of those is not an innate difference in the scientific ability of boys and girls. But early conditioning does play a

stubborn and subtle role. A recent Nova program, "The Pinks and the Blues," documented how girls and boys are treated differently from birth—the boys always encouraged in more physical kinds of play, more active explorations of their environments. Sheila Tobias, in her book, *Math Anxiety*, showed how the games boys play help them to develop an intuitive understanding of speed, motion and mass. The main sorting out of the girls from the boys in science seems to happen in junior high school. As a friend who teaches in a science museum said, "By the time we get to electricity, the boys already have had some experience with it. But it's unfamiliar to the girls." Science books draw on boys' experiences. "The examples are all about throwing a baseball at such and such a speed," said my step daughter, who barely escaped being a science drop-out.

8   The most obvious reason there are not many more women in science is that women are discriminated against as a class, in promotions, salaries and hirings, a conclusion reached by a recent analysis by the National Academy of Sciences.

9   Finally, said Dr. Kistiakowsky, women are simply made to feel out of place in science. Her conclusion was supported by a Ford Foundation study by Lynn H. Fox on the problems of women in mathematics. When students were asked to choose among six reasons accounting for girls lack of interest in math, the girls rated this statement second: "Men do not want girls in the mathematical occupations."

10   A friend of mine remembers winning a Bronxwide mathematics competition in the second grade. Her friends—both boys and girls—warned her that she shouldn't be good at math: "You'll never find a boy who likes you." My friend continued nevertheless to excel in math and science, won many awards during her years at the Bronx High School of Science, and then earned a full scholarship to Harvard. After one year of Harvard science, she decided to major in English.

11   When I asked her why, she mentioned what she called the "macho mores" of science. "It would have been O.K. if I'd had someone to talk to," she said. "But the rules of comportment were such that you never admitted you didn't understand. I later realized that even the boys didn't get everything clearly right away. You had to stick with it until it had time to sink in. But for the boys, there was a payoff in suffering through the hard times, and a kind of punishment—a shame—if they didn't. For the girls it was O.K. not to get it, and the only payoff for

sticking it out was that you'd be considered a freak."

12 Science is undeniably hard. Often, it can seem quite boring. It is unfortunately too often presented as laws to be memorized instead of mysteries to be explored. It is too often kept a secret that science, like art, takes a well developed esthetic sense. Women aren't the only ones who say, "I hate science." That's why everyone who goes into science needs a little help from friends. For the past ten years, I have been getting more than a little help from a friend who is a physicist. But my stepdaughter—who earned the highest grades ever recorded in her California high school on the math Scholastic Aptitude Test—flunked calculus in her first year at Harvard. When my friend the physicist heard about it, he said, "Harvard should be ashamed of itself."

13 What he meant was that she needed that little extra encouragement that makes all the difference. Instead, she got that little extra discouragement that makes all the difference. "In the first place, all the math teachers are men," she explained. "In the second place, when I met a boy I liked and told him I was taking chemistry, he immediately said: 'Oh, you're one of those science types.' In the third place, it's just a kind of social thing. The math clubs are full of boys and you don't feel comfortable joining."

14 In other words, she was made to feel unnecessary, and out of place.

15 A few months ago, I accompanied a male colleague from the science museum where I sometimes work to a lunch of the history of science faculty at the University of California. I was the only woman there, and my presence for the most part was obviously and rudely ignored. I was so surprised and hurt by this that I made an extra effort to speak knowledgeably and well. At the end of the lunch, one of the professors turned to me in all seriousness and said: "Well, K. C., what do the women think of Carl Sagan?" I replied that I had no idea what "the women" thought about anything. But now I know what I should have said: I should have told him that his comment was unnecessary, injurious and out of place.

Suggestions for Discussion and Writing

1. From your own experiences, do you believe that ability in science and math depends more on encouragement and education than inborn ability? What incidents from your own life

can you remember that support your opinion?

    2. What are the reasons Cole includes to support her thesis? What kinds of evidence does she use to back up those reasons? Do you find her argument convincing?

    3. Science and math are very precise, factual fields, and they rely on facts and data to draw conclusions. So why does Cole use personal narrative and anecdotes as the heart of her argument?

    4. Based on standardized test scores, while men excel at science and math, women excel in reading and writing. Can you think of reasons why they would outperform men in these school subjects?

    5. Look up some of the articles and books Cole mentions, and compare them to more recently-published research. What are the current beliefs as to why fewer women than men excel at science and math?

Phyllis Schlafly
Understanding the Difference

PHYLLIS SCHLAFLY (born in 1924) projects the image of a typical middle-class housewife, but her credentials are far from average: she has earned bachelor's, master's, law, and doctor of law degrees. Schlafly is one of the United States' most recognizable conservative voices, opposing the Equal Rights Amendment, pornography, and the destruction of the typical American family. A member of the Daughters of the American Revolution, she was named to the President's Defense Policy Advisory Group in 1980; her recent books include *Equal Pay for Unequal Work* (1984), *Who Will Rock the Cradle?* (1989), and *Stronger Families or Bigger Government* (1990). This essay is taken from her book *The Power of the Positive Woman* (1977).

The first requirement for the acquisition of power by the Positive Woman is to understand the differences between men and women. Your outlook on life, your faith, your behavior, your potential for fulfillment, all are determined by the parameters of your original premise. The Positive Woman starts with the assumption that the world is her oyster. She rejoices in the creative capability within her body and the power potential of her mind and spirit. She understands that men and women are different, and that those very differences provide the key to her success as a person and fulfillment as a woman.

2   The women's liberationist, on the other hand, is imprisoned by her own negative view of herself and of her place in the world around her. This view of women was most succinctly expressed in an advertisement designed by the principal women's liberationist organization, the National Organization for Women (NOW), and run in many magazines and newspapers and as spot announcements on many television stations. The advertisement showed a darling curlyheaded girl with the caption: "This healthy, normal baby has a handicap. She was born female."

3   This is the self-articulated dog-in-the-manger, chip-on-the-shoulder, fundamental dogma of women's liberation movement. Someone—it is not clear who, perhaps God, perhaps the "Establishment," perhaps a conspiracy of male chauvinist pigs—dealt women a foul blow by making them female. It becomes necessary, therefore, for women to agitate and demonstrate and hurl demands on society in order to wrest from an oppressive male-dominated social structure the status that has been wrongfully denied to women through the centuries.

4   By its very nature, therefore, the women's liberation movement precipitates a series of conflict situations—in the legislatures, in the courts, in the schools, in industry—with man targeted as the enemy. Confrontation replaces cooperation as the watchword of all relationships. Women and men become adversaries instead of partners.

5   The second dogma of the women's liberationists is that, of all the injustices perpetrated upon women through the centuries, the most oppressive is the cruel fact that women have babies and men do not. Within the confines of the women's liberationist ideology, therefore,

the abolition of this overriding inequality of women becomes the primary goal. This goal must be achieved at any and all costs—to the woman herself, to the baby, to the family, and to society. Women must be made equal to men in their ability *not* to become pregnant and *not* to be expected to care for babies they may bring into the world.

6   This is why women's liberationists are compulsively involved in the drive to make abortion and child-care centers for all women, regardless of religion or income, both socially acceptable and government-financed. Former Congresswoman Bella Abzug has defined the goal: "to enforce the constitutional right of females to terminate pregnancies that they do not wish to continue."

7   If man is targeted as the enemy, and the ultimate goal of women's liberation is independence from men and the avoidance of pregnancy and its consequences, then lesbianism is logically the highest form in the ritual of women's liberation. Many, such as Kate Millett, come to this conclusion, although many others do not.

8   The Positive Woman will never travel that dead-end road. It is self-evident to the Positive Woman that the female body with its baby-producing organs was not designed by a conspiracy of men but by the Divine Architect of the human race. Those who think it is unfair that women have babies, whereas men cannot, will have to take up their complaint with God because no other power is capable of changing that fundamental fact. On some college campuses, I have been assured that other methods of reproduction will be developed. But most of us must deal with the real world rather than with the imagination of dreamers.

9   Another feature of the woman's natural role is the obvious fact that women can breast-feed babies and men cannot. This functional role was not imposed by conspiratorial males seeking to burden women with confining chores, but must be recognized as part of the plan of the Divine Architect for the survival of the human race through the centuries and in the countries that know no pasteurization of milk or sterilization of bottles.

10   The Positive Woman looks upon her femaleness and her fertility as part of her purpose, her potential, and her power. She rejoices that she has a capability for creativity that men can never have.

11   The third basic dogma of the women's liberation movement is that there is no difference between male and female except the sex organs, and that all those physical, cognitive, and emotional differ-

ences you *think* are there, are merely the result of centuries of restraints imposed by a male-dominated society and sex-stereotyped schooling. The role imposed on women is, by definition, inferior, according to the women's liberationists.

12   The Positive Woman knows that, while there are some physical competitions in which women are better and can command more money than men, including those that put a premium on grace and beauty, such as figure skating, the superior physical strength of males over females in competitions of strength, speed, and short-term endurance is beyond rational dispute.

13   In the Olympic Games, women not only cannot win any medals in competition with men, the gulf between them is so great that they cannot even qualify for the contests with men. No amount of training from infancy can enable women to throw the discus as far as men, or to match men in push-ups or in lifting weights. In track and field events, individual male records surpass those of women by 10 to 20 percent.

14   Female swimmers today are beating Johnny Weissmuller's records, but today's male swimmers are better still. Chris Evert can never win a tennis match against Jimmy Connors. If we removed lady's tees from golf courses, women would be out of the game. Putting women in football or wrestling matches can only be an exercise in laughs.

15   The Olympic Games, whose rules require strict verification to ascertain that no male enters a female contest and, with his masculine advantage, unfairly captures a woman's medal, formerly insisted on a visual inspection of the contestants' bodies. Science, however, has discovered that men and women are so innately different physically that their maleness/femaleness can be conclusively established by means of a simple skin test of fully clothed persons.

16   If there is *anyone* who should oppose enforced sex-equality, it is the women athletes. Babe Didrickson, who played and defeated some of the great male athletes of her time, is unique in the history of sports.

17   If sex equality were enforced in professional sports, it would mean that men could enter the women's tournaments and win most of the money. Bobby Riggs has already threatened: "I think that men 55 years and over should be allowed to play women's tournaments—like the Virginia Slims. Everybody ought to know there's no sex after 55 anyway."

18   The Positive Woman remembers the essential validity of the old prayer: "Lord, give me the strength to change what I can change, the serenity to accept what I cannot change, and the wisdom to discern the difference." The women's liberationists are expending their time and energies erecting a make-believe world in which they hypothesize that *if* schooling were gender-free, and *if* the same money were spent on male and female sports programs, and *if* women were permitted to compete on equal terms, *then* they would prove themselves to be physically equal. Meanwhile, the Positive Woman has put the ineradicable physical differences into her mental computer, programmed her plan of action, and is already on the way to personal achievement.

19   Thus, while some militant women spend their time demanding more money for professional sports, ice skater Janet Lynn, a truly Positive Woman, quietly signed the most profitable financial contract in the history of women's athletics. It was not the strident demands of the women's liberationists that brought high prizes to women's tennis but the discovery by sports promoters that beautiful female legs gracefully moving around the court made women's tennis a highly marketable television production to delight male audiences.

20   Many people thought that the remarkable filly named Ruffian would prove that a female race horse could compete equally with a male. Even with the handicap of extra weights placed on the male horse, the race was a disaster for the female. The gallant Ruffian gave her all in a noble effort to compete, but broke a leg in the race and, despite the immediate attention of top veterinarians, had to be put away.

21   Despite the claims of the women's liberation movement, there are countless physical differences between men and women. The female body is 50 to 60 percent water, the male 60 to 70 percent water, which explains why males can dilute alcohol better than women and delay its effect. The average woman is about 25 percent fatty tissue, while the male is 15 percent, making women more buoyant in water and able to swim with less effort. Males have a tendency to color blindness. Only 5 percent of persons who get gout are female. Boys are born bigger. Women live longer in most countries of the world, not only in the United States where we have a hard-driving competitive pace. Women excel in manual dexterity, verbal skills, and memory recall.

22   Arianna Stassinopoulos in her book *The Female Woman* has done a good job of spelling out the many specific physical differences

that are so innate and so all-pervasive that

> even if Women's Lib was given a hundred, a thousand, ten thousand years in which to eradicate all the differences between the sexes, it would still be an impossible undertaking . . .
>
> It is inconceivable that millions of years of evolutionary selection during a period of marked sexual division of labor have not left pronounced traces on the innate character of men and women. Aggressiveness, and mechanical and spatial skills, a sense of direction, and physical strength—all masculine characteristics—are the qualities essential for a hunter; even food gatherers need these same qualities for defense and exploration. The prolonged period of dependence of human children, the difficulty of carrying the peculiarly heavy and inert human baby—a much heavier, clumsier burden than the monkey infant and much less able to cling on for safety—meant that women could not both look after their children and be hunters and explorers. Early humans learned to take advantage of this period of dependence to transmit rules, knowledge and skills to their offspring—women needed to develop verbal skills, a talent for personal relationships, and a predilection for nurturing going even beyond the maternal instinct.

23   Does the physical advantage of men doom women to a life of servility and subservience? The Positive Woman knows that she has a complementary advantage which is at least as great—and, in the hands of a skillful woman, far greater. The Divine Architect who gave men a superior strength to lift weights also gave women a different kind of superior strength.

24   The women's liberationists and their dupes who try to tell each other that the sexual drive of men and women is really the same, and that it is only societal restraints that inhibit women from an equal desire, an equal enjoyment, and an equal freedom from the consequences, are doomed to frustration forever. It just isn't so, and pretending cannot make it so. The differences are not a woman's weakness but her strength.

25   Dr. Robert Collins, who has had ten years' experience in listening to and advising young women at a large eastern university, put his finger on the reason why casual "sexual activity" is such a cheat on women:

> A basic flaw in this new morality is the assumption that males and females are the same sexually. The simplicity of the male anatomy and its operation suggest that to a man, sex can be an activity apart from

his whole being, a drive related to the organs themselves.

In a woman, the complex internal organization, correlated with her other hormonal systems, indicates her sexuality must involve her total self. On the other hand, the man is orgasm-oriented with a drive that ignores most other aspects of the relationship. The woman is almost totally different. She is engulfed in romanticism and tries to find and express her total feelings for her partner.

A study at a midwestern school shows that 80 percent of the women who had intercourse hoped to marry their partner. Only 12 percent of the men expected the same.

Women say that soft, warm promises and tender touches are delightful, but that the act itself usually leads to a "Is that all there is to it?" reaction . . .

[A typical reaction is]: "It sure wasn't worth it. It was no fun at the time. I've been worried ever since. . . ."

The new morality is a fad. It ignores history, it denies the physical and mental compositions of human beings, it is intolerant, exploitative, and is oriented toward intercourse, not love.

26   The new generation can brag all it wants about the new liberation of the new morality, but it is still the woman who is hurt most. The new morality isn't just a "fad"—it is a cheat and a thief. It robs the woman of her virtue, her youth, her beauty, and her love—for nothing, just nothing. It has produced a generation of young women searching for their identity, bored with sexual freedom, and despondent from the loneliness of living a life without commitment. They have abandoned the old commandments, but they can't find any new rules that work.

27   The Positive Woman recognizes the fact that, when it comes to sex, women are simply not the equal of men. The sexual drive of men is much stronger than that of women. That is how the human race was designed in order that it might perpetuate itself. The other side of the coin is that it is easier for women to control their sexual appetites. A Positive Woman cannot defeat a man in a wrestling or boxing match, but she can motivate him, inspire him, encourage him, teach him, restrain him, reward him, and have power over him that he can never achieve over her with all his muscle. How or whether a Positive Woman uses her power is determined solely by the way she alone defines her goals and develops her skills.

28   The differences between men and women are also emotional and psychological. Without woman's innate maternal instinct, the human

race would have died out centuries ago. There is nothing so helpless in all earthly life as the newborn infant. It will die within hours if not cared for. Even in the most primitive, uneducated societies, women have always cared for their newborn babies. They didn't need any schooling to teach them how. They didn't need any welfare workers to tell them it is their social obligation. Even in societies to whom such concepts as "ought," "social responsibility," and "compassion for the helpless" were unknown, mothers cared for their new babies.

29   Why? Because caring for a baby serves the natural maternal need of a woman. Although not nearly so total as the baby's need, the woman's need is nonetheless real.

30   The overriding psychological need of a woman is to love something alive. A baby fulfills this need in the lives of most women. If a baby is not available to fill that need, women search for a baby-substitute. This is the reason why women have traditionally gone into teaching and nursing careers. They are doing what comes naturally to the female psyche. The schoolchild or the patient of any age provides an outlet for woman to express her natural maternal need.

31   This maternal need in women is the reason why mothers whose children have grown up and flown from the nest are sometimes cut loose from their psychological moorings. The maternal need in women can show itself in love for grandchildren, nieces, nephews, or even neighbors' children. The maternal need in some women has even manifested itself in an extraordinary affection lavished on a dog, a cat or a parakeet.

32   This is not to say that every woman must have a baby in order to be fulfilled. But it is to say that fulfillment for most women involves expressing their natural maternal urge by loving and caring for someone.

33   The women's liberation movement complains that traditional stereotyped roles assume that women are "passive" and that men are "aggressive." The anomaly is that a woman's most fundamental emotional need is not passive at all, but active. A woman naturally seeks to love affirmatively and to show that love in an active way by caring for the object of her affections.

34   The Positive Woman finds somebody on whom she can lavish her maternal love so that it doesn't well up inside her and cause psychological frustrations. Surely no woman is so isolated by geography or insulated by spirit that she cannot find someone worthy of her

maternal love. All persons, men and women, gain by sharing something of themselves with their fellow humans, but women profit most of all because it is part of their very nature.

35   One of the strangest quirks of women's liberationists is their complaint that societal restraints prevent men from crying in public or showing their emotions, but permit women to do so, and that therefore we should "liberate" men to enable them, too, to cry in public. The public display of fear, sorrow, anger, and irritation reveals a lack of self-discipline that should be avoided by the Positive Woman just as much as by the Positive Man. Maternal love, however, is not a weakness but a manifestation of strength and service, and it should be nurtured by the Positive Woman.

36   Most women's organizations, recognizing the preference of most women to avoid hard-driving competition, handle the matter of succession of officers by the device of a nominating committee. This eliminates the unpleasantness and the tension of a competitive confrontation every year or two. Many women's organizations customarily use a prayer attributed to Mary, Queen of Scots, which is an excellent analysis by a woman of women's faults:

> Keep us, O God, from pettiness; let us be large in thought, in word, in deed. Let us be done with fault-finding and leave off self-seeking . . . Grant that we may realize it is the little things that create differences, that in the big things of life we are at one.

37   Another silliness of the women's liberationists is their frenetic desire to force all women to accept the title *Ms* in place of *Miss* or *Mrs.* If Gloria Steinem and Betty Friedan want to call themselves *Ms* in order to conceal their marital status, their wishes should be respected.

38   But that doesn't satisfy the women's liberationists. They want all women to be compelled to use *Ms* whether they like it or not. The women's liberation movement has been waging a persistent campaign to browbeat the media into using *Ms* as the standard title for all women. The women's liberationists have already succeeding in getting the Department of Health, Education and Welfare to forbid schools and colleges from identifying women students as *Miss* or *Mrs.*

39   All polls show that the majority of women do not care to be called *Ms.* A Roper poll indicated that 81 percent of the women questioned said they prefer *Miss* or *Mrs.* to *Ms.* Most married women feel

they worked hard for the r in their names, and they don't care to be gratuitously deprived of it. Most single women don't care to have their name changed to an unfamiliar title that at best conveys overtones of feminist ideology and is polemical in meaning, and at worst connotes misery instead of joy. Thus, Kate Smith, a very Positive Woman, proudly proclaimed on television that she is "Miss Kate Smith, not Ms." Like other Positive Women, she has been succeeding while negative women have been complaining.

40   Finally, women are different from men in dealing with the fundamentals of life itself. Men are philosophers, women are practical, and 'twas ever thus. Men may philosophize about how life began and where we are heading; women are concerned about feeding the kids today. No woman would ever, as Karl Marx did, spend years reading political philosophy in the British Museum while her child starved to death. Women don't take naturally to a search for the intangible and the abstract. The Positive Woman knows who she is and where she is going, and she will reach her goal because the longest journey starts with a very practical first step.

41   Amaury de Riencourt, in his book *Sex and Power in History*, shows that a successful society depends on a delicate balancing of male and female factors, and that the women's liberation movement, which promotes unisexual values and androgyny, contains within it "a social and cultural death wish and the end of the civilization that endorses it."

42   One of the few scholarly works dealing with woman's role, *Sex and Power in History* synthesizes research from a variety of disciplines—sociology, biology, history, anthropology, religion, philosophy, and psychology. De Riencourt traces distinguishable types of women in different periods in history, from prehistoric to modern times. The "liberated" Roman matron, who is most similar to the present-day feminist, helped bring about the fall of Rome through her unnatural emulation of masculine qualities, which resulted in a large-scale breakdown of the family and ultimately of the empire.

43   De Riencourt examines the fundamental, inherent differences between men and women. He argues that man is the more aggressive, rational, mentally creative, analytical-minded sex because of his early biological role as hunter and provider. Woman, on the other hand, represents stability, flexibility, reliance on intuition, and harmony with nature, stemming from her procreative function.

44   Where man is discursive, logical, abstract, or philosophical, woman tends to be emotional, personal, practical, or mystical. Each set of qualities is vital and complements the other. Among the many differences explained in de Riencourt's book are the following:

> Women tend more toward conformity than men—which is why they often excel in such disciplines as spelling and punctuation where there is only one correct answer, determined by social authority. Higher intellectual activities, however, require a mental independence and power of abstraction that they usually lack, not to mention a certain form of aggressive boldness of the imagination which can only exist in a sex that is basically aggressive for biological reasons.
>
>   To sum up: The masculine proclivity in problem solving is analytical and categorical; the feminine, synthetic and contextual. . . Deep down, man tends to focus on the object, on external results and achievements; woman focuses on subjective motives and feelings. If life can be compared to a play, man focuses on the theme and structure of the play, woman on the innermost feelings displayed by the actors.

45   De Riencourt provides impressive refutation of two of the basic errors of the women's liberation movement: (1) that there are no emotional or cognitive differences between the sexes, and (2) that women should strive to be like men.

46   A more colloquial way of expressing the de Riencourt conclusion that men are more analytical and women more personal and practical is in the different answers that one is likely to get to the question, "Where did you get that steak?" A man will reply, "At the corner market," or wherever he bought it. A woman will usually answer, "Why? What's the matter with it?"

47   An effort to eliminate the differences by social engineering or legislative or constitutional tinkering cannot succeed, which is fortunate, but social relationships and spiritual values can be ruptured in the attempt. Thus the role reversals being forced upon high school students, under which guidance counselors urge reluctant girls to take "shop" and boys to take "home economics," further confuse a generation already unsure about its identity. They are as wrong as efforts to make a left-handed child right-handed.

Suggestions for Discussion and Writing

    1. Schlafly's essay provokes either violent admiration or

violent opposition from its readers. Do you think she is making a serious argument, or just trying to provoke responses. What stylistic elements of her writing make readers react in such a way?

2. In Schlafly's world-view, there are only two kinds of women: positive women and feminists. Does this absolute division work? Are there any kinds of women she leaves out?

3. Look carefully at the examples Schlafly uses to support her argument. Are these biased or neutral witnesses? What is the effect of their inclusion on you as readers?

4. How does Schlafly define feminism? Do you think this is an accurate definition? If you would modify her definition, how would you do so?

5. Schlafly's argument about sports is a provocative one. Research the background of the "physical strength" argument. Do you believe it has merit? Are the Olympics, or figure skaters, accurate models for the roles sports and athletes play in our culture? What happens in Olympic sports (for example equestrianism, sailing, riflery, archery) where men and women compete as equals?

Anthony Burgess
Grunts from a Sexist Pig

ANTHONY BURGESS, born in England in 1917, began writing novels in his early forties after service in the Army and English-teaching stints for the British Colonial Service in Gibraltar, Malaysia, and Borneo. He loves to play language games, filling his books with punning and quibbles on the meanings of words; the only three authors he claims to admire are Shakespeare, James Joyce, and Vladimir Nabokov. The author of *A Clockwork Orange*, he wrote in the magazine *Modern Fiction Studies* (1981) that "language is extremely dangerous. (It) probably bears no relation to ultimate reality. It's a ritual making device. It's a ritual making *process*." This essay is taken from his collection *But Do Blondes Prefer Gentlemen?* (1986).

Cleaning out my son's bedroom the other day (he has gone to Paris to work as an apprentice fish chef in the all-male kitchens of Le Fouquet) I came across a partly eaten pig in pink marzipan. It had come, apparently, in the Christmas mail and was so ill-wrapped that neither its provenance nor purpose was apparent. My son thought it was an eccentric gift from one of his friends. Now, quite by chance, I discover (a matter of an old *Punch* in a thanatologist's waiting room) that it was a trophy sent by the Female Publishers of Great Britain to myself as one of the Sexist Pigs of the year. I forget who the others were, but I think one of them published a picture book on the beauty of the female breast. What my own sin against woman was I am not sure, but I'm told that it may have been a published objection to the name the Virago Press (women publishers publishing women) had chosen for itself.

2   Now all my dictionaries tell me that a virago is a noisy, violent, ill-tempered woman, a scold or a shrew. There is, true, an archaic meaning which makes a virago a kind of amazon, a woman strong, brave and warlike. But the etymology insists on a derivation from Latin *vir*, a man, and no amount of semantic twisting can force the word into a meaning which denotes intrinsic female virtues as opposed to ones borrowed from the other sex. I think it was a silly piece of naming, and it damages what is a brave and valuable venture. The Virago Press has earned my unassailable gratitude for reprinting the *Pilgrimage* of Dorothy Richardson, and I said so publicly. But I get from its warlike officers only a rude and stupid insult, and I cannot laugh it off. Women should not behave like that, nor men either.

3   It has already been said, perhaps too often, that militant organizations pleading the rights of the supposedly oppressed—blacks, homosexuals, women—begin with reason but soon fly from it. On this basic level of language they claim the right to distort words to their own ends. I object to the delimitation of "gay." American blacks are not the only blacks in the world: the Tamils of India and Sri Lanka are far blacker. "Chauvinistic" stands for excessive patriotism

and not for other kinds of sectional arrogance. "Pig" is an abusive word which libels a clean and tasty animal: it is silly, and it can be ignored. But "sexist" is intended to have a precise meaning, and, on learning that I was a sexist pig, I felt it necessary to start thinking about the term.

4   As far as I can make out, one *ought* to be a sexist if one preaches or practises discrimination of any kind towards members of the other sex. In practice, a sexist is always male, and his sexism consists in his unwillingness to accept the world view of women in one or other or several or all of its aspects. This means, in my instance, that if I will not accept the meaning the Virago Press imposes on its chosen name, I qualify, by feminist logic, for the pink pig. But I cannot really believe it is as simple as that. The feminists must have other things against me but none of them will speak out and say what they are.

5   In the *Harvard Guide to Contemporary American Writing*, Elizabeth Janeway, discussing women's literature, considers a book by Mary Ellmann called *Thinking About Women*. She says: "It is worth being reminded of how widespread and how respectable has been the unquestioned assumption of women's inevitable, innate, and significant 'otherness,' and Ellmann here collects utterances on the subject not only from those we might expect (Norman Mailer, Leslie Fiedler, Anthony Burgess) but from Robert Lowell, Malamud, Beckett, and Reinhold Niebuhr." Note both the vagueness and the obliqueness. There can be no vaguer word in the world than "otherness." The vagueness is a weapon. Since it is not defined, the term "otherness" can mean whatever its users wish, rather like "virago." The position of people like Mailer and Burgess and Fiedler vis-a-vis this "otherness" does not have to be defined either: we have an intuitive knowledge of their qualities, and, between women, no more need be said.

6   That women are "other," meaning different from men, is one of the great maxims of the feminists. They are biologically different, think and feel differently. But men must not say so, for with men the notion of difference implies a value judgement: women are not like us, therefore they must be inferior to us. I myself have never said or written or even thought this. What I am prepared to see as a virtue in myself (as also in Mailer and Fiedler and other pigs) is—because of the feminist insistence on this damnable otherness—automatically transformed by such women as read me into a vice. I mean the fact that

I admire women, love the qualities in them that are different from my own male ones, but will not be seduced by their magic into accepting their values in areas where only neutral values should apply. Here, of course, the trouble lies. Women don't believe there are neutral zones: what males call neutral they call male.

7   I believe, for instance, that in matters of art we are in a zone where judgements have nothing to do with sex. In considering the first book the Virago Press brought out—the masterpiece of Dorothy Richardson—I did not say that here we had a great work of women's literature, but rather here we had a great work which anticipated some of the innovations of James Joyce. I should have stressed that this was a work by a woman, and the womanly aspect of the thing didn't seem to me to be important. I believe that the sex of an author is irrelevant, because any good writer contains both sexes. But what we are hearing a lot of now, especially in American colleges, is the heresy that *Madame Bovary* and *Anna Karenina* can't be good portraits of women because they were written by men. These are not aesthetic judgements: they are based on an a priori position which refuses to be modified by looking at the facts. The feminists just don't want men to be able to understand women. On the other hand, women are quite sure that they understand men, and nobody finds fault with the male creations of the Brontës or of Jane Austen.

8   Let's get out of literature and into life. I think I am quite capable of seeing the feminist point of view with regard to men's sexual attitude to women. I am strongly aware of the biological polarity, and it intrudes where women say it shouldn't. I am incapable of having *neutral* dealings with a woman. Consulting a woman doctor or lawyer, shaking hands with a woman prime minister, listening to a sermon by a woman minister of religion, I cannot help letting the daydream of a possible sexual relationship intrude. That this diminishes the woman in question I cannot deny. It depersonalizes her, since the whole sexual process necessarily involves depersonalization: this is nature's fault, not man's. Women object to their reduction into "sex objects," but this is what nature decrees when the erotic process gets to work. While writing this I am intermittently watching a most ravishing lady on French television. She is talking about Kirkegaard, but I am not taking much of that in. Aware of her charms as she must be, she ought to do what that beautiful lady professor of mathematics did at the University of Bologna in the Middle Ages—talk from behind a

screen, meaning talk on the radio. But then the voice itself, a potent sex signal, would get in the way.

9   This awareness of the sexual power of women, I confess, induces attitudes which àre, from the feminist angle, unworthy. At Brown's Hotel a woman porter proposed carrying my bags upstairs. It was her job, she said, but I could not let her do it. Old as I am, I still give up my seat to women far younger when on a bus or tube train. This is a protective tenderness wholly biological in origin. How can I apologize for it when it is built into my glands? Women are traditionally (but this is, I admit, possibly a man-imposed tradition) slower to be sexually moved than are men, and this enables them to maintain a neutral relationship with the other sex in offices and consulting rooms.

10   I believe what women tell me to believe—namely, that they can do anything men can do except impregnate and carry heavy loads (though this latter was contradicted by the girl at Brown's Hotel). Nevertheless, I have to carry this belief against weighty evidence to the contrary. Take music, for instance. Women have never been denied professional musical instruction—indeed, they used to be encouraged to have it—but they have not yet produced a Mozart or a Beethoven. I am told by feminists that all this will change some day, when women have learned how to create like women composers, a thing men have prevented their doing in the past. This seems to me to be nonsense, and it would be denied by composers like Thea Musgrave and the shade of the late Dame Ethel Smyth (a great feminist herself, the composer of *The March of the Women* as well as *The Wreckers* and *The Prison*, which the liberationists ought to do something about reviving). I believe that artistic creativity is a male surrogate for biological creativity, and that if women do so well in literature it may be that literature is, as Mary McCarthy said, closer to gossip than to art. But no one will be happier than I to see women produce the greatest art of all time, so long as women themselves recognize that the art is more important than the artist.

11   I see that most, if not all, of what I say above is likely to cause feminist rage and encourage further orders to pink-pig manufacturers (did the Virago Press search for a *woman* confectioner?). But, wearily, I recognize that anything a man says is liable to provoke womanly hostility in these bad and irrational times. A man, by his very nature, is incapable of saying the right thing to a woman unless he indues the

drag of hypocrisy. Freud, bewildered, said: "What does a woman *want*?" I don't think, despite the writings of Simone de Beauvoir, Caroline Bird, Sara Evans, Betty Friedan, Germaine Greer, Elizabeth Janeway, Kate Millett, Juliet Mitchell, Sarah B. Pomeroy, Marian Ramelson, Alice Rossi, Sheila Rowbotham, Dora Russell, Edith Thomas, Mary Wollstonecraft and the great Virginia herself, the question has yet been answered, except negatively. What women *don't* want is clear—their subjection to the patriarchal image, male sexual exploitation, and all the rest of it. When positive programmes emerge—like the proposed "desexualization" of language—we men have an uneasy intimation of the possible absurdity of the whole militant movement. I refuse to say Ms, which is not a real vocable, and I object to "chairperson" and the substitution of "ovarimony" for "testimony". And I maintain (a) that a virago is a detestable kind of woman and (b) that feminist militancy should not condone bad manners. If that pink pig had not been thrown in the garbage bin I should tell the women publishers of Britain what to do with it.

Suggestions for Discussion and Writing

1. Why do you think Virago Press chose its name? Do you think Burgess' objections to the name of the press are valid? Does it matter what a publishing house is called?

2. Is there such a thing as a female chauvinist sow? What might her characteristics be? Do you think Burgess' definition of such a person might differ from yours? How?

3. Burgess objects that a critic uses "vagueness" as a weapon. Are there any words or language strategies that he uses as weapons? Is there anything wrong with using words as weapons?

4. Burgess' interpretations of several words rely very strongly on their roots and original meanings in foreign languages. Is he right to use such a strict interpretation? Can words change meaning? Is it possible for a negative word like *virago* to acquire some positive meanings? Can you think of other examples where this might have happened?

5. Is it true that men always think about sex when they are dealing with a woman? Can you find any research or evidence to prove or disprove Burgess' claims?

James M. Dubik
An Officer and a Feminist

JAMES M. DUBIK was a major in the U.S. Army and stationed in Savannah, Georgia, when he wrote this essay for *Newsweek* in 1987. The Rangers are the Army's elite fighting force, front line troops specializing in jungle warfare and airborne attacks. To qualify for the Rangers, a soldier must have excellent performance ratings in the regular Army, pass a difficult screening process, and endure long periods of additional intensive training. The Rangers played an important and distinguished role in Operation Desert Storm. Since they are a combat unit, U.S. law allows the Rangers to exclude women as members.

I'm a member of a last bastion of male chauvinism. I'm an infantry officer, and there are no women in the infantry. I'm a Ranger and no women go to Ranger School. I'm a member of America's special-operation forces—and there, although women are involved in intelligence, planning and clerical work, only men can be operators, or "shooters." Women can become paratroopers and jump out of airplanes alongside me—yet not many do. All this is as it should be, according to what I learned while growing up.

2   Not many women I knew in high school and college in the '60s and early '70s pushed themselves to their physical or mental limits or had serious career dreams of their own. If they did, few talked about them. So I concluded they were exceptions to the rule. Then two things happened. First, I was assigned to West Point, where I became a philosophy instructor. Second, my two daughters grew up.

3   I arrived at the Academy with a master's degree from Johns Hopkins University in Baltimore and a graduation certificate from the U.S. Army Command and General Staff College at Fort

Leavenworth. I was ready to teach, but instead, I was the one who got an education.

4   The women cadets, in the classroom and out, did not fit my stereotype of female behavior. They took themselves and their futures seriously. They persevered in a very competitive environment. Often they took charge and seized control of a situation. They gave orders; they were punctual and organized. They played sports hard. They survived, even thrived, under real pressure. During field exercises, women cadets were calm and unemotional even when they were dirty, cold, wet, tired and hungry. They didn't fold or give up.

5   Most important, such conduct seemed natural to them. From my perspective all this was extraordinary; to them it was ordinary. While I had read a good bit of "feminist literature" and, intellectually, accepted many of the arguments against stereotyping, this was the first time my real-life experience supported such ideas. And seeing is believing.

6   Enter two daughters: Kerith, 12; Katie, 10.

7   Kerith and Katie read a lot, and they write, too—poems, stories, paragraphs and answers to "thought questions" in school. In what they read and in what they write, I can see their adventurousness, their inquisitiveness and their ambition. They discover clues and solve mysteries. They take risks, brave dangers, fight villains—and prevail. Their schoolwork reveals their pride in themselves. Their taste for reading is boundless; they're interested in everything. "Why?" is forever on their lips. Their eyes are set on personal goals that they, as individuals, aspire to achieve: Olympic gold, owning their own business, public office.

8   Both play sports. I've witnessed a wholesome, aggressive, competitive spirit born in Kerith. She played her first basketball season last year, and when she started, she was too polite to bump anyone, too nice to steal anything, especially if some other girl already had the ball. By the end of the season, however, Kerith was taking bumps and dishing them out. She plays softball with the intensity of a Baltimore Oriole. She rides and jumps her horse in competitive shows. Now she "can't imagine" not playing a sport, especially one that didn't have a little rough play and risk.

9   In Katie's face, I've seen Olympic intensity as she passed a runner in the last 50 yards of a mile relay. Gasping for air, knees shaking, lungs bursting, she dipped into her well of courage and "gutted out" a

final kick. Her comment after the race: "I kept thinking I was Mary Decker beating the Russians." For the first time she experienced the thrill of pushing herself to the limit. She rides and jumps, too. And her basketball team was a tournament champion. The joy and excitement and pride that shone in the eyes of each member of the team was equal to that in any NCAA winner's locker room. To each sport Katie brings her dedication to doing her best, her drive to excel and her desire to win.

10   Both girls are learning lessons that, when my wife and I were their age, were encouraged only in boys. Fame, aggressiveness, achievement, self-confidence—these were territories into which very few women (the exception, not the rule) dared enter. Kerith and Katie, most of their friends, many of their generation and the generations to come are redefining the social game. Their lives contradict the stereotypes with which I grew up. Many of the characteristics I thought were "male" are, in fact, "human." Given a chance, anyone can, and will, acquire them.

11   My daughters and the girls of their generation are lucky. They receive a lot of institutional support not available to women of past generations: from women executives, women athletes, women authors, women politicians, women adventurers, women Olympians. Old categories, old stereotypes and old territories don't fit the current generation of young women; and they won't fit the next generation, either. As Kerith said, "I can't even imagine not being allowed to do something or be something just because I am a girl."

12   All this does not negate what I knew to be true during my own high-school and college years. But what I've learned from both the women cadets at West Point and from my daughters supports a different conclusion about today's women and the women of tomorrow from the beliefs I was raised with. Ultimately we will be compelled to align our social and political institutions with what is already becoming a fact of American life. Or more precisely, whenever biological difference is used to segregate a person from an area of human endeavor, we will be required to demonstrate that biological difference is relevant to the issue at hand.

Suggestions for Discussion and Writing

1. Dubik begins by listing his own background and training

to explain his attitudes about women. What effect does this have on your reading of the essay?

2. Dubik's two daughters, Katie and Kerith, have led him to redefine some of his conclusions about "male" characteristics. Why?

3. Dubik gives more detail about his own daughters than he does about the female West Point cadets. Why do you think he made this choice? Would more examples of how the women soldiers performed have led you, or him, to different conclusions?

4. The last two sentences of Dubik's essay make predictions about how our society may have to change its perception of gender roles. Do you agree with his predictions? Do you see any evidence that they are happening?

5. In the wake of the Persian Gulf War, there has been renewed debate as to what roles women should be allowed to play in the military. In the Gulf, women served near the front lines, were captured by the enemy, and died in battle. Research the current regulations involving women in combat. Should women be allowed to perform all roles? Should exceptions be made for mothers? Does the United States' policy on women in the military match the policies used in other countries?

3 Stereotypes of Men

"Manhood" is an item in vogue in conversations these days, as the new Men's Movement evolves and men explore what it means in our culture to be a man. (You can tell how popular the subject is: it's been satirized on *Murphy Brown*, *Cheers*, *In Living Color*, and *Saturday Night Live*, and discussed seriously on all the talk shows.) In these essays, four distinguished American writers reflect on the various aspects of manhood in our society, reaching very different conclusions. Paul Theroux begins by identifying the problems our society has in defining manhood. Mark Gerzon examines the difficulties faced by boys in becoming men. Wallace Stegner describes the idea of manhood promoted in the American West, and John McMurtry looks at football and war, and how these shape our ideas of manhood. As you read and consider these essays, ask, "How do I define manhood? Should I change my definition in any way? Why? Who is my role model of the ideal man?"

Paul Theroux
Being a Man

PAUL THEROUX was born in Massachusetts in 1941,
but has lived abroad a great part of his life. A novelist, essayist, and noted travel writer, he offers a
mildly ironic look at what happens to people when
they are taken out of their native environments. This
essay is taken from *Sunrise With Seamonsters: Travels
and Discoveries 1964-1984*; here his irony is trained
on his own culture. Among his many books are
Riding the Iron Rooster (1988), *Travelling the World*
(1990), *Chicago Loop* (1990), *To the Ends of the Earth*
(1991), and *The Happy Isle of Oceania* (1992).

There is a pathetic sentence in the chapter "Fetishism" in Dr.
Norman Cameron's book *Personality Development and
Psychopathology*. It goes, "Fetishists are nearly always men; and their
commonest fetish is a woman's shoe." I cannot read that sentence without thinking that it is just one more awful thing about being a man—
and perhaps it is an important thing to know about us.

2   I have always disliked being a man. The whole idea of manhood
in America is pitiful, in my opinion. This version of masculinity is a
little like having to wear an ill-fitting coat for one's entire life (by
contrast, I imagine femininity to be an oppressive sense of nakedness).
Even the expression "Be a man!" strikes me as insulting and abusive. It
means: Be stupid, be unfeeling, obedient, soldierly and stop thinking.
Man means "manly"—how can one think about men without considering the terrible ambition of manliness? And yet it is part of every
man's life. It is a hideous and crippling lie; it not only insists on difference and connives at superiority, it is also by its very nature destructive, emotionally damaging, and socially harmful. The youth who is
subverted, as most are, into believing in the masculine ideal is effec-

tively separated from women and he spends the rest of his life finding women a riddle and a nuisance. Of course, there is a female version of this male affliction. It begins with mothers encouraging little girls to say (to other adults) "Do you like my new dress?" In a sense, little girls are traditionally urged to please adults with a kind of coquettishness while boys are enjoined to behave like monkeys towards each other. The nine-year-old coquette proceeds to become womanish in a subtle power game in which she learns to be sexually indispensable, socially decorative and always alert to a man's sense of inadequacy.

3   Femininity—being lady-like—implies needing a man as witness and seducer; but masculinity celebrates the exclusive company of men. That is why it is so grotesque; and that is also why there is no manliness without inadequacy—because it denies men the natural friendship of women.

4   It is very hard to imagine any concept of manliness that does not belittle women, and it begins very early. At an age when I wanted to meet girls— let's say the treacherous years of thirteen to sixteen—I was told to take up a sport, get more fresh air, join the Boy Scouts, and I was urged not to read so much. It was the 1950s and if you asked too many questions about sex you were sent to camp—boy's camp, of course: the nightmare. Nothing is more unnatural or prison-like than a boy's camp, but if it were not for them we would have no Elks' Lodges, no pool rooms, no boxing matches, no Marines.

5   And perhaps no sports as we know them. Everyone is aware of how few in number are the athletes who behave like gentlemen. Just as high school basketball teaches you how to be a poor loser, the manly attitude towards sports seems to be little more than a recipe for creating bad marriages, social misfits, moral degenerates, sadists, latent rapists and just plain louts. I regard high school sports as a drug far worse than marijuana, and it is the reason that the average tennis champion, say, is a pathetic oaf.

6   Any objective study would find the quest for manliness essentially right-wing, puritanical, cowardly, neurotic and fueled largely by a fear of women. It is also certainly philistine. There is no book-hater like a Little League coach. But indeed all the creative arts are obnoxious to the manly ideal, because at their best the arts are pursued by uncompetitive and essentially solitary people. It makes it very hard for a creative youngster, for any boy who expresses the desire to be alone seems to be saying that there is something wrong with him.

7   It ought to be clear by now that I have something of an objection
to the way we turn boys into men. It does not surprise me that when the
President of the United States has his customary weekend off he dresses
like a cowboy—it is both a measure of his insecurity and his willingness to please. In many ways, American culture does little more for a
man than prepare him for modeling clothes in the L. L. Bean cata-
logue. I take this as a personal insult because for many years I found it
impossible to admit to myself that I wanted to be a writer. It was my
guilty secret, because being a writer was incompatible with being a
man. There are people who might deny this, but that is because the
American writer, typically, has been so at pains to prove his manliness
that we have come to see literariness and manliness as mingled qualities. But first there was a fear that writing was not a manly profession—indeed, not a profession at all. (The paradox in American letters is that it has always been easier for a woman to write and for a man
to be published.) Growing up, I had thought of sports as wasteful and
humiliating, and the idea of manliness was a bore. My wanting to
become a writer was not a flight from that oppressive role-playing,
but I quickly saw that it was at odds with it. Everything in stereotyped
manliness goes against the life of the mind. The Hemingway personality is too tedious to go into here, and in any case his exertions are
well-known, but certainly it was not until this aberrant behavior was
examined by feminists in the 1960s that any male writer dared question the pugnacity in Hemingway's fiction. All the bullfighting and
arm wrestling and elephant shooting diminished Hemingway as a
writer, but it is consistent with a prevailing attitude in American
writing: one cannot be a male writer without first proving that one is
a man.

8   It is normal in America for a man to be dismissive or even
somewhat apologetic about being a writer. Various factors make it
easier. There is a heartiness about journalism that makes it acceptable—journalism is the manliest form of American writing and,
therefore, the profession the most independent-minded women seek
(yes, it is an illusion, but that is my point). Fiction-writing is equated
with a kind of dispirited failure and is only manly when it produces
wealth—money is masculinity. So is drinking. Being a drunkard is
another assertion, if misplaced, of manliness. The American male
writer is traditionally proud of his heavy drinking. But we are also a
very literal-minded people. A man proves his manhood in America in

old-fashioned ways. He kills lions, like Hemingway; or he hunts ducks, like Nathanael West; or he makes pronouncements like, "A man should carry enough knife to defend himself with," as James Jones once said to a *Life* interviewer. Or he says he can drink you under the table. But even tiny drunken William Faulkner loved to mount a horse and go fox hunting, and Jack Kerouac roistered up and down Manhattan in a lumberjack shirt (and spent every night of *The Subterraneans* with his mother in Queens). And we are familiar with the lengths to which Norman Mailer is prepared, in his endearing way, to prove that he is just as much a monster as the next man.

9   When the novelist John Irving was revealed as a wrestler, people took him to be a very serious writer, and even a bubble reputation like Eric *(Love Story)* Segal's was enhanced by the news that he ran the marathon in a respectable time. How surprised we would be if Joyce Carol Oates were revealed as a sumo wrestler or Joan Didion active in pumping iron. "Lives in New York City with her three children" is the typical woman writer's biographical note, for just as the male writer must prove he has achieved a sort of muscular manhood, the woman writer—or rather her publicists—must prove her motherhood.

10   There would be no point in saying any of this if it were not generally accepted that to be a man is somehow—even now in feminist-infuenced America—a privilege. It is on the contrary an unmerciful and punishing burden. Being a man is bad enough; being manly is appalling (in this sense, women's lib has done much more for men than for women). It is the sinister silliness of men's fashions, and a clubby attitude in the arts. It is the subversion of good students. It is the so-called "Dress Code" of the Ritz-Carlton Hotel in Boston, and it is the institutionalized cheating in college sports. It is the most primitive insecurity.

11   And this is also why men often object to feminism but are afraid to explain why: of course women have a justified grievance, but most men believe—and with reason—that their lives are just as bad.

Suggestions for Discussion and Writing

1. Theroux insists that the American idea of manhood is "a hideous and crippling lie." What are the reasons he uses to support this controversial thesis?

2. Do you agree that femininity requires a male witness, but that masculinity excludes women altogether? What arguments can you make to support or attack this opinion?

3. Why does Theroux use boys' camps and organized sports as the chief examples in this essay? Can you think of other examples he might have used as well?

4. Take the opposite side of Theroux's argument: what's good about the ways American culture turns boys into men?

5. The "men's movement" of the late 1980s and early 1990s is re-examining the American definition of masculinity. Explore magazine and newspaper articles about this movement and explain how it is redefining manhood. (You might want to look up Robert Bly's book *Iron John* in your card catalog as an excellent first source.)

Mark Gerzon
Manhood: The Elusive Goal

MARK GERZON came of age in the 1960s and has been writing about American society ever since. Much of his work focuses on rites of passage, the ways in which members of a society move from one social level to another (e.g. from adolescent to adult or from single to married). He is the author of *The Whole World is Watching: A Young Man Looks at Youth's Dissent* (1969) and *A Childhood for Every Child: The Politics of Parenthood* (1973). This essay is excerpted from *A Choice of Heroes* (1982), in which he argues that the five traditional American male heroes (the frontiersman, the soldier, the breadwinner, the expert, and the Lord) will be replaced by new stereotypes: the healer, the mediator, the companion, the colleague, and the nurturer. His latest book, *Coming Into Our Own*, appeared in 1992.

> There is no steady unretracing progress in this life ... Once gone
> through, we trace the round again; and are infants, boys, and men, and
> Ifs eternally.
>
> Herman Melville
> *Moby Dick*

It was not coincidence that when love entered my life so did violence. I fell in love for the first time with a high school classmate, Diana. She was a cheerleader, the most feminine of all roles. Even now, almost twenty years later, I think of her when I see cheerleaders practicing. In one cheer, they would shout each letter of each member of the starting line-up's name as they ran onto the basketball court heralding them as if they were heroes. They had mastered the art of feminine support: they remained on the sidelines while acclaiming the men who played the game.

2   In this, Diana was wholehearted. In winter, her face would glow when the ball swished through the hoop; she would look crestfallen when it fell short. In autumn, chanting "Hit 'em again, hit 'em again, harder, harder," her body pulsed to the rhythm of her words. Even if she was not the most beautiful cheerleader, she was certainly the most magnetic. She made us feel like men.

3   Before she and I started dating, she went with a fellow two years my senior, a leading figure in one of the male clubs known for its toughness. Since he and Diana had broken up (or so she said), I felt no qualms when our study dates became romantic. Soon she and I were together almost constantly. When she invited me to a party sponsored by her club, I accepted. After all, she was "mine."

4   Midway through the evening, however, her former beau arrived with several of his hefty club brothers behind him. "They want you," a friend warned me, then quickly disappeared. My strategy, which was to pretend that I had not noticed their arrival, became impractical when three of them had me cornered. And I had no club brothers to back me up.

5   "Let's go outside," said Diana's old beau.

6   "What for?" I was still playing dumb.

7   The purpose of our outing was to settle with our fists who Diana

belonged to. He obviously felt that he had staked his claim first and that I was trespassing on his territory. I believed that she had the right to choose for herself to whom she wanted to belong. Neither of us, perhaps not even Diana herself, considered it odd that at the age of sixteen she should belong to anyone.

8   As it turned out, the other boy friend and I didn't fight, at least not that night. "Why'd you let him talk you out of it?" one of his buddies asked him. He was outraged at being deprived of what was to be the high point of his evening.

9   A few weeks later, after a basketball game, my adversary and I passed each other under the bleachers. Without warning, he punched me hard in my right eye. My fist was raised to return the blow when several arms pressed me back against the wall.

10   "Whatsa matter?" he shouted at me contemptuously. "Are you gonna cry?"

11   The impatient crowd pushed us in opposite directions. Stunned, I felt my eye to check if it was bleeding. Only then did I feel the telltale moistness. Although no tears trickled down my cheeks, they were still evidence against my manliness. First, I had weaseled out of a fight. Next, I let him hit me without ever returning the blow. But the most damaging evidence of all were my barely averted tears. To be hit and to cry was the ultimate violation of the code of masculine conduct.

12   That happened half a lifetime ago. I no longer see my unwillingness to fight as an indictment of my character. Had I been as old and as tough as my adversary, perhaps I would have handled our conflict differently. Perhaps I would have fought. Perhaps I even might have won. Instead, aware of my relative weakness and inexperience, I chose not to. I wanted to protect my eyes, my mouth, my groin. I thought I might need them in the future. But the deeper reason had nothing to do with self-protection but with love. I could not understand what the winner of a fight would gain. Would Diana accept the verdict of our brawl? Like a Kewpie doll at the fairgrounds, would she let herself be claimed by whichever contestant came out on top? If her love could be won by violence, I was not sure I wanted it. I wanted her to love me for who I was, not for how I fought.

13   My problem, my friends told me then, was that I was too sensitive.

14   Strange how things change. The image of manhood against which I am measured has changed so much that now, almost twenty

years later, I am told I am not sensitive *enough*. When tensions build in our relationship, Shelley will admonish me for being out of touch with my feelings. "You are always so defensive, always trying to protect yourself," she will say. "Why can't you be more open to your feelings?"

15   How can I explain it to her? How can any man explain it to any woman? Women are not raised to abort all tears. They are not measured by their toughness. They are not expected to bang against each other on hockey rinks and football fields and basketball courts. They do not go out into the woods to play soldiers. They do not settle disagreements by punching each other. For them, tears are a badge of femininity. For us, they are a masculine demerit.

16   Nothing has made me see this more clearly than talking with Richard Ryan, a former alcoholic. Sitting in the sun one afternoon by a lake near his home, Richard reminded me of a masculine rite of passage I had almost forgotten.

17   "After I gave this rap about alcoholism at the high school, this kid came up to me and said, 'Can I talk with you privately, Mr. Ryan?' Usually that means that either the kid's parents are alcoholic or he is. But not this kid. He said to me, 'Mr. Ryan, I've never been drunk, never smoked a joint. What's wrong with me?'

18   "So I said to him, 'Nothing's wrong with you, man. You're doin' fine.'

19   "'But why do I feel I have to lie to my friends about it?' he asked. 'If they'd knew I didn't drink or smoke they'd make fun of me.'"

20   Richard Ryan rolled over onto his stomach as he finished the story. Either the sun or his emotions made him hide his face.

21   "I always felt like I had to lie as a kid," Ryan told me. "I liked to bake cookies. I liked to watch my kid brothers and sisters. I liked to write poetry. But my dad made me feel that was wrong somehow. So I started to pretend I *didn't* want to do it."

22   I had heard the lament so often now that I pushed him for specifics. "But what did your dad do? Did he walk in and say, 'Get out of the kitchen' or 'That's women's work'?"

23   "No, no. Nothing like that. It was more subtle." He thought for a moment. "For example, when my mother's mother died, I wanted to be her pallbearer. Grandma had been very special to me. I felt like she'd carried me all my life. When she died, I wanted to carry her once. So I asked my dad if I could be a pallbearer. He said, 'Only if you

promise not to cry. Pallbearers can't cry!' I knew if I lied and said I wouldn't, he'd let me. But I felt like that'd be betraying her. How could I go to her funeral and not cry? Since I wouldn't promise, my dad refused to let me do it."

24   Now in his mid-thirties, Ryan runs a project called Creative Drug Education. He visits high schools and talks about alcohol and drug abuse. But he doesn't preach. He tells his own story:

25   "When I used to go out and get bombed, guys would say, 'He drinks like a man' or 'He holds it like a man.' Being drunk, I really felt like I was something great. The other guys and I, we were like a pack, and drinking was our bond. We'd get together and, because we drank, we'd say stuff and hug each other and do all sorts of things we'd never let ourselves do if we were sober."

26   Only after reaching the age of thirty did Richard realize he was an alcoholic. "I've only recently felt I can be who I am," he continues. "All those years I felt I had to blot out a whole side of myself. I used alcohol to make myself feel good about myself. After I quit drinking, I thought I was free. But then I realized I was addicted to smoking. And I mean *addicted*. My withdrawal from nicotine was almost as bad as from booze—the shakes, sweating, couldn't sleep. I found it hard to be around people without a cigarette in my hand. It was the whole Marlboro man thing—it made me look cool, made me feel like a man. When a friend told me I should stop, I told him, 'Anybody can quit smoking. It takes a real man to face cancer.' I said it as a joke, but I meant it. That's how sick I was."

27   Richard no longer looks sick. He is big and muscular. We swam out to the middle of the lake and back and, when we dried off, he wasn't even out of breath. He is respected by the people with whom he works. Teachers tell me he is more effective with young people who use drugs than anyone they've ever met.

28   As we walked back to the car, I saw a sadness in him, a wound that had not yet healed.

29   "What you thinking about?" I asked, not knowing a better way to probe.

30   He laughed. "Oh, I was just thinking about Grandma's funeral. You know what? Every one of those pallbearers cried."

31   In Western societies, there are clearly no longer any rites of passage. The very existence of terms such as teenager (the German word is

Halbwüchsiger, half-grown) shows that the absence of this social institution results in an in-between stage. All too often adult society avoids this whole question by regarding those in their teens in terms of the high school health book definition. Adolescence, it says, is the period when the person is no longer a child, but not yet an adult. This is defining the concept of adolescence by avoiding it altogether. This is why we have a youth culture. It is where adolescents go (and sometimes stay) before they become grownups.

32   Despite the absence of any established initiation rite, young men need one. By default, other institutions take the place of these missing rites. Some commentators on growing up in America point to sports or fraternities for example, to demonstrate that our culture does have various kinds of initiation rites. But they are wrong.

33   Sports, for instance, can hardly serve as the means for gaining manhood. Sports are games. Except for the professionals who make their living from them, these games have little connection with real life. Moreover, only a small minority of males in American high schools and colleges can participate in athletics. As dozens of articles document, sports play a key role in enabling boys and young men to test their physical prowess, but they do not alone make a boy a man.

34   Fraternities, too, are a painfully inadequate means for gaining manhood. Except for token community service projects once a year, most fraternities are disconnected from society. How can they provide a socially recognized initiation rite when they involve only members of the younger generation? Frat members do not go off into seclusion with the adults of the "tribe." They go off into seclusion with themselves. They are initiated into youth culture, perhaps, but not into the world of adults. .

35   The young man facing adulthood cannot reach across this great divide. He has only rites of impasse. There is no ritual—not sexual, economic, military, or generational—that can confirm his masculinity. Maturity eludes him. Our culture is famous for its male adolescent pain. From James Dean in *Rebel Without a Cause* and Dustin Hoffman in *The Graduate* to the more recent box office hits *Breaking Away*, *My Bodyguard*, and *Ordinary People*, young men try to prove they are grown men. But to no avail. None of the surrogate initiation rites—car duels, college diplomas, after-work drinking rituals, first paychecks, sports trophies—answers their deepest needs. None has proven to be what William James called the "moral equiv-

alent of war."

36   The only rituals that confirm manhood now are imitations of war. The military academies, for example, like boot camp itself, involve many of the ingredients of primitive rites of passage. Young men are secluded with older men. They must endure tests of psychological or physical endurance.

37   Pat Conroy's novel *The Lords of Discipline*, which depicts life in a southern military academy, and Lucian K. Truscott IV's *Dress Gray*, which portrays West Point, showed how boys are turned into men—the kind of men the military needs. But, as we have recognized, the Soldier is no longer the hero. The Vietnam war was "billed on the marquee as a John Wayne shoot-'em-up test of manhood," wrote Mark Baker in *Nam*, but it ended up "a warped version of *Peter Pan*. . . a brutal Never Never Land where little boys didn't have to grow up. They just grew old before their time." Similarly, the heroes of Conroy's and Truscott's tales are not the brave soldier but the dissenter. Nevertheless, because military service is the only rite of passage available, men are drawn to it like moths to light. We need to prove our manhood and will take whatever paths our culture offers.

38   With the option of going to war foreclosed, young men seek to prove themselves by performing other manly deeds. The most obvious surrogates for war often involve violence too. It is not directed at the enemy, but at each other, and ourselves.

39   Each week, the news media overflow with accounts of young men between the ages of fifteen and twenty-five who have committed acts of violence. Too old to be boys, too young to have proven themselves men, they are finding their own rites of passage. Here are three, culled from the newspapers:

40   A Boy Scout leader smashes his new car on a country road at 100 miles per hour: he is "showing off" to the four scouts who were riding with him. Now they are all dead.

41   A 16-year-old who lives in a comfortable suburb throws a large rock from a freeway overpass through the windshield of a car. The victim, a 31-year-old housewife, suffers a concussion but survives. "You do it for the thrill," the boy says. "It's a boring town," says one of his classmates.

42   A teenage boy is so upset that his girl friend has jilted him that he threatens to kill himself. Talking to her on the phone, he says he will drive over to her house and smash his car into the tree in her front

yard if she will not go out with him. She refuses. So he does it, killing himself.

43   Many movies are made as surrogate rites of passage for young men. They are designed for the guy who, in actor Clint Eastwood's words, "sits alone in the theater. He's young and he's scared. He doesn't know what he's going to do with his life. He wishes he could be self-sufficient, like the man he sees up there on the screen, somebody who can look out for himself, solve his own problems." The heroes of these films are men who are tough and hard, quick to use violence, wary of women. Whether cowboys, cops, or superheroes, they dominate everything—women, nature, and other men. Young men cannot outmaneuver the Nazis as Indiana Jones did in *Raiders of the Lost Ark*, or battle Darth Vader, or outsmart Dr. No with James Bond's derring-do. To feel like heroes they turn to the other sex. They ask young women for more than companionship, or sex, or marriage. They ask women to give them what their culture could not—their manhood.

44   Half the nation's teenagers have had sex before they graduate from high school. The easiest way to prove oneself a man today is to make it with a girl. First we make out or put the make on her. Then we make it. We are not, like our "primitive" forebears, joining together with a woman as adults. We are coming together in order to become adults, if not in society's eyes, then in our own.

45   "You in her pants yet?" one of the high school jocks asks his classmate in *Ordinary People*, the Academy Award-winning movie directed by Robert Redford. We prove our manhood on the football field or the basketball court by scoring points against other men. We prove our manhood in sex by scoring with women.

46   The young man, armed with lines like "Don't you love me?" is always ready for action. He wants to forge ahead, explore new territory. After all, he has nothing to lose. He has no hymen, no uterus. He is free to play the role of bold adventurer, coaxing the reluctant girl to let him sow his wild oats in her still virgin land. "I love you, but I don't feel ready," she may say. She may be afraid that her refusal may jeopardize her relationship with her young explorer, but she is even more afraid to get pregnant. She may feel less mature than her sex-hungry companion. But the emotional reality may be precisely the opposite. Certain of her femininity and of her pregnability, she dares to wait until the time is right. Insecure about his masculinity and obsessed with proving it—to himself and his buddies, if not to her—

he needs to score in order to feel that he has made the team.

47   Sonny Burns, the sexually insecure hero of Dan Wakefield's *Going All the Way*, finds himself engaged in an amorous overture on a double date. But he admits to himself, and to a generation of readers, that he is doing so not because he finds his date exciting. On the contrary, she bores him. He does so because he wants to impress his buddy in the front seat. He must prove he is a man, and a man takes whatever "pussy" he can get. Pretending to be passionate, he thinks about the high school rating system, according to which boys reported their sexual scores: "The next day, when the guys asked you what you got the night before, you could say you got finger action inside the pants. That wasn't as good as really fucking but it rated right along with dry-humping and was much better than just the necking stuff like frenching and getting covered-tit or bare-tit. It was really pretty much of a failure if you parked with a girl and got only covered-tit."

48   Even if he wins, the victory is private. There are no fans in the bleachers as he crosses home plate and scores. He has not proved himself a man to adult males, as did young men in traditional rites of passage. His sexual conquest is a rite of passage only in his own mind. If adult society were to pass judgment on these back-seat gymnastics, it would probably be negative. The responsible adult would ask him if he was ready for marriage. Could he support her if he had to? And of course the answers are no. He has become an adult sexually, not socially. He has proved his virility in the dark of night. By the light of day, the proof has vanished.

49   As Margaret Mead pointed out in *Male and Female*, our culture leaves adolescents in a quandary. We give them extraordinary freedom but tell them not to use it. "We permit and encourage situations in which young people can indulge in any sort of sex behavior that they elect," wrote Mead a generation ago. "We actually place our young people in a virtually intolerable situation, giving them the entire setting for behaviour for which we then punish them when it occurs." It is a cultural arrangement for which some young women pay an awful price.

50   Whether veiled in fiction or revealed in autobiography, women recall the ritual of modern courtship with caustic humor at best, more often with bitterness. So objectified do they feel that they develop a detached attitude toward their bodies. Reports the cheerleader heroine in Lisa Alther's *Kinflicks*: "Joe Bob would dutifully knead my breasts

through my uniform jacket and padded bra, as though he were a housewife poking plums to determine their ripeness." Later, she would observe him sucking "at my nipples while I tried to decide what to do with my hands to indicate my continuing involvement in the project."

51   But Alther's good-natured response is not typical. Other sagas of car-seat courtships and apartment affairs leave their heroines harboring a deep distaste for men. Some declare themselves feminists or lesbians. Some become depressed. Others, as in Judith Rossner's *Looking for Mr. Goodbar*, are killed by their lovers. And a few, after great turmoil, find a man who will treat them gently, with genuine care.

52   The movie theater, that public living room for a nation of young lovers, reflects this yearning too. For those who have grown weary of the macho hero whose physical prowess is enough, Hollywood has provided a countertype. For those who are not infatuated with the Soldier, there are now movies about the anti-soldier. "In what may be an emerging genre in the movies," wrote Paul Starr in his review of *Coming Home*, *An Unmarried Woman*, and *Alice Doesn't Live Here Anymore*, "there appears a character who expresses in his personality and in his relations with the heroine a new idea of masculinity. He might be described as the emotionally competent hero. . . He is the man to whom women turn as they try to change their own lives: someone who is strong and affectionate, capable of intimacy. . . masculine without being dominating." The new hero, though perhaps not rugged and tough in the familiar mold, can be intimate. He can feel. "The new softer image of masculinity seems to represent what is distinctive and significant in recent films, and I expect we will see more of the post-feminist hero because the old, strong, silent type no longer seems adequate as lover—or as person."

53   Who, then, is to be the young man's hero? The gentle, post-feminist figure extolled by the new genre of films and by the roughly five thousand men's consciousness-raising groups across America? Or the self-sufficient, hard-hitting tough that Eastwood tries to embody and that the military breeds? Faced with such polarized and politicized choices, how does a boy become a man? By being hard or by being soft?

54   From the sensible to the absurd, we have answers. We have so many shifting, contradictory criteria for manhood that they confuse rather than inspire.

55   American boys coming of age encounter sexual chaos. A chorus of liberation advocates, now with bass as well as soprano voices, encourages them to free themselves from the oppressive male role, to become softer, and to consider themselves women's equals. But another vociferous group beckons them in another direction. For every pro-feminist man, there is his counterpart, who denounces those "fuzzy-headed housemales, purporting to represent 'men's liberation,' but sponsored by NOW." One Minnesota men's rights leader argued, for example, that men who support women's liberation are "eunuchs," motivated by an "urge to slip into a pair of panties." According to him and his followers: "Men's liberation means establishing the right of males to be men, not to liberate them from being men."

56   The hard-liners and soft-liners both have their respective magazines, organizations, and conferences. Repulsed by the cacophony, most young men try to ignore it. But the questions gnaw at them anyway. Although the pro- and anti-feminist activists irritate them, young men cannot deny their own uncertainty. They are caught between the competing ideals of chauvinism and liberation. The old archetypes do not work; the new ones remain vague and incomplete. If we are not to be John Wayne, then who?

57   Into the vacuum created by the demise of the old archetypes rush myriad images. Each hopes to inspire a following. Masculinity becomes the target for everyone from toothpaste advertisers to Hollwood superstars. These salesmen of self-help all have their diagnoses for the young man struggling to find his own identity. Some take the pose of proud aging lions, defending the traditional masculine role as Western civilization enters a precipitous, psychosexual decline. In *Sexual Suicide*, George Gilder warned of the imminent feminization of man and masculinization of woman and called on men to reassert their superiority.

58   Others do not oppose liberation but rather seem to exploit it. Cynically catering to masculine insecurity, they describe the world of white-collar commuters as a stark and brutal asphalt jungle in which men must constantly flex their aggressive personalities in order to survive. According to Michael Korda, author of *Power!* and *Success!*, life is nothing more than a series of encounters in which one dominates or is dominated, intimidates or is intimidated, achieves power over or is oneself overpowered. "Your gain is inevitably someone else's loss," philosophizes this latter-day Nietzsche, "your failure

someone else's victory."

59   There are also the advocates of liberation who seek to free us from the manacles of machismo. Although they are constructive in intent, they too increase the confusion. In their attempt to free us from one-sidedness, they double our load. They now want us to be "assertive *and* yielding, independent *and* dependent, job *and* people oriented, strong *and* gentle, in short, both masculine *and* feminine." The prescriptions are not wrong, just overwhelming. Their lists of do's and don'ts, like Gail Sheehy's *Passages*, seem too neat, too tidy. They write of "masculinity in crisis" with such certainty. They encourage us to cry with such stoicism. They advise us to "be personal, be intimate with men" with such authority. It is all too much.

60   Whichever model young men choose, they know the traditional expectation of their culture. At least until the seventies, Americans of all ages and of all educational and income levels were in wide agreement about what traits are masculine. According to one study, based on more than a thousand interviews, men are expected to be very aggressive, not at all emotional, very dominant, not excitable, very competitive, rough, and unaware of others' feelings. And women are expected to be more or less the opposite.

61   If this is what maleness is, then a young man must find ways to demonstrate those traits. Without a rite of passage he can only prove what he is not. Not a faggot, a pussy, a queer. Not a pushover, a loser, or a lightweight. Not a dimwit or a dunce or a jerk or a nobody. Not a prick or a pansy. Not above all, anything that is feminine. Indeed, without clear rites of passage, the only way to be a man is essentially negative: to not be a woman.

62   If we are to be masculine, then they must be feminine. We convince ourselves that women are yielding, that they are more interested in our careers than in their own, that they are interested in sex whenever we are, that they are fulfilled by raising children. That, we assume, is who they are. Should one of them act differently, then something is wrong, not with our assumptions, but with her.

63   Having entered physical manhood, we are nevertheless emotionally unsure of ourselves. The more unsure we are, the more we stress that we are not "feminine" and the more we are threatened when women act "masculine." We try to rid ourselves of any soft, effeminate qualities. We gravitate toward all-male cliques in the form of sports teams, social clubs, or professional groups. When we are with a

woman, it is virtually always in a sexually charged atmosphere. To be merely friends is nearly impossible because it suggests that we have something in common. We are trying, after all, to prove precisely the opposite, which is why so many marriages fail.

Suggestions for Discussion and Writing

1. Why does Gerzon attach such importance to the incident with the cheerleader? Does he do now so for the same reasons he did as when he was a teenager?

2. What are the possible "rites of passage" for young men? Do young women have similar rites? If so, what are they?

3. Why does Gerzon choose movies as an example of the way in which our culture teaches boys to be men? Are there other forms of media that serve the same purpose?

4. Why does Gerzon use the example of the alcoholic in this essay? How does his analogy affect you as a reader?

5. Gerzon suggests that our culture forces young men into violence as a way of proving their manhood. Do statistics on violence prove him correct? If this is true, what efforts can you find in our society to remedy this problem?

Wallace Stegner
Specifications for a Hero

WALLACE STEGNER, novelist, essayist, and professor, was born in Iowa in 1909. His writings deal with the development of the American West and people's struggle to come to terms with the lack of Eastern American "culture" on the frontier. Among his best-known works are *The Big Rock Candy Mountain* (1943) and *A Shooting Star* (1961). *This is Dinosaur* (1955) is an early conservationist plea for the preservation of western historical sites; *Wolf Willow: A History, a Story, and a Memory of the Plains Frontier*

(1962), from which the excerpt below is taken, is both
a personal memoir and a public history of the settling
of the frontiers of Montana and Saskatchewan.
Stegner was awarded a Pulitzer Prize in 1972.

In our town, as in most towns, everybody had two names—the one
his parents had given him and the one the community chose to call him
by. Our nicknames were an expression of the folk culture, and they
were more descriptive than honorific. If you were underweight, you
were called Skinny or Slim or Sliver; if Overweight, Fat or Chubby;
if left-handed, Lefty; if spectacled, Four Eyes. If your father was the
minister, your name was Preacher Kid, and according to the condition
and color of your hair you were Whitey, Blacky, Red, Rusty, Baldy,
Fuzzy, or Pinky. If you had a habit of walking girls in the brush after
dusk, you were known as Town Bull or T.B. If you were small for
your age, as I was, your name was Runt or Peewee. The revelation of
your shape at the town swimming hole by the footbridge could tag you
for life with the label Birdlegs. The man who for a while ran one of
our two grocery stores was universally known as Jew Meyer.

2   Like the lingo we spoke, our nicknames were at odds with the
traditional and educational formalisms; along with them went a set of
standard frontier attitudes. What was appropriate for Jimmy Craig in
his home or in church or in school would have been shameful to
Preacher Kid Craig down at the bare-naked hole. When we were digging a cave in the cutbank back of my house, and someone for a joke
climbed up on top and jumped up and down, and the roof caved in on
P.K. and he had to be dug out and revived by artificial respiration,
even P.K. thought the hullabaloo excessive. He did not blame us, and
he did not tattle on anyone. His notions of fortitude and propriety—
which were at the other end of the scale from those of his parents—
would not have let him.

3   When we first arrived in Whitemud the Lazy-S was still a
working ranch, with corrals, and calves, and a bunkhouse inhabited by
heroes named Big Horn, Little Horn, Slivers, Rusty, and Slippers.
There was a Chinese cook named Mah Li, who had been abused in
imaginative ways ever since he had arrived back at the turn of the century. In the first district poll for a territorial election, in 1902,
someone had taken Mah Li to the polls and enfranchised him on the

ground that, having been born in Hong Kong, he could swear that he was a British subject and was not an Indian, and was hence eligible to vote. When I knew him, he was a jabbering, good-natured soul with a pigtail and a loose blue blouse, and I don't suppose a single day of his life went by that he was not victimized somehow. He couldn't pass anybody, indoors or out, without having his pigtail yanked or his shirt tails set on fire. Once I saw the cowboys talk him into licking a frosty doorknob when the temperature was fifteen or twenty below, and I saw the tears in his eyes, too, after he tore himself loose. Another time a couple of Scandinavians tried to get him onto a pair of skis on the North Bench hill. They demonstrated how easy it was, climbed up and came zipping by, and then offered to help his toes into the straps. But Mah Li was too many for them that time. "Sssssssssss!" he said in scorn. "Walkee half a mile back!" When I was ten or eleven Mah Li was a friend of mine. I gave him suckers I caught in the river, and once he made me a present of a magpie he had taught to talk. The only thing it could say was our laundry mark, the number O Five, but it was more than any other magpie in town could say, and I had a special feeling for Mah Li because of it. Nevertheless I would have been ashamed not to take part in the teasing, baiting, and candy-stealing that made his life miserable after the Lazy-S closed up and Mah Li opened a restaurant. I helped tip over his backhouse on Hallowe'en; I was part of a war party that sneaked to the crest of a knoll and with .22 rifles potted two of his white ducks as they rode a mud puddle near his shack in the east bend.

4   The folk culture sponsored every sort of crude practical joke, as it permitted the cruelest and ugliest prejudices and persecutions. Any visible difference was enough to get an individual picked on. Impartially and systematically we persecuted Mah Li and his brother Mah Jim, Jew Meyer and his family, any Indians who came down into the valley in their wobble-wheeled buckboards, anyone with a pronounced English accent or fancy clothes or affected manners, any crybaby, any woman who kept a poodle dog and put on airs, any child with glasses, anyone afflicted with crossed eyes, St. Vitus's dance, feeblemindedness, or a game leg. Systematically the strong bullied the weak, and the weak did their best to persuade their persecutors, by feats of courage or endurance or by picking on someone still weaker, that they were tough and strong.

5   Immune, because they conformed to what the folk culture valued,

were people with Texas or Montana or merely Canadian accents, people who wore overalls and worked with their hands, people who snickered at Englishmen or joined the bedevilment of Chinamen, women who let their children grow up wild and unwashed. Indignation swept the school one fall day when the Carpenter kids were sent home by the new teacher from Ontario. She sent a note along with them saying they had pediculosis and should not return to school until they were cured. Their mother in bewildered alarm brought them in to the doctor, and when she discovered that pediculosis meant only the condition of being lousy, she had to be restrained from going over and pulling the smart-alec teacher's hair out. We sympathized completely. That teacher never did get our confidence, for she had convicted herself of being both over-cleanly and pompous.

6   Honored and imitated among us were those with special skills, so long as the skills were not too civilized. We admired good shots, good riders, tough fighters, dirty talkers, stoical endurers of pain. My mother won the whole town because once, riding our flighty mare Daisy up Main Street, she got piled hard in front of Christenson's pool hall with half a dozen men watching, and before they could recover from laughing and go to help her, had caught the mare and remounted and ridden off, tightly smiling. The fact that her hair was red did not hurt: among us, red hair was the sign of a sassy temper.

7   She was one of the immune, and so was my father, for both had been brought up on midwestern farms, had lived on the Dakota frontier, and accepted without question—though my mother would have supplemented it—the code of the stiff upper lip. She had sympathy for anyone's weakness except her own; he went strictly by the code.

8   I remember one Victoria Day when there was a baseball game between our town and Shaunavon. Alfie Carpenter, from a river-bottom ranch just west of town, was catching for the Whitemud team. He was a boy who had abused me and my kind for years, shoving us off the footbridge, tripping us unexpectedly, giving us the hip, breaking up our hideouts in the brush, stampeding the town herd that was in our charge, and generally making himself lovable. This day I looked up from something just in time to see the batter swing and a foul tip catch Alfie full in the face. For a second he stayed bent over with a hand over his mouth; I saw the blood start in a quick stream through his fingers. My feelings were very badly mixed, for I had dreamed often enough of doing just that to Alfie Carpenter's face, but I was

somewhat squeamish about human pain and I couldn't enjoy seeing the dream come true. Moreover I knew with a cold certainty that the ball had hit Alfie at least four times as hard as I had ever imagined hitting him, and there he stood, still on his feet and obviously conscious. A couple of players came up and took his arms and he shook them off, straightened up, spat out a splatter of blood and teeth and picked up his mitt as if to go on with the game. Of course they would not let him— but what a gesture! said my envious and appalled soul. There was a two-tooth hole when Alfie said something; he freed his elbows and swaggered to the side of the field. Watching him, my father broke out in a short, incredulous laugh. "Tough kid!" he said to the man next, and the tone of his voice goose-pimpled me like a breeze on a sweaty skin, for in all my life he had never spoken either to or of me in that voice of approval. Alfie Carpenter, with his broken nose and bloody mouth, was a boy I hated and feared, but most of all I envied his competence to be what his masculine and semi-barbarous world said a man should be.

9   As for me, I was a crybaby. My circulation was poor and my hands always got blue and white in the cold. I always had a runny nose. I was skinny and small, so that my mother anxiously doctored me with Scott's Emulsion, sulphur and molasses, calomel, and other doses. To compound my frail health, I was always getting hurt. Once I lost both big-toe nails in the same week, and from characteristically incompatible causes. The first one turned black and came off because I had accidentally shot myself through the big toe with a .22 shot; the second because, sickly thing that I was, I had dropped a ten-pound bottle of Scott's Emulsion on it.

10   I grew up hating my weakness and despising my cowardice and trying to pretend that neither existed. The usual result of that kind of condition is bragging. I bragged, and sometimes I got called. Once in Sunday School I said that I was not afraid to jump off the high diving board that the editor of the Leader had projected out over the highest cut-bank. The editor, who had been a soldier and a hero, was the only person in town who dared use it. It did not matter that the boys who called my bluff would not have dared to jump off it themselves. I was the one who had bragged, and so after Sunday School I found myself out on that thing, a mile above the water, with the wind very cold around my knees. The tea-brown whirlpools went spinning slowly around the deep water of the bend, looking as impossible to jump into as if they had been whorls in cement. A half dozen times I sucked in

my breath and grabbed my courage with both hands and inched out to the burlap pad on the end of the board. Every time, the vibrations of the board started such sympathetic vibrations in my knees that I had to creep back for fear of falling off. The crowd on the bank got scornful, and then ribald, and then insulting; I could not rouse (even the courage to answer back, but went on creeping out, quaking back, creeping out again, until they finally all got tired and left for their Sunday dinners. Then at once I walked out to the end and jumped.

11   I think I must have come down through thirty or forty feet of air, bent over toward the water, with my eyes out on stems like a lobster's and I hit the water just so, with my face and chest, a tremendous belly-flopper that drove my eyes out through the back of my head and flattened me out on the water to the thickness of an oil film. The air was full of colored lights; I came to enough to realize I was strangling on weed-tasting river water, and moved my arms and legs feebly toward shore. About four hours and twenty deaths later, I grounded on the mud and lay there gasping and retching, sick for the hero I was not, for the humiliation I had endured, for the mess I had made of the jump when I finally made it—even for the fact that no one had been around to see me, and that I would never be able to convince any of them that I really had, at the risk of drowning, done what I had bragged I would do.

12   Contempt is a hard thing to bear, especially one's own. Because I was what I was, and because the town went by the code it went by, I was never quite out of sight of self-contempt or the contempt of my father or Alfie Carpenter or some other whose right to contempt I had to grant. School, and success therein, never fully compensated for the lacks I felt in myself. I found early that I could shine in class, and I always had a piece to speak in school entertainments, and teachers found me reliable at cleaning blackboards, but teachers were women, and school was a woman's world, the booby prize for those not capable of being men. The worst of it was that I liked school, and liked a good many things about the womanish world, but I wouldn't have dared admit it, and I could not respect the praise of my teachers any more than I could that of my music teacher or my mother.

13   "He has the arteestic tempera*ment*," said Madame Dujardin while collecting her pay for my piano lessons. "He's *sensitive*," my mother would tell her friends, afternoons when they sat around drinking coffee and eating Norwegian coffee cake, and I hung around inside, partly for the sake of coffee cake and partly to hear them talk

about me. The moment they did talk about me, I was enraged. *Women* speaking up for me, noticing my "sensitivity," observing me with that appraising female stare and remarking that I seemed to like songs such as "Sweet and Low" better than "Men of Harlech," which was *their* sons' favorite—my mother interpolating half with pride and half with worry that sometimes she had to drive me out to play, I'd rather stay in and read Ridpath's *History of the World*. Women giving me the praise I would have liked to get from my father or Slivers or the Assiniboine halfbreed down at the Lazy-S. I wanted to be made of whang leather.

14   Little as I want to acknowledge them, the effects of those years remain in me like the beach terraces of a dead lake. Having been weak, and having hated my weakness, I am as impatient with the weakness of others as my father ever was. Pity embarrasses me for the person I am pitying, for I know how it feels to be pitied. Incompetence exasperates me, a big show of pain or grief or any other feeling makes me uneasy, affectations still inspire in me a mirth I have grown too mannerly to show. I cannot sympathize with the self-pitiers, for I have been there, or with the braggarts, for I have been there too. I even at times find myself reacting against conversation, that highest test of the civilized man, because where I came from it was unfashionable to be "mouthy."

15   An inhumane and limited code, the value system of a life more limited and cruder than in fact ours was. We got most of it by inheritance from the harsher frontiers that had preceded ours—got it, I suppose, mainly from our contacts with what was left of the cattle industry.

16   So far as the Cypress Hills were concerned, that industry began with the Mounted Police beef herd at Fort Walsh, and was later amplified by herds brought in to feed treaty Indians during the starving winters after 1879. In practice, the Indians ate a good deal of beef that hadn't been intended for them; it took a while to teach them that the white man's spotted buffalo were not fair game when a man was hungry. The raiding of cattle and horse herds was never controlled until the Canadian Indians were moved to reservations far north of the Line after 1882. Nevertheless it was the Indians who first stimulated the raising of cattle on that range, and the departure of the Indians which left the Whitemud River country open to become the last great cattle country.

17   In some ways, the overlapping of the cattle and homesteading

phases of the plains frontier was similar to the overlapping of the horse and gun cultures earlier, and in each case the overlapping occurred latest around the Cypress Hills. Cattle came in from the south, homesteaders from the east and southeast. Among the homesteaders—Ontario men, Scandinavians and Americans working up from the Dakotas, and Englishmen, Scots, and Ukrainians straight off the immigrant boats—there was a heavy percentage of greenhorns and city men. Even the experienced dryland farmers from the States were a prosaic and law-abiding lot by comparison with the cowboys they displaced. As it turned out, the homesteaders, by appropriating and fencing and plowing the range, squeezed out a way of life that was better adapted to the country than their own, and came close to ruining both the cattlemen and themselves in the process, but that is a later story. What succeeded the meeting and overlapping of the two cultures was a long and difficult period of adaptation in which each would modify the other until a sort of amalgamation could result. But while the adaptations were taking place, during the years of uneasy meeting and mixture, it was the cowboy tradition, the horseback culture, that impressed itself as image, as romance, and as ethical system upon boys like me. There were both good and bad reasons why that should have been true.

18   Read the history of the northern cattle ranges in such an antiAmerican historian as John Peter Turner and you hear that the "Texas men" who brought the cattle industry to Canada were all bravos, rustlers, murderers, gamblers, thugs, and highwaymen; that their life was divided among monte, poker, six-guns, and dancehall girls; and that their law was the gun-law that they made for themselves and enforced by hand. Allow sixty or seventy per cent of error for patriotic fervor, and Mr. Turner's generalizations may be accepted. But it is likewise true that American cow outfits left their gun-law cheerfully behind them when they found the country north of the Line well policed, that they cheerfully cooperated with the Mounted Police, took out Canadian brands, paid for grazing leases, and generally conformed to the customs of the country. They were indistinguishable from Canadian ranchers, to whom they taught the whole business. Many Canadian ranches, among them the 76, the Matador, the Turkey Track, and the T-Down-Bar, were simply Canadian extensions of cattle empires below the border.

19   So was the culture, in the anthropological sense, that accom-

panied the cattle. It was an adaptation to the arid Plains that had begun along the Rio Grande and had spread north, like gas expanding to fill a vacuum, as the buffalo and Indians were destroyed or driven out in the years following the Civil War. Like the patterns of hunting and war that had been adopted by every plains tribe as soon as it acquired the horse, the cowboy culture made itself at home all the way from the Rio Grande to the North Saskatchewan. The outfit, the costume, the practices, the terminology, the state of mind, came into Canada ready-made, and nothing they encountered on the northern Plains enforced any real modifications. The Texas men made it certain that nobody would ever be thrown from a horse in Saskatchewan; he would be piled. They made it sure that no Canadian steer would ever be angry or stubborn; he would be o'nery or ringy or on the prod. Bull Durham was as native to the Whitemud range as to the Pecos, and it was used for the same purposes: smoking, eating, and spitting in the eye of a ringy steer. The Stetson was as useful north as south, could be used to fan the fire or dip up a drink from a stream, could shade a man's eyes or be clapped over the eyes of a bronc to gentle him down. Boots, bandanna, stock saddle, rope, the ways of busting broncs, the institution of the spring and fall roundup, the bowlegs in batwing or goatskin chaps— they all came north intact. About the only thing that changed was the name for the cowboy's favorite diversion, which down south they would have called a rodeo but which we called a stampede.

20   It was a nearly womanless culture, nomadic, harsh, dangerous, essentially romantic. It had the same contempt for the dirtgrubbers that Scythian and Cossack had, and Canadian tillers of the soil tended to look upon it with the same suspicion and fear and envy that tillers of the soil have always expressed toward the herdsmen. As we knew it, it had a lot of Confederate prejudices left in it, and it had the cal-lousness and recklessness that a masculine life full of activity and ad-venture is sure to produce. I got it in my eyes like stardust almost as soon as we arrived in Whitemud, when the town staged its first stam-pede down in the western bend. Reno Dodds, known as Slivers, won the saddle bronc competition and set me up a model for my life. I would grow up to be about five feet six and weigh about a hundred and thirty pounds. I would be bowlegged and taciturn, with deep creases in my cheeks and a hide like stained saddle leather. I would be the quietest and most dangerous man around, best rider, best shot, the one who couldn't be buffaloed. Men twice my size, beginning some brag or

other, would catch my cold eye and begin to wilt, and when I had
stared them into impotence I would turn my back contemptuous, hook
onto my pony in one bowlegged arc, and ride off. I thought it tremendous that anyone as small and skinny as Slivers could be a top hand and
a champion rider. I don't think I could have survived without his example, and he was still on my mind years later when, sixteen years old
and six feet tall and weighing a hundred and twenty-five pounds, I
went every afternoon to the university gym and worked out on the
weights for an hour and ran wind sprints around the track. If I
couldn't be big I could be *hard*.

21   We hung around the Lazy-S corrals a good deal that first year or
two, and the cowpunchers, when they had no one else to pester, would
egg us into what they called shit-fights, with green cow manure for
snowballs; or they would put a surcingle around a calf and set us
aboard. After my try I concluded that I would not do any more of it
just at that time and I limped to the fence and sat on the top rail nursing my sprains and bruises and smiling to keep from bawling out
loud. From there I watched Spot Orullian, a Syrian boy a couple of
years older than I ride a wildly pitching whiteface calf clear around
the corral and halfway around again, and get piled hard, and come up
wiping the cow dung off himself, swearing like a pirate. They
cheered him, he was a favorite at once, perhaps all the more because he
had a big brown birthmark on his nose and so could be kidded. And I
sat on the corral rail hunching my winglike shoulder-blades, smiling
and smiling and smiling to conceal the black envy that I knew was just
under the skin of my face. It was always boys like Spot Orullian who
managed to be and do what I wanted to do and be.

22   Many things that those cowboys represented I would have done
well to get over quickly, or never catch: the prejudice, the callousness,
the destructive practical joking, the tendency to judge everyone by the
same raw standard. Nevertheless, what they themselves most respected,
and what as a boy I most yearned to grow up to, was as noble as it was
limited. They honored courage, competence, self-reliance, and they
honored them tacitly. They took them for granted. It was their absence,
not their presence, that was cause for remark. Practising comradeship
in a rough and dangerous job, they lived a life calculated to make a
man careless of everything except the few things he really valued.

23   In the fall of 1906 it must have seemed that the cowboy life was
certain to last a good while, for the Canadian range still lay wide

open, and stockmen from the western states had prospected it and laid large plans for moving bigger herds across the Line to escape the nesters and sheepmen who had already broken up the Montana ranges. Probably the entire country from Wood Mountain to the Alberta line would have been leased for grazing, at the favorable Canadian rate of a few cents an acre, if the winter of 1906-07 had not happened.

24   That winter has remained ever since, in the minds of all who went through it, as the true measure of catastrophe. Some might cite the winter of 1886-87, the year of the Big Die-Up on the American range, but that winter did not affect the Whitemud country, where cattle came in numbers only after 1887. Some who had punched cows in Alberta in the early days might cast a vote for the fatal Cochran drive of 1881, when 8,000 out of 12,000 cattle died over by Lethbridge; and some would certainly, just as weather, mention the April blizzard of 1892, or the winter that followed it, or the big May blizzard of 1903. But after 1907 no one would seriously value those earlier disasters. The winter of 1906-07 was the real one, the year of the blue snow. After it, the leases that might have been taken up were allowed to lapse, the herds that might have been augmented were sold for what they would bring—fifteen to twenty dollars a head with suckling calves thrown in. Old cattlemen who had ridden every range from Texas north took a good long look around in the spring and decided to retire.

25   The ranches that survived were primarily the hill ranches with shelter plus an access to bench or prairie hay land where winter feed could be cut. The net effect of the winter of 1906-07 was to make stock farmers out of ranchers. Almost as suddenly as the disappearance of the buffalo, it changed the way of life of the region. A great event, it had the force in the history of the Cypress Hills country that a defeat in war has upon a nation. When it was over, the protected Hills might harbor a few cowboys, and one or two of the big ranches such as the 76 might go on, but most of the prairie would be laid open to homesteading and another sort of frontier.

26   That new frontier, of which my family was a part, very soon squeezed out the Lazy-S. The hay lands in the bottoms were broken up into town lots, my father was growing potatoes where whitefaces had used to graze, the punchers were drifting off to Alberta. But while we had them around, we made the most of them, imitating their talk and their walk and their songs and their rough-handed jokes; admiring

them for the way they tormented Mah Li; hanging around in the shade of the bunkhouse listening to Rusty, who was supposed to be the second son of an earl, play the mouth organ; watching the halfbreed Assiniboine braid leather or horsehair into halter ropes and hack-amores. I heard some stories about the winter of 1906-07, but I never heard enough. Long afterward, digging in the middens where historians customarily dig, I found and read some more, some of them the reminiscences of men I knew. What they record is an ordeal by weather. The manner of recording is laconic, deceptively matter of fact. It does not give much idea of how it feels to ride sixty or eighty miles on a freezing and exhausted pony, or how cold thirty below is when a fifty-mile wind is driving it into your face, or how demoralizing it is to be lost in a freezing fog where north, south, east, west, even up and down, swim and shift before the slitted and frost-stuck eyes.

27   They do not tell their stories in Technicolor; they would not want to seem to adorn a tale or brag themselves up. The calluses of a life of hardship blunt their sensibilities to their own experience. If we want to know what it was like on the Whitemud River range during that winter when the hopes of a cattle empire died, we had better see it through the eyes of some tenderfoot, perhaps someone fresh from the old country, a boy without the wonder rubbed off him and with something to prove about himself. If in inventing this individual I put into him a little of Corky Jones, and some of the boy Rusty whose mouth organ used to sweeten the dusty summer shade of the Lazy-S bunkhouse, let it be admitted that I have also put into him something of myself, the me who sat on a corral bar wetting with spit my smarting skinned places, and wishing I was as tough as Spot Orullian.

Suggestions for Discussion and Writing

1. The author's title "Specifications for a Hero" suggests an objective recipe for a role model. Instead, he provides a series of anecdotes about his own growing up. How do these anecdotes live up to the title? How do they affect you as a reader?

2. What were the values of Western society that most strongly affected Stegner and his peers? Which ones does he

now see as most damaging? Why?

3. Stegner seems to identify similar masculine stereotypes to those identified by other writers in this section. What does this tell you about our culture's traditional definition of masculinity? Do you see any indication that this definition is changing today?

4. Why does Stegner stress the collision of cowboy and farm cultures?

5. Does the "code of the stiff upper lip" still exist? Where does it come from? What are its rules? Where do you see it happening in modern life?

John McMurtry
Kill 'Em! Crush 'Em! Eat 'Em Raw!

JOHN MCMURTRY (born in 1939) defies the stereotype of the "dumb jock." He was a professional linebacker with the Calgary Stampeders of the Canadian Football League. A succession of injuries ended his football career and sent him back to academics, and he received a Ph.D. in philosophy at the University of London. His book *The Structure of Marx's World View* was published in 1978. This essay was originally published in 1971, at the height of protests against the Vietnam War.

A few months ago my neck got a hard crick in it. I couldn't turn my head; to look left or right I'd have to turn my whole body. But I'd had cricks in my neck since I started playing grade-school football and hockey, so I just ignored it. Then I began to notice that when I reached for any sort of large book (which I do pretty often as a philosophy teacher at the University of Guelph) I had trouble lifting it with one hand. I was losing the strength in my left arm, and I had such a steady pain in my back I often had to stretch out on the floor of the room I was in to relieve the pressure.

2   A few weeks later I mentioned to my brother, an orthopedic surgeon, that I'd lost the power in my arm since my neck began to hurt. Twenty-four hours later I was in a Toronto hospital not sure whether I might end up with a wasted upper limb. Apparently the steady pounding I had received playing college and professional football in the late Fifties and early Sixties had driven my head into my backbone so that the discs had crumpled together at the neck—"acute herniation"—and had cut the nerves to my left arm like a pinched telephone wire (without nerve stimulation, of course, the muscles atrophy, leaving the arm crippled). So I spent my Christmas holidays in the hospital in heavy traction and much of the next three months with my neck in a brace. Today most of the pain has gone, and I've recovered most of the strength in my arm. But from time to time I still have to don the brace, and surgery remains a possibility.

3   Not much of this will surprise anyone who knows football. It is a sport in which body wreckage is one of the leading conventions. A few days after I went into the hospital for that crick in my neck, another brother, an outstanding football player in college, was undergoing spinal surgery in the same hospital two floors above me. In his case it was a lower, more massive herniation, which every now and again buckled him so that he was unable to lift himself off his back for days at a time. By the time he entered the hospital for surgery he had already spent several months in bed. The operation was successful, but, as in all such cases, it will take him a year to recover fully.

4   These aren't isolated experiences. Just about anybody who has ever played football for any length of time, in high school, college or one of the professional leagues, has suffered for it later physically.

5   Indeed, it is arguable that body shattering is the very *point* of football, as killing and maiming are of war. (In the United States, for example, the game results in 15 to 20 deaths a year and about 50,000 major operations on knees alone.) To grasp some of the more conspicuous similarities between football and war, it is instructive to listen to the imperatives most frequently issued to the players by their coaches, teammates and fans. "Hurt 'em!" "Level 'em!" "Kill 'em!" "Take 'em apart!" Or watch for the plays that are most enthusiastically

applauded by the fans. Where someone is "smeared," "knocked silly," "creamed," "nailed," "broken in two," or even "crucified." (One of my coaches when I played corner linebacker with the Calgary Stampeders in 1961 elaborated, often very inventively, on this language of destruction: admonishing us to "unjoin" the opponent, "make 'im remember you" and "stomp 'im like a bug.") Just as in hockey, where a fight will bring fans to their feet more often than a skillful play, so in football the mouth waters most of all for the really crippling block or tackle. For the kill. Thus the good teams are "hungry," the best players are "mean," and "casualties" are as much a part of the game as they are of a war.

6   The family resemblance between football and war is, indeed, striking. Their languages are similar: "field general," "long bomb," "blitz," "take a shot," "front line," "pursuit," "good hit," "the draft" and so on. Their principles and practices are alike: mass hysteria, the art of intimidation, absolute command and total obedience, territorial aggression, censorship, inflated insignia and propaganda, blackboard maneuvers and strategies, drills, uniforms, formations, marching bands and training camps. And the virtues they celebrate are almost identical: hyper-aggressiveness, coolness under fire and suicidal bravery. All this has been implicitly recognized by such jock-loving Americans as media stars General Patton and President Nixon, who have talked about war as a football game. Patton wanted to make his Second World War tank men look like football players. And Nixon, as we know, was fond of comparing attacks on Vietnam to football plays and drawing coachly diagrams on a blackboard for TV war fans.

7   One difference between war and football, though, is that there is little or no protest against football. Perhaps the most extraordinary thing about the game is that the systematic infliction of injuries excites in people not concern, as would be the case if they were sustained at, say, a rock festival, but a collective rejoicing and euphoria. Players and fans alike revel in the spectacle of a combatant felled into semiconsciousness, "blindsided," "clotheslined" or "decapitated." I can remember, in fact, being chided by a coach in pro ball for not "getting my hat" injuriously into a player who was already lying helpless on the ground. (On another occasion, after the Stampeders had traded the celebrated Joe Kapp to BC, we were playing the Lions in Vancouver and Kapp was forced on one play to run with the ball. He was coming

"down the chute," his bad knee wobbling uncertainly, so I simply dropped on him like a blanket. After I returned to the bench I was reproved for not exploiting the opportunity to unhinge his bad knee.)

8   After every game, of course, the papers are full of reports on the day's injuries, a sort of post-battle "body count," and the respective teams go to work with doctors and trainers, tape, whirlpool baths, cortisone and morphine to patch and deaden the wounds before the next game. Then the whole drama is reenacted—injured athletes held together by adhesive, braces and drugs—and the days following it are filled with even more feverish activity to put on the show yet again at the end of the next week. (I remember being so taped up in college that I earned the nickname "mummy.") The team that survives this merry-go-round spectacle of skilled masochism with the fewest incapacitating injuries usually wins. It is a sort of victory by ordeal: "We hurt them more than they hurt us."

9   My own initiation into this brutal circus was typical. I loved the game from the moment I could run with a ball. Played shoeless on a green open field with no one keeping score and in a spirit of reckless abandon and laughter, it's a very different sport. Almost no one gets hurt and it's rugged, open and exciting (it still is for me). But then, like everything else, it starts to be regulated and institutionalized by adult authorities. And the fun is over.

10   So it was as I began the long march through organized football. Now there was a coach and elders to make it clear by their behavior that beating other people was the only thing to celebrate and that trying to shake someone up every play was the only thing to be really proud of. Now there were severe rule enforcers, audiences, formally recorded victors and losers, and heavy equipment to permit crippling bodily moves and collisions (according to one American survey, more than 80% of all football injuries occur to fully equipped players). And now there was the official "given" that the only way to keep playing was to wear suffocating armor, to play to defeat, to follow orders silently and to renounce spontaneity for joyless drill. The game had been, in short, ruined. But because I loved to play and play skillfully, I stayed. And progressively and inexorably, as I moved through high school, college and pro leagues, my body was dismantled. Piece by piece.

11   I started off with torn ligaments in my knee at 13. Then, as the organization and the competition increased, the injuries came faster

and harder. Broken nose (three times), broken jaw (fractured in the first half and dismissed as a "bad wisdom tooth," so I played with it for the rest of the game), ripped knee ligaments again. Torn ligaments in one ankle and a fracture in the other (which I remember feeling relieved about because it meant I could honorably stop drill-blocking a 270-pound defensive end). Repeated rib fractures and cartilage tears (usually carried, again, through the remainder of the game). More dislocations of the left shoulder than I can remember (the last one I played with because, as the Calgary Stampeder doctor said, it "couldn't be damaged any more"). Occasional broken or dislocated fingers and toes. Chronically hurt lower back (I still can't lift with it or change a tire without worrying about folding). Separated right shoulder (as with many other injuries, like badly bruised hips and legs, needled with morphine for the games). And so on. The last pro game I played—against Winnipeg Blue Bombers in the Western finals in 1961—I had a recently dislocated left shoulder, a more recently wrenched right shoulder and a chronic pain centre in one leg. I was so tied up with soreness I couldn't drive my car to the airport. But it never occurred to me or anyone else that I miss a play as a corner linebacker.

12   By the end of my football career, I had learned that physical injury—giving it and taking it—is the real currency of the sport. And that in the final analysis the "winner" is the man who can hit to kill even if only half his limbs are working. In brief, a warrior game with a warrior ethos into which (like almost everyone else I played with) my original boyish enthusiasm had been relentlessly taunted and conditioned.

13   In thinking back on how all this happened, though, I can pick out no villains. As with the social system as a whole, the game has a life of its own. Everyone grows up inside it, accepts it and fulfills its dictates as obediently as helots. Far from ever questioning the principles of the activity, people simply concentrate on executing these principles more aggressively than anybody around them. The result is a group of people who, as the leagues become of a higher and higher class, are progressively insensitive to the possibility that things could be otherwise. Thus, in football, anyone who might question the wisdom or enjoyment of putting on heavy equipment on a hot day and running full speed at someone else with the intention of knocking him senseless would be regarded simply as not really a devoted athlete

and probably "chicken." The choice is made straightforward. Either you, too, do your very utmost to efficiently smash and be smashed, or you admit incompetence or cowardice and quit. Since neither of these admissions is very pleasant, people generally keep any doubts they have to themselves and carry on.

14   Of course, it would be a mistake to suppose that there is more blind acceptance of brutal practices in organized football than elsewhere. On the contrary, a recent Harvard study has approvingly argued that football's characteristics of "impersonal acceptance of inflicted injury," an overriding "organization goal," the "ability to turn oneself on and off" and being, above all, "out to win" are of "inestimable value" to big corporations. Clearly, our sort of football is no sicker than the rest of our society. Even its organized destruction of physical well-being is not anomalous. A very large part of our wealth, work and time is, after all, spent in systematically destroying and harming human life. Manufacturing, selling and using weapons that tear opponents to pieces. Making ever bigger and faster predator-named cars with which to kill and injure one another by the million every year. And devoting our very lives to outgunning one another for power in an ever more destructive rat race. Yet these practices are accepted without question by most people, even zealously defended and honored. Competitive, organized injuring is integral to our way of life, and football is simply one of the more intelligible mirrors of the whole process: a sort of colorful morality play showing us how exciting and rewarding it is to Smash Thy Neighbor.

15   Now it is fashionable to rationalize our collaboration in all this by arguing that, well, man *likes* to fight and injure his fellows and such games as football should be encouraged to discharge this original-sin urge into less harmful channels than, say, war. Public-show football, this line goes, plays the same sort of cathartic role as Aristotle said stage tragedy does: without real blood (or not much), it releases players and audience from unhealthy feelings stored up inside them.

16   As an ex-player in this seasonal coast-to-coast drama, I see little to recommend such a view. What organized football did to me was make me *suppress* my natural urges and re-express them in an alienating, vicious form. Spontaneous desires for free bodily exuberance and fraternization with competitors were shamed and forced under ("If it ain't hurtin' it ain't helpin' ") and in their place were demanded ar-

mored mechanical moves and cool hatred of all opposition. Endless authoritarian drill and dressing-room harangues (ever wonder why competing teams can't prepare for a game in the same dressing room?) were the kinds of mechanisms employed to reconstruct joyful energies into mean and alien shapes. I am quite certain that everyone else around me was being similarly forced into this heavily equipped military precision and angry antagonism, because there was always a mutinous attitude about full-dress practices, and everybody (the pros included) had to concentrate incredibly hard for days to whip themselves into just one hour's hostility a week against another club. The players never speak of these things, of course, because everyone is so anxious to appear tough.

17   The claim that men like seriously to battle one another to some sort of finish is a myth. It only endures because it wears one of the oldest and most propagandized of masks—the romantic combatant. I sometimes wonder whether the violence all around us doesn't depend for its survival on the existence and preservation of this tough-guy disguise.

18   As for the effect of organized football on the spectator, the fan is not released from supposed feelings of violent aggression by watching his athletic heroes perform it so much as encouraged in the view that people-smashing is an admirable mode of self-expression. The most savage attackers, after all, are, by general agreement, the most efficient and worthy players of all (the biggest applause I ever received as a football player occurred when I ran over people or slammed them so hard they couldn't get up). Such circumstances can hardly be said to lessen the spectators' martial tendencies. Indeed it seems likely that the whole show just further develops and titillates the North American addiction for violent self-assertion. . . . Perhaps, as well, it helps explain why the greater the zeal of U.S. political leaders as football fans (Johnson, Nixon, Agnew), the more enthusiastic the commitment to hard-line politics. At any rate there seems to be a strong correlation between people who relish tough football and people who relish intimidating and beating the hell out of commies, hippies, protest marchers and other opposition groups.

19   Watching well-advertised strong men knock other people around, make them hurt, is in the end like other tastes. It does not weaken with feeding and variation in form. It grows.

20   I got out of football in 1962. I had asked to be traded after Cal-

gary had offered me a $25-a-week-plus-commissions off-season job as a clothing-store salesman. ("Dear Mr. Finks:" I wrote. [Jim Finks was then the Stampeders' general manager.] "Somehow I do not think the dialectical subtleties of Hegel, Marx and Plato would be suitably oriented amidst the environmental stimuli of jockey shorts and herringbone suits. I hope you make a profitable sale or trade of my contract to the East.") So the Stampeders traded me to Montreal. In a preseason intersquad game with the Alouettes I ripped the cartilages in my ribs on the hardest block I'd ever thrown. I had trouble breathing and I had to shufflewalk with my torso on a tilt. The doctor in the local hospital said three weeks rest, the coach said scrimmage in two days. Three days later I was back home reading philosophy.

Suggestions for Discussion and Writing

1. McMurtry contends that "body shattering is the very *point* of football, as killing and maiming are of war." Is his analogy correct? Give your reasons for agreeing or disagreeing with him.

2. Unlike the other authors in this section, McMurtry doesn't specifically talk about the concept of manhood in his essay. What is he implying about it through his discussion of other subjects?

3. Whom do you think McMurtry intended as his original audience? Can you find specific clues in the essay that led you to that conclusion?

4. Why do you think McMurtry chose to use football as an illustration of our "sick" society? What sorts of effects does that choice have on you as a reader?

5. Is football—or are organized sports in general—too violent? Does research support his contention that violent sports promote violence in the spectators? What can be done about this problem?

4 Work vs. Women's Work

Like it or not, our culture has certain very fixed notions about what is "women's work" and "men's work". That's why we can find humor in movies like "Mr. Mom" or "Working Girl": they play off what those fixed notions are. But underneath the humor, there are some very real concerns about the notion of who does what work in our country. The Supreme Court recently considered the notion that employers ought to be able to ban women from some jobs to prevent them from suing if they became pregnant and the their unborn babies suffered birth defects resulting from their mothers' jobs. Everywhere in this country, two-job families wrestle with the questions of who will raise the children, do the yardwork, empty the catboxes, stay home with a sick child. These essays contribute to that discussion. Virginia Woolf begins with a classic look at the attitudes that may hamper women from succeeding in careers outside the home. Ellen Goodman looks at the strains placed on our society when most mothers go back to work. Ruth Schwartz Cowan asks how much labor "labor-saving devices" really save. Lester C. Thurow offers some hard answers for why women earn less than men. And Judy Brady offers a job description for wives, from a very different point of view. As you read and consider these essays, ask, "Are there jobs I think of as 'a man's job' or 'women's work'? Why do I think so? Is the job I want (or have) a man's job or a woman's job? Should sex play a role in determining who gets this job?"

Virginia Woolf

Professions for Women

The novelist VIRGINIA WOOLF (1882-1941) is one of the most influential writers of the twentieth century. She writes not only about what women have to give to each other and to men, but what men and women have, and should give to each other. If she finds women sometimes superior to men, it is in their ability to take the first step, to try to overcome male-imposed standards such as she describes in the essay below. The essay below was first given as a speech in 1936 to a group of women in upper-class London, many of whom had begun careers.

When your secretary invited me to come here, she told me that your Society is concerned with the employment of women and she suggested that I might tell you something about my own professional experiences. It is true I am a woman; it is true I am employed; but what professional experiences have I had? It is difficult to say. My profession is literature; and in that profession there are fewer experiences for women than in any other, with the exception of the stage—fewer, I mean, that are peculiar to women. For the road was cut many years ago—by Fanny Burney, by Aphra Behn, by Harriet Martineau, by Jane Austen, by George Eliot—many famous women, and many more unknown and forgotten, have been before me, making the path smooth, and regulating my steps. Thus, when I came to write, there were very few material obstacles in my way. Writing was a reputable and harmless occupation. The family peace was not broken by the scratching of a pen. No demand was made upon the family purse. For ten and six-pence one can buy paper enough to write all the plays of Shakespeare—if one has a mind that way. Pianos and models, Paris, Vienna and Ber-lin, masters and mistresses, are not needed by a writer. The cheapness of writing paper is, of course, the reason why women have succeeded as writers before they have succeeded in the other professions.

2   But to tell you my story—it is a simple one. You have only got to figure to yourselves a girl in a bedroom with a pen in her hand. She had only to move that pen from left to right—from ten o'clock to one. Then it occurred to her to do what is simple and cheap enough after all—to slip a few of those pages into an envelope, fix a penny stamp in the corner, and drop the envelope into the red box at the corner. It was thus that I became a journalist; and my effort was rewarded on the first day of the following month—a very glorious day it was for me—by a letter from an editor containing a cheque for one pound ten shillings and sixpence. But to show you how little I deserve to be called a pro-fessional woman, how little I know of the struggles and difficulties of such lives, I have to admit that instead of spending that sum upon bread and butter, rent, shoes and stockings, or butcher's bills, I went out and bought a cat—a beautiful cat, a Persian cat, which very soon involved me in bitter disputes with my neighbours.

3   What could be easier than to write articles and to buy Persian cats with the profits? But wait a moment. Articles have to be about some-thing. Mine, I seem to remember, was about a novel by a famous man. And while I was writing this review, I discovered that if I were going to review books I should need to do battle with a certain phantom. And the phantom was a woman, and when I came to know her better I called her after the heroine of a famous poem, The Angel in the House. It was she who used to come between me and my paper when I was writing reviews. It was she who bothered me and wasted my time and so tormented me that at last I killed her. You who come of a younger and happier generation may not have heard of her—you may not know what I mean by the Angel in the House. I will describe her as shortly as I can. She was intensely sympathetic. She was immensely charming. She was utterly unselfish. She excelled in the difficult arts of family life. She sacrificed herself daily. If there was chicken, she took the leg; if there was a draught she sat in it—in short she was so constituted that she never had a mind or a wish of her own, but preferred to sympathize

always with the minds and wishes of others. Above all—I need not say
it—she was pure. Her purity was supposed to be her chief beauty—her
blushes, her great grace. In those days—the last of Queen Victoria—
every house had its Angel. And when I came to write I encountered her
with the very first words. The shadow of her wings fell on my page; I
heard the rustling of her skirts in the room. Directly, that is to say, I
took my pen in hand to review that novel by a famous man, she slipped
behind me and whispered: "My dear, you are a young woman. You are
writing about a book that has been written by a man. Be sympathetic; be
tender; flatter; deceive; use all the arts and wiles of our sex. Never let
anybody guess that you have a mind of your own. Above all, be pure."
And she made as if to guide my pen. I now record the one act for which
I take some credit to myself, though the credit rightly belongs to some
excellent ancestors of mine who left me a certain sum of money—
shall we say five hundred pounds a year?—so that it was not necessary
for me to depend solely on charm for my living. I turned upon her and
caught her by the throat. I did my best to kill her. My excuse, if I were
to be had up in a court of law, would be that I acted in self-defense.
Had I not killed her she would have killed me. She would have
plucked the heart out of my writing. For, as I found, directly I put pen
to paper, you cannot review even a novel without having a mind of
your own, without expressing what you think to be the truth about
human relations, morality, sex. And all these questions, according to
the Angel in the House, cannot be dealt with freely and openly by
women; they must charm, they must conciliate, they must—to put it
bluntly—tell lies if they are to succeed. Thus, whenever I felt the
shadow of her wing or the radiance of her halo upon my page, I took
up the inkpot and flung it at her. She died hard. Her fictitious nature
was of great assistance to her. It is far harder to kill a phantom than a
reality. She was always creeping back when I thought I had dispatched
her. Though I flatter myself that I killed her in the end, the struggle
was severe; it took much time that had better have been spent upon
learning Greek grammar; or in roaming the world in search of adventures. But it was a real experience; it was an experience that was bound
to befall all women writers at that time. Killing the Angel in the
House was part of the occupation of a woman writer.

4   But to continue my story. The Angel was dead; what then
remained? You may say that what remained was a simple and common
object—a young woman in a bedroom with an inkpot. In other words,

now that she had rid herself of falsehood, that young woman had only to be herself. Ah, but what is "herself"? I mean, what is a woman? I assure you, I do not know. I do not believe that you know. I do not believe that anybody can know until she has expressed herself in all the arts and professions open to human skill. That indeed is one of the reasons why I have come here—out of respect for you, who are in process of showing us by your experiments what a woman is, who are in process of providing us, by your failures and successes, with that extremely important piece of information

5   But to continue the story of my professional experiences. I made one pound ten and six by my first review; and I bought a Persian cat with the proceeds. Then I grew ambitious. A Persian cat is all very well, I said; but a Persian cat is not enough. I must have a motor car. And it was thus that I became a novelist—for it is a very strange thing that people will give you a motor car if you will tell them a story. It is a still stranger thing that there is nothing so delightful in the world as telling stories. It is far pleasanter than writing reviews of famous novels. And yet, if I am to obey your secretary and tell you my professional experiences as a novelist, I must tell you about a very strange experience that befell me as a novelist. And to understand it you must try first to imagine a novelist's state of mind. I hope I am not giving away professional secrets if I say that a novelist's chief desire is to be as unconscious as possible. He has to induce in himself a state of perpetual lethargy. He wants life to proceed with the utmost quiet and regularity. He wants to see the same faces, to read the same books, to do the same things day after day, month after month, while he is writing, so that nothing may break the illusion in which he is living—so that nothing may disturb or disquiet the mysterious nosings about, feelings round, darts, dashes and sudden discoveries of that very shy and illusive spirit, the imagination. I suspect that this state is the same both for men and women. Be that as it may, I want you to imagine me writing a novel in a state of trance. I want you to figure to yourselves a girl sitting with a pen in her hand, which for minutes, and indeed for hours, she never dips into the inkpot. The image that comes to my mind when I think of this girl is the image of a fisherman lying sunk in dreams on the verge of a deep lake with a rod held out over the water. She was letting her imagination sweep unchecked round every rock and cranny of the world that lies submerged in the depths of our unconscious being. Now came the experience, the experience that I

believe to be far commoner with women writers than with men. The line raced through the girl's fingers. Her imagination had rushed away. It had sought the pools, the depths, the dark places where the largest fish slumber. And then there was a smash. There was an explosion. There was foam and confusion. The imagination had dashed itself against something hard. The girl was roused from her dream. She was indeed in a state of the most acute and difficult distress. To speak without figure she had thought of something, something about the body, about the passions which it was unfitting for her as a woman to say. Men, her reason told her, would be shocked. The consciousness of what men will say of a woman who speaks the truth about her passions had roused her from her artist's state of unconsciousness. She could write no more. The trance was over. Her imagination could work no longer. This I believe to be a very common experience with women writers—they are impeded by the extreme conventionality of the other sex. For though men sensibly allow themselves great freedom in these respects, I doubt that they realize or can control the extreme severity with which they condemn such freedom in women.

6   These then were two very genuine experiences of my own. These were two of the adventures of my professional life. The first— killing the Angel in the House—I think I solved. She died. But the second, telling the truth about my own experiences as a body, I do not think I solved. I doubt that any woman has solved it yet. The obstacles against her are still immensely powerful—and yet they are very difficult to define. Outwardly, what is simpler than to write books? Outwardly, what obstacles are there for a woman rather than for a man? Inwardly, I think, the case is very different; she has still many ghosts to fight, many prejudices to overcome. Indeed it will be a long time still, I think, before a woman can sit down to write a book without finding a phantom to be slain, a rock to be dashed against. And if this is so in literature, the freest of all professions for women, how is it in the new professions which you are now for the first time entering?

7   Those are the questions that I should like, had I time, to ask you. And indeed, if I have laid stress upon these professional experiences of mine, it is because I believe that they are, though in different forms, yours also. Even when the path is nominally open—when there is nothing to prevent a woman from being a doctor, a lawyer, a civil servant—there are many phantoms and obstacles, as I believe, looming in

her way. To discuss and define them is I think of great value and importance; for thus only can the labour be shared, the difficulties be solved. But besides this, it is necessary also to discuss the ends and the aims for which we are fighting, for which we are doing battle with these formidable obstacles. Those aims cannot be taken for granted; they must be perpetually questioned and examined. The whole position, as I see it—here in this hall surrounded by women practising for the first time in history I know not how many different professions—is one of extraordinary interest and importance. You have won rooms of your own in the house hitherto exclusively owned by men. You are able, though not without great labour and effort, to pay the rent. You are earning your five hundred pounds a year. But this freedom is only a beginning; the room is your own, but it is still bare. It has to be furnished; it has to be decorated; it has to be shared. How are you going to furnish it, how are you going to decorate it? With whom are you going to share it, and upon what terms? These, I think are questions of the utmost importance and interest. For the first time in history you are able to ask for them; for the first time you are able to decide for yourselves what the answers should be. Willingly would I stay and discuss those questions and answers—but not tonight. My time is up; and I must cease.

Suggestions for Discussion and Writing

1. Woolf's strategy in the introduction seems to be one protesting her *inability* to address this subject. As a reader, do you believe her, or do you get some other message from what she has to say?

2. Who is the Angel in the House? In what forms does she still exist? Is there a masculine equivalent for her? What sources in modern culture still promote the image of the Angel?

3. What Angels "loom. . . in the way" of women who pursue professions today? Do men face similar Angels?

4. Why, according to Woolf, are women supposed to leave writing about "human relations, morality, sex" to men? Do those attitudes still prevail today? Are there any taboo subjects for male or female writers today?

5. *The Angel in the House* is the title of a famous nineteenth-century British poem by Coventry Patmore (1823-1896).

If your library has a copy of this poem, read it, and analyze why Woolf made it the central image in her essay.

Ellen Goodman
The Neighborhood Mom

ELLEN GOODMAN (born in Massachusetts in 1941) sees her writings appear frequently in newspapers and magazines throughout the country. She graduated with honors from Radcliffe in 1963, and has been a writer and journalist as well as a nationally-syndicated columnist and, since 1986, associate editor of the Boston *Globe*. She won the Pulitzer Prize for commentary in 1980 and the Hubert H. Humphrey Civil Rights Award in 1988; her most recent collection of essays is *Making Sense* (1989). This column first appeared in 1987.

It was the fourth no-school day of the year. The Neighborhood Mother had just heard from two of those she refers to privately as her "clients."

2   One of these clients was the mother of Jason. The other was the mother of Andrew. The boys were friends of her own 6-year-old son, Matthew, and the mothers all knew each other through that chain that connects the parents of classmates by a Xeroxed telephone list. The Neighborhood Mother was familiar with that school list because she had typed it.

3   The first of her clients was a single working mother, the second was half of a two-working-parent family. Both these work lives were inflexible enough that the very first flake threatened them with disaster. But because there is no Red Cross for working parents faced with a no-school day, they called The Neighborhood Mother.

4   So it was that by 9 A.M., the N.M. had the boots, snowsuits and energy level of five children, including Jason's brother, under her

roof for the entire day. At times like this the woman, who had not worked outside her home since her second child was born, nostalgically remembered mornings when she took a cup of coffee to her desk and worried about the sales campaign for a line of natural shampoos.

5   The N.M. didn't mind taking on her small extras. She understood the lives of her neighbor-clients. She knew that some longed for her option. Certainly she knew the alternative for her young visitors was to spend the day alone.

6   Yet there was something bothering her when we talked. Maybe it was the way Jason's mother had anxiously said, "since you're home anyway." Maybe it was the way a man at the last PTA meeting had asked her the classic question, "Are you working?" Or was it because even her clients regarded her as a volunteer?

7   It occurred to the N.M. that as fewer women could or did make the choice to stay home with their own children, more and more was expected of them. In the past year, she had been room mother, PTA representative, had gone on three school trips as bus monitor, and brought cookies and juice for as many birthdays. Because she was home. Anyway.

8   The N.M.'s name was listed under "In Case of Emergency" for no fewer than half-a-dozen kids, including her own nieces, who had spent two sick days on her daybed. Two or three times, when the baby sitter hadn't shown up at a friend's, she had done after-school care for two or three more.

9   It wasn't just child care, mind you. In the weeks before Christmas, the United Parcel delivery man had been at her door often enough to start a rumor, if there had been any neighbors around to gossip. He left a streetful of packages for pickup by their owners. She also held keys to the houses next door, and at one time or another had let in a repairer or deliverer to each of them.

10   The woman was not oppressed by this. She could and did say no. But she wondered sometimes whether anyone knew about her multi-service center. Knew how many depended on the few women who were home. Anyway.

11   The N.M. thought about all this especially hard because next year she would in all probability be closing down her center and re-entering the work world. This endangered species would lose another member due to the environmental pressures on a single paycheck. How would she replace herself?

12   Was it possible, she wondered, to create a semi-professional net-
work of Neighborhood Mothers and Fathers each on a retainer for
school trips and no-school days, with a fee schedule that might include
sick days? Was that too mercenary?

13   What about swapping, or compensatory time off, as they say in the
business world? For every car pool and after-school project, every sick
or snow day, each client could return the favor with equal hours of
child care or maybe even—this is her fantasy—an occasional house-
cleaning. And what about a work place that accommodates in snow, not
to mention a place that accommodates children?

14   Her point is that we are running the 1980s world along the
1950s model. Once, almost every family had its wife and mother.
Now there is, at most, one per neighborhood. Yet the same rules, the
same expectations, the same needs exist. There has been no real
replacement.

15   So, she says, as the five snowed-in children play in the background, that next year she will be part of the problem and cannot
figure out a proper solution. All she knows for sure is one thing. If she
calls for help, she swears, she will never, ever, say to another N.M.,
"because you are home, anyway."

Suggestions for Discussion and Writing

1. How would Goodman define "the neighborhood
mom"? What are the chief duties in her job description? Does
she have a male counterpart?

2. Do you agree with the Neighborhood Mom "that we
are running the 1980s (and 1990s) world along the 1950s
model"? Who is the "we" in that statement?

3. Many of the words used in conjunction with the Neighborhood Mom have to do with money: mercenary, retainer,
option, client, compensation. Do you believe that Neighborhood Mom should be a paying job? If so, who should pay?

4. In our culture, why do we assume that women should
do the kinds of activities assigned to the Neighborhood Mom?
What does that say about the values we place on men's and
women's time? on parenting?

5. Several solutions have been offered to the problem of
the Neighborhood Mom shortage, including shared jobs, day

care, flexible time schedules, and working at home. Explore the possibilities of one of these solutions, or a solution of your own. Are they offered in your community, and do they work? Why or why not?

Ruth Schwartz Cowan
Less Work for Mother?

RUTH SCHWARTZ COWAN, born in 1941, is a professor of history and has been Director of Women's Studies at the State University of New York at Stony Brook. Her groundbreaking book, *More Work for Mother: The Ironies of Household Technology from the Open Hearth to the Microwave* (1983) documents how women found themselves doing more housework as household tasks became less physically demanding, so that labor-saving devices ended up causing homemakers more work. With Neil M. Cowan, she is also the author of *Our Parents' Lives* (1989). This essay, which appeared in *The Journal of Invention and Technology* in 1987, continues her explorations into the history and politics of housework.

T hings are never what they seem. Skimmed milk masquerades as cream. And laborsaving household appliances often do not save labor. This is the surprising conclusion reached by a small army of historians, sociologists, and home economists who have undertaken, in recent years, to study the one form of work that has turned out to be most resistant to inquiry and analysis—namely, housework.

2   During the first half of the twentieth century, the average American household was transformed by the introduction of a group of machines that profoundly altered the daily lives of housewives; the forty years between 1920 and 1960 witnessed what might be aptly called the "industrial revolution in the home." Where once there had

been a wood- or coal-burning stove there now was a gas or electric range. Clothes that had once been scrubbed on a metal washboard were now tossed into a tub and cleansed by an electrically driven agitator. The dryer replaced the clothesline; the vacuum cleaner replaced the broom; the refrigerator replaced the icebox and the root cellar; an automatic pump, some piping, and a tap replaced the hand pump, the bucket, and the well. No one had to chop and haul wood any more. No one had to shovel out ashes or beat rugs or carry water; no one even had to toss egg whites with a fork for an hour to make an angel food cake.

3   And yet American housewives in 1960, 1970, and even 1980 continued to log about the same number of hours at their work as their grandmothers and mothers had in 1910, 1920, and 1930. The earliest time studies of housewives date from the very same period in which time studies of other workers were becoming popular—the first three decades of the twentieth century. The sample sizes of these studies were usually quite small, and they did not always define housework in precisely the same way (some counted an hour spent taking children to the playground as "work," while others called it "leisure"), but their results were more or less consistent: whether rural or urban, the average American housewife performed fifty to sixty hours of unpaid work in her home every week, and the only variable that significantly altered this was the number of small children.

4   A half century later not much had changed. Survey research had become much more sophisticated, and sample sizes had grown considerably, but the results of the time studies remained surprisingly consistent. The average American housewife, now armed with dozens of motors and thousands of electronic chips, still spends fifty to sixty hours a week doing housework. The only variable that significantly altered the size of that number was full time employment in the labor force; "working" housewives cut down the average number of hours that they spend cooking and cleaning, shopping and chauffeuring, to a not insignificant thirty-five—virtually the equivalent of another full-time job.

5   How can this be true? Surely even the most sophisticated advertising copywriter of all times could not fool almost the entire American population over the course of at least three generations. Labor-saving devices must be saving something, or Americans would not continue, year after year, to plunk down their hard-earned dollars for them.

6   And if laborsaving devices have not saved labor in the home, then what is it that has suddenly made it possible for more than 70 percent of the wives and mothers in the American population to enter the work force and stay there? A brief glance at the histories of some of the technologies that have transformed housework in the twentieth century will help us answer some of these questions.

7   The portable vacuum cleaner was one of the earliest electric appliances to make its appearance in American homes, and reasonably priced models appeared on the retail market as early as 1910. For decades prior to the turn of the century, inventors had been trying to create a carper-cleaning system that would improve on the carpet sweeper with adjustable rotary brushes (patented by Melville Bissell in 1876) or the semiannual ritual of hauling rugs outside and beating them, or the practice of regularly sweeping the dirt out of a rug that had been covered with dampened, torn newspapers. Early efforts to solve the problem had focused on the use of large steam, gasoline, or electric motors attached to piston-type pumps and lots of hoses. Many of these "stationary" vacuum-cleaning systems were installed in apartment houses or hotels, but some were hauled around the streets in horse-drawn carriages by entrepreneurs hoping to establish themselves as "professional house-cleaners."

8   In the first decade of the twentieth century, when fractional-horsepower electric motors became widely—and inexpensively—available, the portable vacuum cleaner intended for use in an individual household was born. One early model—invented by a woman, Corrine Dufour—consisted of a rotary brush, an electrically driven fan, and a wet sponge for absorbing the dust and dirt. Another, patented by David E. Kenney in 1907, had a twelve-inch nozzle, attached to a metal tube, attached to a flexible hose that led to a vacuum pump and separating devices. The Hoover, which was based on a brush, a fan, and a collecting bag, was on the market by 1908. The Electrolux, the first of the canister types of cleaner, which could vacuum something above the level of the floor, was brought over from Sweden in 1924 and met with immediate success.

9   These early vacuum cleaners were hardly a breeze to operate. All were heavy, and most were extremely cumbersome to boot. One early home economist mounted a basal metabolism machine on the back of one of her hapless students and proceeded to determine that more energy was expended in the effort to clean a sample carpet with a vacuum

cleaner than when the same carpet was attacked with a hard broom. The difference, of course, was that the vacuum cleaner did a better job, at least on carpets, because a good deal of what the broom stirred up simply resettled a foot or two away from where it had first been lodged. Whatever the liabilities of the early vacuum cleaners may have been, Americans nonetheless appreciated their virtues; according to a market survey done in Zanesville, Ohio, in 1926, slightly more than half the households owned one. Eventually improvements in the design made these devices easier to operate. By 1960 vacuum cleaners could be found in 70 percent of the nation's homes.

10   When the vacuum cleaner is viewed in a historical context, however, it is easy to see why it did not save housewifely labor. Its introduction coincided almost precisely with the disappearance of the domestic servant. The number of persons engaged in household service dropped from 1,851,000 in 1910 to 1,411,000 in 1920, while the number of households enumerated in the census rose from 20.3 million to 24.4 million. Moreover, between 1900 and 1920 the number of household servants per thousand persons dropped from 98.9 to 58.0, while during the 1920s the decline was even more precipitous as the restrictive immigration acts dried up what had once been the single most abundant source of domestic labor.

11   For the most economically comfortable segment of the population, this meant just one thing: the adult female head of the household was doing more housework than she had ever done before. What Maggie had once done with a broom, Mrs. Smith was now doing with a vacuum cleaner. Knowing that this was happening, several early copywriters for vacuum cleaner advertisements focused on its implications. The vacuum cleaner, General Electric announced in 1918, is better than a maid: it doesn't quit, get drunk, or demand higher wages. The switch from Maggie to Mrs. Smith shows up, in time-study statistics, as an increase in the time that Mrs. Smith is spending at her work.

12   For those—and they were the vast majority of the population—who were not economically comfortable, the vacuum cleaner implied something else again: not an increase in the time spent in housework but an increase in the standard of living. In many households across the country, acquisition of a vacuum cleaner was connected to an expansion of living space, the move from a small apartment to a small house, the purchase of wall-to-wall carpeting. If this did not happen

during the difficult 1930s, it became more possible during the expansive 1950s. As living quarters grew larger, standards for their upkeep increased; rugs had to be vacuumed every week, in some households every day, rather than semiannually, as had been customary. The net result, of course, was that when armed with a vacuum cleaner, housewives whose parents had been poor could keep more space cleaner than their mothers and grandmothers would have ever believed possible. We might put this everyday phenomenon in language that economists can understand: The introduction of the vacuum cleaner led to improvements in productivity but not to any significant decrease in the amount of time expended by each worker.

13   The history of the washing machine illustrates a similar phenomenon. "Blue Monday" had traditionally been, as its name implies, the bane of a housewife's existence—especially when Monday turned out to be "Monday. . . and Tuesday to do the ironing." Thousands of patents for "new and improved" washers were issued during the nineteenth century in an effort to cash in on the housewife's despair. Most of these early washing machines were wooden or metal tubs combined with some kind of hand-cranked mechanism that would rub or push or twirl laundry when the tub was filled with water and soap. At the end of the century, the Sears catalog offered four such washing machines, ranging in price from $2.50 to $4.25, all sold in combination with hand-cranked wringers.

14   These early machines may have saved time in the laundering process (four shirts could be washed at once instead of each having to be rubbed separately against a washboard), but they probably didn't save much energy. Lacking taps and drains, the tubs still had to be filled and emptied by hand, and each piece still had to be run through a wringer and hung up to dry.

15   Not long after the appearance of fractional-horsepower motors, several enterprising manufacturers had the idea of hooking them up to the crank mechanisms of washers and wringers—and the electric washer was born. By the 1920s, when mass production of such machines began, both the general structure of the machine (a central-shaft agitator rotating within a cylindrical tub, hooked up to the household water supply) and the general structure of the industry (oligopolistic—with a very few firms holding most of the patents and controlling most of the market) had achieved their final form. By 1926 just over a quarter of the families in Zanesville had an electric

washer, but by 1941 fully 52 percent of all American households either owned or had interior access (which means that they could use coin-operated models installed in the basements of apartment houses) to such a machine. The automatic washer, which consisted of a vertically rotating washer cylinder that could also act as a centrifugal extractor, was introduced by the Bendix Home Appliance Corporation in 1938, but it remained expensive, and therefore inaccessible, until after World War II. This machine contained timing devices that allowed it to proceed through its various cycles automatically; by spinning the clothes around in the extractor phase of its cycle, it also eliminated the wringer. Although the Bendix subsequently disappeared from the retail market (versions of this sturdy machine may still be found in Laundromats), its design principles are replicated in the agitator washers that currently chug away in millions of American homes.

16   Both the early wringer washers and their more recent automatic cousins have released American women from the burden of drudgery. No one who has ever tried to launder a sheet by hand, and without the benefits of hot running water, would want to return to the days of the scrub-board and tub. But "labor" is composed of both "energy expenditure" and "time expenditure," and the history of laundry work demonstrates that the one may be conserved while the other is not.

17   The reason for this is, as with the vacuum cleaner, twofold. In the early decades of the century, many households employed laundresses to do their wash; this was true, surprisingly enough, even for some very poor households when wives and mothers were disabled or employed full-time in field or factory. Other households—rich and poor—used commercial laundry services. Large, mechanized "steam" laundries were first constructed in this country in the 1860s, and by the 1920s they could be found in virtually every urban neighborhood and many rural ones as well.

18   But the advent of the electric home washer spelled doom both for the laundress and for the commercial laundry; since the housewife's labor was unpaid, and since the washer took so much of the drudgery out of washday, the one-time expenditure for a machine seemed, in many families, a more sensible arrangement than continuous expenditure for domestic services. In the process, of course, the time spent on laundry work by the individual housewife, who had previously employed either a laundress or a service, was bound to increase.

19   For those who had not previously enjoyed the benefits of relief from washday drudgery, the electric washer meant something quite different but equally significant: an upgrading of household cleanliness. Men stopped wearing removable collars and cuffs, which meant that the whole of their shirts had to be washed and then ironed. Housewives began changing two sheets every week, instead of moving the top sheet to the bottom and adding only one that was fresh. Teenagers began changing their underwear every day instead of every weekend. In the early 1960s, when synthetic no-iron fabrics were introduced, the size of the household laundry load increased again; shirts and skirts, sheets and blouses that had once been sent out to the dry cleaner or the corner laundry were now being tossed into the household wash basket. By the 1980s the average American housewife, armed now with an automatic washing machine and an automatic dryer, was processing roughly ten times (by weight) the amount of laundry that her mother had been accustomed to. Drudgery had disappeared, but the laundry hadn't. The average time spent on this chore in 1925 had been 5.8 hours per week; in 1964 it was 6.2.

20   And then there is the automobile. We do not usually think of our cars as household appliances, but that is precisely what they are since housework, as currently understood, could not possibly be performed without them. The average American housewife is today more likely to be found behind a steering wheel than in front of a stove. While writing this article I interrupted myself five times: once to take a child to field-hockey practice, then a second time, to bring her back when practice was finished; once to pick up some groceries at the supermarket; once to retrieve my husband, who was stranded at the train station; once for a trip to a doctor's office. Each time I was doing housework, and each time I had to use my car.

21   Like the washing machine and the vacuum cleaner, the automobile started to transform the nature of housework in the 1920s. Until the introduction of the Model T in 1908, automobiles had been playthings for the idle rich, and although many wealthy women learned to drive early in the century (and several participated in well-publicized auto races), they were hardly the women who were likely to be using their cars to haul groceries.

22   But by 1920, and certainly by 1930, all this had changed. Helen and Robert Lynd, who conducted an intensive study of Muncie, Indiana, between 1923 and 1925 (reported in their famous book Middle-

town), estimated that in Muncie in the 1890s only 125 families, all members of the "elite," owned a horse and buggy, but by 1923 there were 6,222 passenger cars in the city, "roughly one for every 7.1 persons, or two for every three families." By 1930, according to national statistics, there were roughly 30 million households in the United States—and 26 million registered automobiles.

23   What did the automobile mean for the housewife? Unlike public transportation systems, it was convenient. Located right at her doorstep, it could deposit her at the doorstep that she wanted or needed to visit. And unlike the bicycle or her own two feet, the automobile could carry bulky packages as well as several additional people. Acquisition of an automobile therefore meant that a housewife, once she had learned how to drive, could become her own door-to-door delivery service. And as more housewives acquired automobiles, more businessmen discovered the joys of dispensing with delivery services—particularly during the Depression.

24   To make a long story short, the iceman does not cometh anymore. Neither does the milkman, the bakery truck, the butcher, the grocer, the knife sharpener, the seamstress, or the doctor. Like many other businessmen, doctors discovered that their earnings increased when they stayed in their offices and transferred the responsibility for transportation to their ambulatory patients.

25   Thus a new category was added to the housewife's traditional job description: chauffeur. The suburban station wagon is now "Mom's Taxi." Children who once walked to school now have to be transported by their mothers; husbands who once walked home from work now have to be picked up by their wives; groceries that once were dispensed from pushcarts or horse-drawn wagons now have to be packed into paper bags and hauled home in family cars. "Contemporary women," one time-study expert reported in 1974 "spend about one full working day per week on the road and in stores compared with less than two hours per week for women in the 1920s." If everything we needed to maintain our homes and sustain our families were delivered right to our doorsteps—and every member of the family had independent means for getting where she or he wanted to go—the hours spent on housework by American housewives would decrease dramatically.

26   The histories of the vacuum cleaner, the washing machine, and the automobile illustrate the varied reasons why the time spent in

housework has not markedly decreased in the United States during the last half century despite the introduction of so many ostensibly labor-saving appliances. But these histories do not help us understand what has made it possible for so many American wives and mothers to enter the labor force full-time during those same years. Until recently, one of the explanations most often offered for the startling increase in the participation of married women in the work force (up from 24.8 percent in 1950 to 50.1 percent in 1980) was household technology. What with microwave ovens and frozen foods, washer and dryer combinations and paper diapers, the reasoning goes, housework can now be done in no time at all, and women have so much time on their hands that they find they must go out and look for a job for fear of going stark, raving mad.

27   As every "working" housewife knows, this pattern of reasoning is itself stark, raving mad. Most adult women are in the work force today quite simply because they need the money. Indeed most "working" housewives today hold down not one but two jobs; they put in what has come to be called a "double day." Secretaries, lab technicians, janitors, sewing machine operators, teachers, nurses, or physicians for eight (or nine or ten) hours, they race home to become chief cook and bottle washer for another five, leaving the cleaning and the marketing for Saturday and Sunday. Housework, as we have seen, still takes a lot of time, modern technology notwithstanding.

28   Yet household technologies have played a major role in facilitating (as opposed to causing) what some observers believe to be the most significant social revolution of our time. They do it in two ways, the first of which we have already noted. By relieving housework of the drudgery that it once entailed, washing machines, vacuum cleaners, dishwashers, and water pumps have made it feasible for a woman to put in a double day without destroying her health, to work full-time and still sustain herself and her family at a reasonably comfortable level.

29   The second relationship between household technology and the participation of married women in the work force is considerably more subtle. It involves the history of some technologies that we rarely think of as technologies at all—and certainly not as household appliances. Instead of being sheathed in stainless steel or porcelain, these devices appear in our kitchens in little brown bottles and bags of flour; instead of using switches and buttons to turn them on, we use

hypodermic needles and sugar cubes. They are various forms of medication, the products not only of modern medicine but also of modern industrial chemistry: polio vaccines and vitamin pills; tetanus toxins and ampicillin; enriched breads and tuberculin tests.

30   Before any of these technologies had made their appearance, nursing may well have been the most time-consuming and most essential aspect of housework. During the eighteenth and nineteenth centuries and even during the first five decades of the twentieth century, it was the woman of the house who was expected (and who had been trained, usually by her mother) to sit up all night cooling and calming a feverish child, to change bandages on suppurating wounds, to clean bed linens stained with excrement, to prepare easily digestible broths, to cradle colicky infants on her lap for hours on end, to prepare bodies for burial. An attack of the measles might mean the care of a bedridden child for a month. Pneumonia might require six months of bed rest. A small knife cut could become infected and produce a fever that would rage for days. Every summer brought the fear of polio epidemics, and every polio epidemic left some group of mothers with the perpetual problem of tending to the needs of a handicapped child. Cholera, diphtheria, typhoid fever—if they weren't fatal—could mean weeks of sleepless nights and hard-pressed days. "Just as soon as the person is attacked," one experienced mother wrote to her worried daughter during a cholera epidemic in Oklahoma in 1885, "be it ever so slightly, he or she ought to go to bed immediately and stay there; put a mustard [plaster] over the bowels and if vomiting over the stomach. See that the feet are kept warm, either by warm iron or brick, or bottles of hot water. If the disease progresses the limbs will begin to cramp, which must be prevented by applying cloths wrung out of hot water and wrapping round them. When one is vomiting so terribly, of course, it is next to impossible to keep medicine down, but in cholera it must be done."

31   These were the routines to which American women were once accustomed, routines regarded as matters of life and death. To gain some sense of the way in which modern medicines have altered not only the routines of housework but also the emotional commitment that often accompanies such work, we need only read out a list of the diseases for which most American children are unlikely to succumb today, remembering how many of them once were fatal or terribly disabling: diphtheria, whooping cough, tetanus, pellagra, rickets,

measles, mumps, tuberculosis, smallpox, cholera, malaria, and polio.

32   And many of today's ordinary childhood complaints, curable within a few days of the ingestion of antibiotics, once might have entailed weeks, or even months, of full-time attention: bronchitis; strep throat; scarlet fever; bacterial pneumonia; infections of the skin, or the eyes, or the ears, or the airways. In the days before the introduction of modern vaccines, antibiotics, and vitamin supplements, a mother who was employed full-time was a serious, sometimes life-endangering threat to the health of her family. This is part of the reason why life expectancy was always low and infant mortality high among the poorest segment of the population—those most likely to be dependent upon a mother's wages.

33   Thus modern technology, especially modern medical technology, has made it possible for married women to enter the work force by releasing housewives not just from drudgery but also from the dreaded emotional equation of female employment with poverty and disease. She may be exhausted at the end of her double day, but the modern "working" housewife can at least fall into bed knowing that her efforts have made it possible to sustain her family at a level of health and comfort that not so long ago was reserved only for those who were very rich.

Suggestions for Discussion and Writing

1. What are some of the reasons why American women still spend so much time doing housework? Can you think of reasons Cowan doesn't account for?

2. Although many women are working full-time and keeping house, they are doing less housework. What factors have allowed them to do so? Do you think Cowan takes these factors sufficiently into account in her argument?

3. Cowan picks three out of many laborsaving devices as her focuses: vacuums, washer/dryers, and cars. Why do you think she chose these three particular illustrations? What might it suggest about the assumptions she is making about you as readers?

4. What kinds of evidence does Cowan give you to convince you to agree with her? Do you find it persuasive? What other kinds of evidence might she have used?

5. The division of household chores is a sore point in many households; some sociologists call the jobs to be done when people come home from work "the second shift." Look up some magazine and newspaper articles on this phenomenon. What is the status of housework in the 1990s? How do the households you are familiar with fit into this national trend?

Lester C. Thurow

Why Women Are Paid Less than Men

LESTER C. THUROW, born in 1938, holds his master's degree from Oxford and his Ph.D. from Harvard. He is a professor and former dean at M.I.T.'s Sloan School of Management, one of the most prestigious business schools in the United States, and since 1978 has served on the Economic Advisory Board of the NAACP. His book *Dangerous Currents: The State of the Economy* (1983) accurately predicted many of our current economic difficulties. "Why Women are Paid Less than Men" first appeared in his column in *The New York Times Magazine* in 1981.

In the 40 years from 1939 to 1979 white women who work full time have with monotonous regularity made slightly less than 60 percent as much as white men. Why?

2   Over the same time period, minorities have made substantial progress in catching up with whites, with minority women making even more progress than minority men. Black men now earn 72 percent as much as white men (up 16 percentage points since the mid-1950's) but black women earn 92 percent as much as white women. Hispanic men make 71 percent of what their white counterparts do, but His-

panic women make 82 percent as much as white women. As a result of their faster progress, fully employed black women make 75 percent as much as fully employed black men while Hispanic women earn 68 percent as much as Hispanic men.

3   This faster progress may, however, end when minority women finally catch up with white women. In the bible of the New Right, George Gilder's *Wealth and Poverty*, the 60 percent is just one of Mother Nature's constants like the speed of light or the force of gravity. Men are programmed to provide for their families economically while women are programmed to take care of their families emotionally and physically. As a result men put more effort into their jobs than women. The net result is a difference in work intensity that leads to that 40 percent gap in earnings. But there is no discrimination against women—only the biological facts of life.

4   The problem with this assertion is just that. It is an assertion with no evidence for it other than the fact that white women have made 60 percent as much as men for a long period of time.

5   "Discrimination against women" is an easy answer but it also has its problems as an adequate explanation. Why is discrimination against women not declining under the same social forces that are leading to a lessening of discrimination against minorities? In recent years women have made more use of the enforcement provisions of the Equal Employment Opportunities Commission and the courts than minorities. Why do the laws that prohibit discrimination against women and minorities work for minorities but not for women?

6   When men discriminate against women, they run into a problem. To discriminate against women is to discriminate against your own wife and to lower your own family income. To prevent women from working is to force men to work more.

7   When whites discriminate against blacks, they can at least think that they are raising their own incomes. When men discriminate against women they have to know that they are lowering their own family income and increasing their own work effort.

8   While discrimination undoubtedly explains part of the male-female earnings differential, one has to believe that men are monumentally stupid or irrational to explain all of the earnings gap in terms of discrimination. There must be something else going on.

9   Back in 1939 it was possible to attribute the earnings gap to large differences in educational attainments. But the educational gap

between men and women has been eliminated since World War II. It is no longer possible to use education as an explanation for the lower earnings of women. Some observers have argued that women earn less money since they are less reliable workers who are more apt to leave the labor force. But it is difficult to maintain this position since women are less apt to quit one job to take another and as a result they tend to work as long, or longer, for any one employer. From any employer's perspective they are more reliable, not less reliable, than men.

10   Part of the answer is visible if you look at the lifetime earnings profile of men. Suppose that you were asked to predict which men in a group of 25-year-olds would become economically successful. At age 25 it is difficult to tell who will be economically successful and your predictions are apt to be highly inaccurate. But suppose that you were asked to predict which men in a group of 35-year-olds would become economically successful. If you are successful at age 35, you are very likely to remain successful for the rest of your life. If you have not become economically successful by age 35, you are very unlikely to do so later.

11   The decade between 25 and 35 is when men either succeed or fail. It is the decade when lawyers become partners in the good firms, when business managers make it onto the "fast track," when academics get tenure at good universities, and when blue collar workers find the job opportunities that will lead to training opportunities and the skills that will generate high earnings. If there is any one decade when it pays to work hard and to be consistently in the labor force, it is the decade between 25 and 35. For those who succeed, earnings will rise rapidly. For those who fail, earnings will remain flat for the rest of their lives.

12   But the decade between 25 and 35 is precisely the decade when women are most apt to leave the labor force or become part-time workers to have children. When they do, the current system of promotion and skill acquisition will extract an enormous lifetime price.

13   This leaves essentially two avenues for equalizing male and female earnings. Families where women who wish to have successful careers, compete with men, and achieve the same earnings should alter their family plans and have their children either before 25 or after 35. Or society can attempt to alter the existing promotion and skill acquisition system so that there is a longer time period in which both men

and women can attempt to successfully enter the labor force. Without some combination of these two factors, a substantial fraction of the male-female earnings differentials are apt to persist for the next 40 years, even if discrimination against women is eliminated.

Suggestions for Discussion and Writing

1. Thurow equates salary differences with discrimination. Do you think this is a fair comparison? What effects does he want his analogy to have on you, the reader?

2. What are the reasons some people give for dismissing the difference in men's and women's earnings? Can you add any to the list Thurow provides?

3. Thurow claims that "for those who succeed (between 25 and 35), earnings will rise rapidly. For those who fail, earnings will remain flat for the rest of their lives." Is this always true?

4. Thurow offers two solutions to the problem of unequal wages. Are either realistic? What are the advantages and disadvantages to each?

5. One solution often offered to women's taking time off to have children is time off—usually called maternity leave, paternity leave, or family leave. Legislation to support family leave exists in some states and is under consideration by the U.S. Congress. Investigate the situation regarding family leave in your area. Is it available? Does it work? Do employees take it? Why or why not?

Judy Brady
Why I Want a Wife

JUDY BRADY, born in San Francisco in 1937, graduated from the University of Iowa. This ironic essay, printed in the first issue of *Ms.* in 1971, is now considered a classic picture of what our society expects

in a wife. Brady published this essay under her married name of Judy Syfers; she is now divorced, and
working as a writer and feminist.

I belong to that classification of people known as wives. I am A
Wife. And, not altogether incidentally, I am a mother.

2   Not too long ago a male friend of mine appeared on the scene
fresh from a recent divorce. He had one child, who is, of course, with
his ex-wife. He is looking for another wife. As I thought about him
while I was ironing one evening, it suddenly occurred to me that I,
too, would like to have a wife. Why do I want a wife?

3   I would like to go back to school so that I can become economically independent, support myself, and if need be, support those
dependent upon me. I want a wife who will work and send me to
school. And while I am going to school I want a wife to take care of
my children. I want a wife to keep track of the children's doctor and
dentist appointments. And to keep track of mine, too. I want a wife to
make sure my children eat properly and are kept clean. I want a wife
who will wash the children's clothes and keep them mended. I want a
wife who is a good nurturant attendant to my children, who arranges
for their schooling, makes sure that they have an adequate social life
with their peers, takes them to the park, the zoo, etc. I want a wife who
takes care of the children when they are sick, a wife who arranges to be
around when the children need special care, because, of course, I cannot
miss classes at school. My wife must arrange to lose time at work and
not lose the job. It may mean a small cut in my wife's income from
time to time, but I guess I can tolerate that. Needless to say, my wife
will arrange and pay for the care of the children while my wife is
working.

4   I want a wife who will take care of *my* physical needs. I want a
wife who will keep my house clean. A wife who will pick up after my
children, a wife who will pick up after me. I want a wife who will
keep my clothes clean, ironed, mended, replaced when need be, and
who will see to it that my personal things are kept in their proper
place so that I can find what I need the minute I need it. I want a wife
who cooks the meals, a wife who is a *good* cook. I want a wife who
will plan the menus, do the necessary grocery shopping, prepare the
meals, serve them pleasantly, and then do the cleaning up while I do

my studying. I want a wife who will care for me when I am sick and sympathize with my pain and loss of time from school. I want a wife to go along when our family takes a vacation so that someone can continue to care for me and my children when I need a rest and change of scene.

5   I want a wife who will not bother me with rambling complaints about a wife's duties. But I want a wife who will listen to me when I feel the need to explain a rather difficult point I have come across in my course of studies. And I want a wife who will type my papers for me when I have written them.

6   I want a wife who will take care of the details of my social life. When my wife and I are invited out by my friends, I want a wife who will take care of the babysitting arrangements. When I meet people at school that I like and want to entertain, I want a wife who will have the house clean, will prepare a special meal, serve it to me and my friends, and not interrupt when I talk about things that interest me and my friends. I want a wife who will have arranged that the children are fed and ready for bed before my guests arrive so that the children do not bother us. I want a wife who takes care of the needs of my guests so that they feel comfortable, who makes sure that they have an ashtray, that they are passed the hors d'oeuvres, that they are offered a second helping of the food, that their wine glasses are replenished when necessary, that their coffee is served to them as they like it. And I want a wife who knows that sometimes I need a night out by myself.

7   I want a wife who is sensitive to my sexual needs, a wife who makes love passionately and eagerly when I feel like it, a wife who makes sure that I am satisfied. And, of course, I want a wife who will not demand sexual attention when I am not in the mood for it. I want a wife who assumes the complete responsibility for birth control, because I do not want more children. I want a wife who will remain sexually faithful to me so that I do not have to clutter up my intellectual life with jealousies. And I want a wife who understands that *my* sexual needs may entail more than strict adherence to monogamy. I must, after all, be able to relate to people as fully as possible.

8   If, by chance, I find another person more suitable as a wife than the wife I already have, I want the liberty to replace my present wife with another one. Naturally, I will expect a fresh, new life; my wife will take the children and be solely responsible for them so that I am left free.

9   When I am through with school and have a job, I want my wife to
quit working and remain at home so that my wife can more fully and
completely take care of a wife's duties.

10   My God, who *wouldn't* want a wife?

Suggestions for Discussion and Writing

1. In the second paragraph, Brady carefully sets the
scene for the creation of her essay: she is home, ironing,
thinking about a divorced male friend's search for a new wife.
What effect does this setting have on the tone of the essay?
On your response as a reader?

2. According to Brady, what are the major categories of
wifely duties? Has she left any out?

3. If Brady wrote "I Want a Husband," what qualities would
she give him? If you wrote that essay, what qualities would you
include?

4. Who is the "I" in this essay?

5. This essay is considered a classic. Why do you think
that's so? What has changed in the twenty years since Brady
wrote it?

5 Sexual Harassment: The Price of Silence

While sexual harassment has been a fact of life for many centuries, and laws to protect its victims have existed for several decades, many Americans didn't really think about harassment until the autumn of 1991. Supreme Court nominee Clarence Thomas, a well-respected African-American conservative Republican lawyer with a record of government service, was about to replace Justice Thurgood Marshall on the nation's highest court. But suddenly allegations about his past conduct arose. After almost a month of investigation and negotiation, Anita Hill, a well-respected African-American conservative Republican lawyer, who was rumored to be in line for a judicial appointment herself, made public the charges her friends had made in private for many years: Clarence Thomas had sexually harassed her when she was his assistant, first at the Equal Employment Opportunity Commission, and then at the Department of Education, in the early 1980s. In a grueling weekend of televised hearings, Hill detailed her charges to a Senate committee, trying to remain calm and dispassionate as she gave her account of the episode. Thomas responded in prime-time with a passionate charge that the hearings were a "high-tech lynching" based on racist stereotypes of African-American men's sexual prowess. When the hearings were over, Thomas became a Supreme Court Justice. Hill, a law professor from Oklahoma, became a hero to many Americans. And the subject of sexual harassment was the hottest topic in the country.

In these essays, we present five reflections on sexual harassment, with some references to the Hill-Thomas case. The staff of *Newsweek* looks at less-famous cases of harassment and their outcomes, with an overview of the law governing harassment. Mary Lee Settle recounts a harrowing personal encounter with sexual intimidation for the first time in thirty years. William Broyles, Jr., expresses the perplexity men feel when trying to establish personal relationships with women without harassing them. Laura Mansnerus, an attorney, reflects that women are right to imitate Hill and *not* press charges. And finally, Adam Gopnik offers a young man's sudden insight into how many women regard harassment. As you read and consider these essays, ask these questions: "How do I approach a member of the opposite sex? Do I sometimes 'come on too strong'? What makes me do that? Do I feel comfortable asking people out on dates? refusing them? establishing non-sexual friendships with a person of the opposite sex?"

Barbara Kantrowitz[*]
Striking a Nerve

BARBARA KANTROWITZ and her coauthors are staff writers for *Newsweek* magazine. Their jobs require them to become "instant experts" on major stories, and to boil down vast masses of sources into orga-

---

[*] with Todd Barrett, Karen Springen, Mary Hager, Lynda Wright, Ginny Carroll, and Debra Rosenberg.

nized essays accessible to most Americans. This essay, which appeared in 1991 during the Anita Hill-Clarence Thomas controversy, is their attempt to put sexual harassment into a nationwide perspective as the country followed Thomas' confirmation process.

They may be neurosurgeons or typists, police officers or telephone operators, construction workers or even members of Congress. Last week women around the country who disagree on a hundred other issues listened to Anita Hill's allegations and heard themselves talking. They remembered the boss who threatened them, the co-worker whose lewd remarks echoed for hours. They remembered how angry they felt and how they pushed that anger down deep and how they tried to forget—and how they couldn't forget.

2   Sexual harassment is a fact of life in the American workplace; 21 percent of women polled by *Newsweek* said they had been harassed at work and 42 percent said they knew someone who had been harassed. Other surveys indicate that more than half of working women have faced the problem at some pint in their careers. The situation tends to be worst in male-dominated workplaces; in a 1990 Defense Department study, 64 percent of military women said they had endured such abuse. Although the severity may vary—from a pattern of obscene joking to outright assault the emotional damage is often profound and long-lasting. Men "don't understand that caged feeling," says University of Texas sociologist Susan Marshall. "But women know what sexual harassment is. It's when your neck hairs stand up, when you feel like you're being stalked."

3   Defining sexual harassment is one of the law's newest frontiers. While some of the boundaries have been set by recent decisions, there is still considerable debate over just what constitutes actionable behavior. Most people understand that when a supervisor demands that a woman sleep with him in order to keep her job, he's stepped over the legal line. But what about aggressive flirting? Or off-color conversation? Often, it's a matter of perception. Some women may find such activities offensive; others may just shrug. And men and women may see things very differently. University of Arizona professor Barbara Gutek surveyed 1,200 men and women for a study on harassment. She asked her subjects whether they considered a sexual proposition flat-

tering. About 67 percent of the men said they would, while only 17 percent of the women agreed. In contrast, 63 percent of women would be insulted by a proposition, compared with 15 percent of men.

4   Even when their cases seem clear-cut, women say they feel ashamed—as though they were to blame for what happened to them. "Do we have to talk about the sex?" asks Mitzie Buckelew, as her eyes redden and tears begin to fall. She would like to forget that night with her boss in a suburban Atlanta hotel five years ago. Buckelew has claimed in state and federal lawsuits that Donald Farrar, the DeKalb County assistant police chief, threatened to fire her from her secretarial job if she did not have sex with him. He calls her charges "ludicrous." Buckelew claims that even after she gave in, hoping that would end the abuse, he persisted; "He would sneak up behind me and grab my breasts and my rear end right in the office," she says. "He would feel up and down my legs." Buckelew also claims Farrar gave her herpes; he has refused to give her lawyers his medical records.

5   Since Buckelew filed a harassment complaint in 1989, her car has been vandalized. Obscene phone calls wake her up in the middle of the night. She's still waiting for a resolution of the state and federal suits she has filed. In the meantime, she's been reassigned: to the county dog pound. Shortly after Buckelew sued, Farrar resigned with a full pension. "You start questioning yourself," Buckelew says. "Maybe I did ask for it. I know I didn't use good judgment . . . I just didn't know what to do."

No objections

6   Until just a few years ago, women had no recourse when confronted with unwanted advances or offensive comments by a boss or coworker. In offices where they were the minority, women thought they had to go along to get along. Palma Formica, a family practitioner in New Jersey, recalls that when she was a medical student more than 30 years ago, it was "standard procedure" for professors to make "male-female jokes, usually genital oriented, with the woman bearing the brunt." Women never objected. "What are you going to do, get up and walk out of class? You want to be a doctor? You want to be in a man's field? Then you swallow hard and pretend you don't hear."

7   But in the past decade, as women have grown to represent nearly half the work force, the courts have begun to strike down what was once "standard procedure." In 1980, the Equal Employment Oppor-

tunity Commission (the federal agency that investigates bias in the workplace) said that making sexual activity a condition of employment or promotion was a violation of the 1964 Civil Rights Act. Also forbidden: the creation of "an intimidating, hostile or offensive working environment."

8   The EEOC rules had little effect on most women's lives until 1986, when the Supreme Court agreed that sexual harassment did indeed violate civil rights. In the landmark case of *Meritor Savings Bank v. Vinson*, Washington, D.C., bank employee Mechelle Vinson claimed that her supervisor fondled her in front of other employees, followed her into the ladies' room, exposed himself and, on several occasions, raped her. The supervisor and the bank denied her claims, but the court sided with Vinson.

9   Two other major federal court decisions in January of this year refined the legal definition. In a Florida case involving a female shipyard worker, the court ruled that nude pinups in the workplace constitute illegal harassment. A week later a three-judge panel in San Francisco stated that in cases where men and women might see a pattern of behavior differently, the deciding factor should be whether a "reasonable woman" might feel threatened. In that case, a female IRS worker turned down a request for a date by a co-worker. He responded by writing unwelcome love letters to her. "Men, who are rarely victims of sexual assault, may view sexual conduct in a vacuum without a full appreciation of the underlying threat of violence that a woman may perceive," wrote Judge Robert R. Beezer.

State Standards

10   States have also been trying to set their own standards. Kent Sezer, general counsel for the Illinois Human Rights Commission, describes one case in that state in which a judge developed what Sezer calls the "stub-your-toe test." An employer had been using profane language; a female employee claimed he had created a hostile environment. The employer said the words were simply expletives and protected as free speech. The judge disagreed. He said that the expletives should be put to a simple test. If the employer had awakened at night and, as he got out of bed, stubbed his toe, would he have shouted, "Oh, cunt!"? The judge didn't think so, and ruled against the employer.

11   These decisions and others have spurred hundreds of public and

private employees to write sexual-harassment policies telling workers exactly how to behave. "Nowadays, it's basically a legal requirement that you have an anti-harassment policy," says Joan Engstrom, equal-employment-opportunity director for General Mills (109,000 employees), based in Minneapolis. Courts may hold employers liable for maintaining a harassment-free environment; the bill for failure can be steep. Although many cases are settled out of court and then sealed, there have been several multimillion-dollar awards in recent years. Avoiding huge payments isn't the only incentive for companies (many awards are, in fact, under $10,000). The publicity surrounding a harassment charge can damage a company's standing with the public.

12   But corporate policies are only as good as the supervisors who enforce them. Freada Klein, who heads a Cambridge, Mass., consulting firm that advises companies on harassment, says that one third of harassers are the victims' immediate supervisors. Another third, she says, are even higher up on the corporate ladder but do not directly supervise their victims. The rest are the victims' peers. Like many companies with well-respected records in this area, General Mills runs regular training sessions for employees, with videos explaining sexual harassment. Engstrom says General Mills tries to give its employees a simple explanation of its policy; "Employees are to be treated with dignity and respect. Unbusinesslike conduct that could be considered offensive or intimidating will not be tolerated."

13   Other companies have more bureaucratic systems in place. At AT&T, whose national work force is 47 percent female, managers must attend an annual training session that includes a discussion of sexual harassment. Nonmanagers learn about the company policy through a book that explains the company's investigation process. Employees also get a copy of the company's code of conduct and many see training tapes on sexual harassment. Company spokesman Burke Stinson says 95 percent of complaints filed with AT&T's personnel office "turn out to be founded." AT&T officials won't give out exact figures, but they say that some employees have been fired and others transferred or sent to counseling.

No Rewards

14   Even if they work for a company with a well-established harassment policy, many women still keep their mouths shut. They don't want to be seen as troublemakers—and they worry about the long-term

consequences of complaining. "The individual who makes the complaint is immediately subjected to scrutiny, criticism and blame," says Carolyn Chalmers, a Minneapolis lawyer who handles harassment cases. "You're immediately put on the defensive to justify your existence and your credibility." It's a rather simple risk-and-reward equation that for many women adds up to one big zero. The number of cases of sexual harassment reported to the EEOC and local bias agencies has increased somewhat in the past few years, from 4,380 in 1984 to 5,694 last year. Yet those numbers represent just a tiny fraction of actual incidents, lawyers say. According to Joan Huwiler of the NOW Legal Defense Fund, only about 6 percent of victims file formal complaints to the EEOC, other anti-bias agencies or their employers.

15   Frances Conley, a neurosurgeon at Stanford Medical School, endured nearly 25 years of insults before she finally quit her job this spring. Her charges of harassment drew national headlines and letters of support from around the country. The university responded by setting up a committee to investigate the charges. Now Conley's back at her job, hoping that things will get better. But the four months since her resignation "have been the worst four months in my life," Conley says. "I hate conflict. I hate people disapproving of me. It's very difficult to go around with people not liking you."

16   Women who take their accusations to court face even more formidable obstacles than public disapproval. The legal process is long and cumbersome—it can be years from first complaint to final verdict—and in the interim, the woman is in a legal, professional and often financial limbo. "A woman will complain and then becomes a pariah." says Judith Vladeck, a New York lawyer who has argued anti-bias cases for 20 years. "If the male is in any way sanctioned, his male cohorts come to his defense, and the woman becomes the wrongdoer, and she's frozen out."

17   Lawyers, too, say the cases are draining. Women are not entitled to collect damages under the Civil Rights Act—just back pay. Often, that's not enough for a lawyer to spend years in litigation. There are larger judgments in civil suits, but the legal proceedings can be time-consuming. Patricia J. Barry, the Los Angeles lawyer who argued the precedent-setting Vinson case before the Supreme Court in 1986, filed for bankruptcy in 1988 and announced she was giving up civil-rights work. Now she's arguing divorce and child-custody cases. "Most judges perceive themselves as identifying with the man no matter how

horrible he is," Barry says. "It becomes the woman versus the man."

Dark Victory

18   Even some of those who win harassment cases say they feel they lost. As a public-information officer for the Illinois Department of Corrections, Lynda Savage earned glowing evaluations and two salary increases in the early 1980s. But, according to court records, her supervisor, Nicholas Howell, commonly used obscenities when referring to women, brought in suggestive lingerie catalogs and asked Savage to pick out something for his wife and even told her she should buy a vibrator for her l-year-old daughter. Howell denies directing obscene comments to Savage. She complained to three different administrators, but nothing happened. For months, she says, Howell's behavior got worse. She was fired just before her second child was born.

10   Nearly five years later, a state court ruled in her favor and awarded her $137,000, along with an offer of reinstatement to her job. Savage did go back, but says her co-workers shunned her so she quit. She has not received another job offer. "In a lot of ways, I have tested my limits. I know where I'm strong and where I'm not," she says. "Some good has come out of it. But was it worth it?" She thinks about the years of strain on her children and her husband, the lost work opportunities. And she concludes: "No."

20   Sexual-harassment cases have been particularly controversial on college campuses. A 1986 survey by the Association of American Colleges reported that 32 percent of tenured faculty women at Harvard and 49 percent of untenured women had reported some form of sexual harassment. Consultant Freada Klein says that 40 percent of undergraduate women and 28 percent of female graduate students say they've been harassed. In 1989, the Minnesota Legislature passed a law requiring all educational institutions in the state to develop sexual-harassment policies. "Some universities have gone so far as to indicate that for a faculty member to date a student is a prima facie case of sexual harassment," says Margaret Neale, a professor at Northwestern's Kellogg Graduate School of Management. "There is no way to separate the power of the faculty member from the rank of the student."

21   Male-dominated campuses, like male-dominated professions, have the most entrenched problems. In early September a sophomore at Texas A&M University was attacked by three male cadets when she

decided to try out for an elite ceremonial unit within the A&M Corps of Cadets. Only three of the unit's 50 members were female. One of the men held her while two others struck her in the breasts and back. One of the attackers threatened her with a knife, dragging the handle against her flesh and warning that he would use the blade on her if she didn't withdraw her application. The university leveled disciplinary charges against 20 cadets, but officials soon found out this was not an isolated incident.

22   Within days A&M president William Mobley met with four women cadets who detailed a pattern of harassment. One woman told Mobley that she had been raped by a senior while his roommate watched. The women got Mobley's attention. He appointed a committee to investigate and named a woman psychologist with no university affiliation to cochair it. "I don't want to destroy the university," says one of the women students who met with Mobley. "But men hide behind the mask of harassment and say it's tradition. That needs to stop."

23   Some experts believe that "hostile environments" extend far beyond the campus and the workplace. Earlier this year, 13 female tenants won an $800,000 settlement against their San Francisco landlord who continued to employ an apartment manager even after they repeatedly notified the landlord that the manager was harassing the women. According to court records, the manager touched one woman's vaginal area and grabbed her breast. He told another woman he would evict her if she had an overnight visitor. He told women who were behind on their rent they would have to pay immediately or model lingerie for him. The women, all single mothers, were usually financially or emotionally vulnerable to his manipulations.

24   While that situation seems extreme, some feminist legal scholars argue that harassment is part of everyday life for most women and should be regulated. Indiana University professor Carol Brooks Gardner, author of a forthcoming book called "Passing By," argues that it should be considered illegal harassment when a man makes an obscene comment to a woman in the street. Of course, not all street comments are threatening. A simple wolf whistle probably wouldn't traumatize most women. "But," says Gardner, "it's not OK for a man to touch me in any way whatsoever or to mutter salacious comments in my ear, or to yell out vulgar verbal evaluations." Any regulations against this type of harassment would be extremely difficult to enforce. For

example, who would detain the assailant? Women in such a situation usually just want to get away as quickly as possible.

"Honor Roll"

25   Whatever happens on the street or in the courts, the publicity surrounding Anita Hill's allegations has brought the issue into the open. "The fact that this claim scuttled the nomination or delayed the nomination helps the cause like nothing else does," says Nancy Gertner, a Boston civil-rights attorney. It shows that charges of sexual harassment can be taken seriously—even in an almost all-male institution like the Senate. In fact, Congress could be the first test of how well the public has been educated by the week's proceedings. Congressional employees are not covered by the Civil Rights Act, and therefore have no protection against harassment. To correct this oversight, the Women's Political Caucus sent a written policy in April to all 535 members of Congress. Those who agreed to run harassment-free offices joined the caucus's "Honor Roll." At the start of last week, there were 200 members. By the end of the week, 12 more had signed up. After listening to Anita Hill, a lot of women voters would like to see Congress put its own House—and Senate—in order.

Suggestions for Discussion and Writing

1. How would you define the tone of this essay? Why do you think the *Newsweek* writers chose to use this tone for such an emotional subject?

2. The essay suggests that it's difficult to file and win sexual harassment cases because of the costs involved. What are some of those costs? How would you change the process to make it more fair, while at the same time protecting the rights of all parties?

3. Is sexual harassment strictly a women's issue? Can you think of instances where men might feel harassed? How are those episodes different from harassment of women? Do men filing complaints find the same discrimination that women do?

4. What kinds of evidence do the *Newsweek* authors use in this essay? Is it enough, and the right kind of evidence, to make you agree that "sexual harassment is a fact of life in the American workplace"?

5. Does your college or university have a policy about

sexual harassment? What is it? How is it enforced? How is it publicized? Do you and your fellow students know about it? Do you feel it is broad enough, or not specific enough? If students file a complaint under that policy, do they suffer the same kinds of consequences this article describes?

Mary Lee Settle
The Genteel Attacker

The novelist and writer MARY LEE SETTLE was born in Charleston, West Virginia, in 1918. She served with the Women's Auxiliary of the Royal Air Force in Britain during World War II and received a National Book Award in 1978 for *Blood Tie* (1977). Settle's most recent books include *The Killing Ground* (1982), *Celebration* (1986), *Charley Bland* (1989), and *Turkish Reflections* (1991). This intensely personal essay appeared in *The New York Times* late in 1991.

Thirty years ago, a man came to my house. He was drunk. He broke china by throwing it against the wall. He hit me. He threatened to keep on beating me. He then raped me. I was six miles out in the country, alone. I had no option but to submit. He was stronger than I was in only one way. Physically. This was not a stranger, a thief, a Willie Horton. It was the husband of a friend of mine, a man known for his politeness, his good manners, his "genteel" way of life.

2   For 30 years, I have submitted to the social dictatorship of silence that women have always had to submit to or be put through the shame, the indignity and the disbelief experienced by women who "make trouble, speak out, rock the boat."

3   Until today, I thought that I was doing it for two reasons. One of them is still valid. I did not want to injure my friend, who was, I'm sure, completely innocent of any knowledge of her husband's hidden

behavior. So, I think, were his friends, the same friends I saw nearly every day. For 30 years, I have been polite to this man, friendly at parties. I knew then and I still know, that doubt would be cast on what I had to say. That is the second reason.

4   I had already experienced this. At my college, Sweet Briar, in Amherst County, Va., I had been a victim of attempted "date rape." I was 18 years old. In the pejorative phrase, I had "to walk home from a car ride." I did, in the middle of the night, in winter, several miles in the rain, to a place where I thought I would be cared for and safe after the ordeal.

5   Instead, I was subjected to doubt, to prurient questioning by faculty and by the student council, even to a physical examination to see if I was still a virgin. I was. But like the lie detector test given to Anita Hill, the examination was not "completely valid," the woman doctor said. The incident was so demeaning that I left the school the next year. This episode I did tell about. I called it a "novel"; it was "The Clam Shell."

6   Now I can speak, not only because public opinion has changed, anger has replaced timidity, truth the polite brutality of "good manners" in a WASP world. The gloss has been torn from the ways a woman, alone, professional, can be victimized by what I call Nice Boy Men, the kind of man your mother wanted you to go out with.

7   I have kept silent because I know what pain it can cause to focus the spotlight of prurient scrutiny on one's person. I know why Anita Hill said nothing, except to close and trusted friends, for so many years. I know why she smiled and was polite and friendly, and submitted to the unwritten social dictatorship of silence.

8   She has, by her heroic stance, given not only me but thousands of women who have been silenced by shame the courage and the need to speak out about what we have tried for so long to bury and forget. She has caused, in this last week, a profound reaction among American women, a healthy opening and healing of old wounds.

9   This process has only just begun. Most of us are not strident women. Perhaps I speak for others when I say I wanted to be left alone. But the sight of that travesty, that avid curiosity, that "judicial" doubt of a brave woman's word, that attempt to diminish her when she finally did speak publicly, was itself akin to the indignities she suffered in the first place.

10   This is all too familiar to us, and we have to see that it does not

happen again—not in a living room, not at a party, not in an office, not in a court of law and, above all, never again in the political arena.

Suggestions for Discussion and Writing

1. Who is Willie Horton? Why does Settle draw a distinction between him and her "genteel" attacker?

2. Settle wrote a novel about her experience with an attempted date rape (*The Clam Shell*) in 1971, but remained silent about this incident for thirty years. What reasons does she give for breaking her silence? Why do you think she chose this form rather than making it into fiction?

3. Settle repeatedly stresses words like "genteel" and "polite" in her essay. What point is she making about the behaviors our society expects from men and women?

4. What does Settle mean by "the social dictatorship of silence"? Does such a code exist? What are its rules? Who enforces it?

5. Many newspapers and television stations will not publish the name of a person who has been raped, even when they publish the name of the accused or convicted rapist. Do you believe that the press should continue to hold back these names? What are the advantages and disadvantages of doing so?

William Broyles Jr.
Public Policy, Private Ritual

WILLIAM BROYLES, JR., was born in Houston in 1944, served as a Marine in Vietnam where he was awarded the Bronze Star, and received a B.A. degree from Rice University and both the B.A. and M.A. degrees from Oxford University. He taught philosophy at the U.S. Naval Academy before turning to journalism; he has been the editor of *Texas Monthly, New West,* and *California* magazine as well

as a columnist for *U.S. News and World Report*. He is
the author of *Brothers in Arms* (1986); in the following
1991 essay, he reflects on some of the issues the Hill-
Thomas controversy raised.

At a birthday party in my office, the celebrant was feted with a
cake in the shape of male genitals. The cake was devoured with great
gusto, to the mirth and entertainment of many of those present and the
intense discomfort of others. The cake was presented to a woman by the
other women in the office. Those most uncomfortable were men.

2   If men had sponsored the party, it could have been considered an
example of insensitivity and the abuse of male power. Since women
did it, the party was all camaraderie and good fun, and any man who
was offended simply kept it to himself.

3   Sex arrived in the workplace when women did, and, ever since,
men have been unsure just what women believe its boundaries are.
Over the past 20 years, I have seen a steady increase in frank language
and sexual innuendo, much of it coming from the women, no matter
whether they were my boss or the lowest subordinate. The tougher the
job and the greater the pressure, the franker the language and the more
intense the sexual atmosphere.

4   Wherever I have worked, sexual relationships among co-workers
have been a fact of life—from hasty couplings in closets, to serious
affairs, to love and marriage. The law can't eliminate sex at work; it
can only try to keep it within reasonable boundaries.

5   During the Senate Judiciary Committee hearings, the senators
fell over themselves to express their horror at the language Clarence
Thomas allegedly used in asking Anita Hill out—language unfortunately not that different from the average hit record, movie or television show, where jokes about male anatomy, suggestive language,
double entendres and frank sexuality have become commonplace. This
pervasiveness of sex in our public life makes determining standards of
acceptable behavior much more difficult.

6   If a man asks a co-worker out, discusses personal matters with her
and in other ways tries to advance the relationship, he can through the
same actions be responsible for consequences ranging from sexual
harassment to beginning a lifetime relationship. What is offensive to
one woman may be obnoxious, amusing or even endearing to another.

7   Where men and women are together, there is misunderstanding and mystery. I have seen highly professional, otherwise respectable men commit sexual harassment, just as I have seen highly professional, otherwise capable women imagine relationships that did not exist (this happened, in fact, to me) and contrive harassment charges to revenge other slights or to advance themselves.

8   It's crucial to legally define sexual harassment as clearly as possible so that the true victims of sexual abuse and discrimination don't have their suffering trivialized. Otherwise we will be treated in our courts to interchanges every bit as bizarre as Senator Joseph Biden and John Doggett arguing over how to ask a woman out. This is not and should never be a matter of law or public policy.

9   One troubling aspect of the Thomas hearings was that they put on public display the private rituals by which men and women come together. The man usually initiates relationships and therefore subjects himself to embarassment, rejection and misunderstanding, particularly since these matters are not always conducted in straightforward, businesslike ways.

10   Men don't get it. That's what the professional feminists tell us. And they are right, we don't. We may get some of it, but not all—not even many of us who have promoted and encouraged our women subordinates and oppose any form of sexual discrimination or harassment.

11   And that's because the rules of sexual harassment are not objective but determined by the reactions of the woman involved. Each woman makes her own law. Women want to be treated equally but don't want to be considered sexless. They want to be sexually attractive but only to the right man and only with the proper approach. That leaves considerable possibility for error. The man must read the woman's signals; the woman must make those signals clear.

12   Women today enrich the workplace at all levels and in all jobs. They are police officers and firefighters. They make a strong case for being qualified to carry arms into combat. If women are tough enough for that, to kill and risk being killed, they are tough enough to handle a dirty joke or a clumsy flirtation without rushing to join the women who are truly victims.

13   Women want to be respected, capable workers without losing their sexual identities, and they should be able to have it both ways. But if a man wants to ask a co-worker out, he shouldn't have to bring his lawyer along.

Suggestions for Discussion and Writing

1. Broyles argues that "it's crucial to legally define sexual harassment as clearly as possible." What difficulties would you predict anyone trying to write such a definition would have?

2. Is it true that in cases of sexual harassment, "Each woman makes her own law"? In what circumstances would you agree with Broyles?

3. Broyles implies that sometimes women file false charges of sexual harassment, and notes parenthetically that he was the victim of such a false accusation. Does this fact affect the way you respond to his argument? How?

4. Do you agree with Broyles that if people are strong enough to "kill and risk being killed," exposure to sexual situations and innuendos should not distress them? Is this a fair comparison to make?

5. Some occupations, such as the military, forbid sexual relationships between officers and enlisted personnel (these are called non-fraternization policies). Do you believe that people who work together ought to become sexually involved? How about professors and students? Doctors and patients? Lawyers and clients? What sorts of rules ought to govern these situations?

Laura Mansnerus
Don't Tell

LAURA MANSNERUS is an attorney and a respected journalist. A noted book reviewer, she is particularly interested in writers who document and adapt the lives of others; among her recent profiles for the *New York Times* are interviews with Margaret Atwood, Shere Hite, and Scott Turow. This essay

*appeared in The New York Times Magazine shortly
after Clarence Thomas was sworn in.*

Sometimes discrimination announces itself like pie in the face
to the most wide-eyed young worker. I know this from a talk I had 18
years ago with the executive editor of the first newspaper I worked for.
I made an appointment with the busy man and asked if he thought I
could ever move from copy editing into a reporting job. He called
for the results of the battery of tests I'd taken as a job applicant, he
frowned over them and then he said no. A machine-scored personality
profile, which he helpfully posed in front of me to let me see that
science compelled his answer, showed that I was much too female a
type to work as a reporter for him.

2   So much for my career plans. The news was a surprise
(Nurturing and compliant? Me?), a non sequitur and an insult, and it
looked like a violation of the employment-discrimination laws. So
what did I do? I chatted up the editor at the press club. At parties, I
pasted on a smile of rapt interest in his anecdotes. With my boyfriend
of the moment, a protégé of the editor—bad coincidence—I went to
dinner at the editor's apartment and surely said, "Wonderful to see
you." The man was widely loathed, but no one, except the poor
boyfriend, heard a word of grievance from me; I was as sweet as the test
said I was. A year later, after I'd quit to take a job that then evaporated,
I wrote the editor a warm, ingratiating letter asking him to take me
back. His response left the door open, but fortunately another job
materialized.

3   I demonstrated a complete failure of moral resolve. Nearly two
decades later, having held many other jobs, having become a lawyer,
having seen the sex-discrimination laws evolve and having watched the
United States Senate recently consider an account of sexual harassment
from the most impeccable witness that a plaintiff's lawyer could
invent, I know I did the right thing.

4   Now, I haven't suffered degradation; the sexual advances I've
received from superiors have consisted mostly of peculiar remarks
from guys who were stranded in the era of pledge formals and hope
chests. But I had plenty of answers for the senators and witnesses who
demanded to know about Anita Hill: Why didn't she report these
incidents? Why didn't she take notes? Why did she continue to speak

highly of Clarence Thomas? Why did she follow him into another job?

5   One answer is that in trying to patch up the humiliations of daily life, you probably do not consult the rules of evidence, even if you're a lawyer, expecting that someday you'll have to explain any lapses in strategy to Senator Specter. Another is that your tormentor can also be your friend, which might or might not stop you from telling the truth if the F.B.I. comes around 10 years later to ask what it was like to work for him.

6   But the easiest answer is that a young woman who brings enthusiasm and hope to a job is going to try, sometimes with heartbreaking docility, to get along. And nobody likes a tattletale. We know now that the uglier the tale, the more savage the raking that the victim gets. But we knew all along that to squeal on one's mentor, or even one's boss, is an idiotic thing to do. (You'd think a senator wouldn't have any trouble understanding that proposition.)

7   A tattletale is by definition a weakling who asks for intervention, which is exactly what the grievance procedures available to workers are all about. The laws and company policies and sensitivity-training seminars are supposed to aid victims and whiners, and that's why the authorities are just as happy that they don't work.

8   Begin with the Equal Employment Opportunity Commission: last year it received about 33,000 sex-discrimination complaints and filed suit in 197 cases. For a woman who is some how able to retain her own lawyer—and the plaintiff, incidentally, has typically already been fired—the odds are better, but not by much.

9   Legislated remedies are fine. They're absolutely necessary. And Congress is stunningly proud of itself for this year's Civil Rights Act, which liberalizes the rules in job-discrimination cases, in ways that a worker can understand if she is also a civil rights lawyer. But most people, civil rights lawyers included, can understand that sworn accusations, discovery motions and depositions are going to have a horrifying effect around the office. Even a discreet inquiry by the company's Human Resources Department will mark the complainer as, well, a complainer—and probably, eventually, as a loser too.

10   What of the view that the woman who speaks up is a fighter rather than a whiner? Well, it's something you might believe if you're very young or extraordinarily aggressive. But fights take place between adversaries, not between the boss man and a pesky underling. That

Anita Hill emerged from the hearings without looking like a perpetually kayoed cartoon character is testament to a dignity that most people don't have.

11 It's clear that the senators didn't view Professor Hill, who found none among them inclined to be combative on her behalf as an actual challenge to Clarence Thomas. After all, they were themselves cowed by Clarence Thomas. Would anybody be cowed by Anita Hill? At best the senators were oily and patronizing.

12 At worst, of course, they blithely slandered her which is usually the case when the charge is the kind that would upset the accused's wife. Delusion and vindictiveness are handy explanations, easier and at the same time more cruel to the aggrieved woman than the traditional defense of calling her a slut.

13 So I look at my own little potential sex-discrimination case from 1973. Suppose I had lodged a complaint. I would not have been cross-examined by Orrin Hatch. I would not have had to watch some preening egomaniac I'd spoken to at a party appear on national television to accuse me of romantic fantasizing. No one would have suggested that I'd asked for whatever was said to me. Not at all. As a union member, I probably wouldn't have lost my boring job. But I wouldn't have got another one, at that newspaper or any other, and that seems like enough of a deterrent to me.

14 Anita Hill, law professor, said hesitantly to her questioners that in declining to invoke the legal process she might have used poor judgment. No, no, no. The 25-year-old who shut up proceeded with a recommendation and no muss or fuss to a university teaching job. Now she has tenure. Her judgment was dead on.

Suggestions for Discussion and Writing

1. Would you call Mansnerus' episode with the executive editor of the newspaper "sexual harassment"? Why or why not? Does Mansnerus do so?

2. What name does Mansnerus give to a person who files a harassment complaint? Do you think she dislikes the people who file such complaints? Why does she use such a word?

3. What reasons does Mansnerus give for Anita Hill's continuing to work for Clarence Thomas? Do you think these are the true reasons? Can you think of others? Do they agree with

the reasons the senators gave? Is there evidence for any of these reasons?

4. Most of us think of lawyers as people eager to bring lawsuits. Yet Mansnerus seems to suggest that people are smart *not* to file suit in sexual harassment cases. What are her reasons? What effect does her legal perspective have on you as a reader?

5. Many young people seek successful people in their fields to act as "mentors" for their careers. (Anita Hill apparently chose Clarence Thomas for her mentor.) Examine the phenomenon of mentoring. Is it a good idea? What are the advantages and drawbacks to having a mentor? What qualities should you seek in a mentor?

Adam Gopnik
The Truths We Choose
Not To Hear

ADAM GOPNIK is a staff writer who writes frequent art reviews and critical pieces for *The New Yorker*. Gopnik, with Kirk Varnedoe, organized a controversial exhibition called "High and Low: Modern Art and Popular Culture" at the Museum of Modern Art in 1990; together, they also wrote *High and Low: Modern Art and Popular Culture* (1990) and edited *Modern Art and Popular Culture: Readings in High and Low Art*. This essay appeared anonymously in *The New Yorker* on October 28, 1991.

I am one of that generation of men who grew up and were educated at a time when the central tenets of feminism were more or less dogma among right-thinking people, and I have spent my whole life among women who identify themselves as feminists. I have four sisters, each of whom is, in one way or another, engaged in living out a feminist life. My wife is a feminist filmmaker. My mother is a feminist professor—one of the first women of her generation to get a Ph.D. in formal logic. And yet, proud as I am of all these women, I had always felt, as almost every man surely does to one degree or another, that to be ardently or uncritically feminist was to become, in a sense, feminized, and I maintained a certain ironic distance from what struck me as the more metaphysical reaches of feminist "theory"—all those claims about women and power, women and language, and women and the male definition of reality which fill feminist texts and papers. But in the last three days, watching the Senate Judiciary Committee hearings on Judge Clarence Thomas, and watching the Senate's (and the press's) treatment of Professor Anita Hill, I have had something like a conversion experience. I have begun to realize that in the past the more "abstract" and the more categorical reaches of the feminist catechism—not to mention its now familiar nuts and bolts—seemed a little unreal to me not because they weren't true but because I had never seen them made concrete and particular.

2   Women, I have long been told, live within a set of double blinds. If a woman makes a charge against a man, the issue will always become not the man's behavior but the woman's character. And a corollary is that if a woman can be shown to have lied in the past about anything at all, the lie will be taken as compelling evidence that she is lying now. On a Saturday-night news program, two male journalists invoked the names of Tawana Brawley and Janet Cooke while discussing the hearings, and then they had a long debate about which woman, Brawley or Cooke, Professor Hill more closely resembled—although no connection could be found between either the frightened teen-ager or the dishonest reporter and the college professor, whose integrity had not yet been impeached. *Of course* the comparison was apt, the two men seemed to assume: they're black, they're women, they lie.

3   Women, my sisters explain, talk to other women not just to solve problems but to share pain, and this is not a difference of "conversational style," but is rooted in women's understanding of the realities of power. "Why didn't you give her advice? Why didn't you counsel her to come forward?" the incredulous senators demanded as the professor's friends tried to explain that after they heard her complaints of sexual harassment they had felt powerless to offer any solu-

tion. They had just tried to offer understanding and an ear, they said—that was what she *wanted* them to do, knowing that any "solution" would do at least as much damage to her as it could do to him. I will never forget the looks on the faces of Professor Hill's women friends—a judge and a welfare administrator—as they tried to explain why their friend hadn't come forward; they were the looks of pained and compassionate grownups trying to explain something to children.

4   Women must always be seen as powerless and passive, my sisters have pointed out, and any action they take will always be reinterpreted by men in this light. Grown men, including Judge Thomas himself, put forward in all seriousness the notion that Professor Hill was merely mouthing a "concocted" story that had been skillfully assembled from disparate sources by "special-interest groups" and then taught to her. In the minds of her accusers, Professor Hill could not even be granted the dignity of strategies of her own, however malicious; in order to be dismissed, she first had to be made a "pawn."

5   A woman's attractiveness will always be held against her, I now understand, and a woman's unattractiveness will always be held against her, too. Professor Hill was good-looking, and therefore it was fair to speculate that she was out to snare Judge Thomas, and that her accusation was the product of her failure to do so. But she wasn't *that* good-looking, and so it was also fair to conclude that the whole thing must be "fantasy." "Quite frankly, Anita Hill is not worth that type of risk," one of the Judge's supporters said—not good-looking enough to throw a career away on.

6   A man's career is assumed—by the man, and by other men—to be the equivalent of a woman's life; a setback to his ambition will be taken as a threat to his very existence. A woman's career, on the other hand, is just a job. Many of the senators couldn't understand why Anita Hill didn't simply give up her career if she didn't like the way she was treated. Clarence Thomas is a judge: what he does for a living is to review the cases of men and women, many of whom believe themselves to be as innocent as he claims to be. Yet when he was asked to bear for a moment a version of the same kind of scrutiny, he saw himself as a martyr—a lynching victim. His rage was thought to be impressive. Had Professor Hill shown the slightest sign of anger, of course, it would have been further proof of her "unstable" and "vindictive" nature.

7   As my sisters long ago explained, in the seemingly distant context of discussions of late-nineteenth-century psychiatry, any woman who is difficult will eventually be called mad. On Saturday afternoon, Senator Arlen Specter blandly accused Professor Hill of perjury. By Sunday night, he had refined this conjecture: it was not that Professor Hill was lying but that she was simply unable to distinguish truth from fantasy. His tone suggested that this change in accusation had been made for her benefit—that she ought to be grateful for the superior male wisdom that recognized her as helpless in the grip of her delusions rather than as a deliberate liar.

8   Men define reality, and women seek refuge within the interstices of those definitions, my sisters have told me; the feminist theorists have written similar things, grandly and abstractly. I now see what this means in terms of practical conduct. Judge Thomas offered nothing except a blanket denial and a raft of wild accusations. Nonetheless, his anger was apparently judged by many other men, and by some women, to be admirable, as a kind of expression of masculinity: so admirable that it enabled him to redefine the hearings in terms of *his* suffering, *his* struggle, *his* career, *his* reality. He turned the discussion to the historical generalities of racial oppression—of which his accuser had certainly had at least as much experience as he had—and was allowed to escape the responsibility of meeting the particular accusations of sexual oppression. The committee had treated Professor in "a very polite and professional way," senator Specter said on Tuesday, and this time he went on to accuse her of both perjury *and* delusional lying. Since she had been treated "politely," her claims could be dismissed, instead of refuted, and she could once again be rendered negligible.

9   Talking to my wife and mother and sisters about the hearings, I heard in their voices not so much anger as resignation and familiarity. "This comes to you as a *surprise?*" they said, in so many words. Watching these women over a lifetime, I realize, I had often been a little surprised when they would burst into rage and indignation about what seemed to me "petty" injustice at the hands of men. They had on tap a vein of anger that bewildered me, rising, as it did, from lives that were so obviously successful and happy. I owe them an apology. They had experienced things that I had not, and had tried to tell me truths that I had chosen not to hear.

Suggestions for Discussion and Writing

1. Gopnik begins with a long description of his "feminist" credentials. Since it's an anonymous essay, why did he choose this strategy for his introduction? What is its effect on you as a reader?

2. What is a "conversion experience"? What are the characteristics of people who have had such experiences? What effect is Gopnik trying to achieve by using this term?

3. Do you believe that "a man's career is assumed—by the man, and by other men—to be the equivalent of a woman's life" and that "a woman's career, on the other hand, is just a job"? Do you think that many people hold this attitude? What features in our society support your opinion?

4. What does this statement mean: "Men define reality, and women seek refuge within the interstices of those definitions"?

5. What was your reaction to the Anita Hill-Clarence Thomas hearings? Did you find yourself taking sides? If so, which side did you take, and why? Now that some time has passed, has your perspective on this issue changed? What new ideas or issues have affected your thinking about sexual harassment?

6 Pornography

Few episodes upset a community like a pornography case. Whether it's an attempt to ban 'adult' bookstores and theatres, or censorship of a controversial art exhibit, or objections to record album covers, pornography brings out some of our deepest reservations about sexuality and gender. The Supreme Court declared in 1973 that pornography was defined by "community standards," but few communities can even agree on what those standards are. For some, it's the half-naked child in the suntan lotion commercial, while for others it's "snuff flicks" (fillms where characters appear to be killed). and "chicken porn" (films exploiting young children). And whatever it is, it may be protected by the Constitution.

These essays reflect the difficulty many people have in defining pornography, in deciding to whom pornography laws apply and in deciding where our society may draw the limits between community standards and censorship. Margaret Atwood offers three controversial analogues to pornography in her argument. Susan Brownmiller and Susan Jacoby disagree over what the First Amendment actually protects. Gloria Steinem tries to separate erotic from pornographic art, and Hugh Hefner equates recent governmental attempts to demonstrate pornography's harmfulness with the anti-Communist witch hunts of the 1950s. As you read and consider these essays, ask: "How would I define pornography? Would I make a distinction between paintings of Greek goddesses and the photographs in sexy magazines? Are TV commercials, music videos, album covers, and the like pornography? What are my standards? My community's?"

Margaret Atwood
Pornography

MARGARET ATWOOD (born in 1939) is one of Canada's most famous authors and a proponent of preserving Canadian literature. A poet, novelist, and lecturer as well as essayist, she is best known for her novels *The Handmaid's Tale* (1983) and *Cat's Eye* (1989). Here she reacts as artist, feminist, and citizen to a subject she has explored in depth in her writings. This essay first appeared in *Chatelaine* magazine in 1983.

When I was in Finland a few years ago for an international writers' conference, I had occasion to say a few paragraphs in public on the subject of pornography. The context was a discussion of political repression, and I was suggesting the possibility of a link between the two. The immediate result was that a male journalist took several large bites out of me. Prudery and pornography are two halves of the same coin, said he, and I was clearly a prude. What could you expect from an Anglo-Canadian? Afterward, a couple of pleasant Scandinavian men asked me what I had been so worked up about. All "pornography" means, they said, is graphic depictions of whores, and what was the harm in that?

2   Not until then did it strike me that the male journalist and I had two entirely different things in mind. By "pornography," he meant naked bodies and sex. I, on the other hand, had recently been doing the research for my novel *Bodily Harm,* and was still in a state of shock

from some of the material I had seen, including the Ontario Board of Film Censors' "outtakes." By "pornography," I meant women getting their nipples snipped off with garden shears, having meat hooks stuck into their vaginas, being disemboweled; little girls being raped; men (yes, there are some men) being smashed to a pulp and forcibly sodomized. The cutting edge of pornography, as far as I could see, was no longer simple old copulation, hanging from the chandelier or otherwise: it was death, messy, explicit and highly sadistic. I explained this to the nice Scandinavian men. "Oh, but that's just the United States," they said. "Everyone knows they're sick." In their country, they said, violent "pornography" of that kind was not permitted on television or in movies; indeed, excessive violence of any kind was not permitted. They had drawn a clear line between erotica, which earlier studies had shown did not incite men to more aggressive and brutal behavior toward women, and violence, which later studies indicated did.

3   Some time after that I was in Saskatchewan, where, because of the scenes in *Bodily Harm, I* found myself on an open-line radio show answering questions about "pornography." Almost no one who phoned in was in favor of it, but again they weren't talking about the same stuff I was, because they hadn't seen it. Some of them were all set to stamp out bathing suits and negligees, and, if possible, any depictions of the female body whatsoever. God, it was implied, did not approve of female bodies, and sex of any kind, including that practised by bumblebees, should be shoved back into the dark, where it belonged. I had more than a suspicion that *Lady Chatterley's Lover,* Margaret Laurence's *The Diviners,* and indeed most books by most serious modern authors would have ended up as confetti if left in the hands of these callers.

4   For me, these two experiences illustrate the two poles of the emotionally heated debate that is now thundering around this issue. They also underline the desirability and even the necessity of defining the terms. "Pornography" is now one of those catchalls, like "Marxism" and "feminism," that have become so broad they can mean almost anything, ranging from certain verses in the Bible, ads for skin lotion and sex tests for children to the contents of Penthouse, Naughty '90s postcards and films with titles containing the word *Nazi* that show vicious scenes of torture and killing. It's easy to say that sensible people can tell the difference. Unfortunately, opinions on what constitutes a sensible person vary.

5   But even sensible people tend to lose their cool when they start talking about this subject. They soon stop talking and start yelling, and the name calling begins. Those in favor of censorship (which may include groups not noticeably in agreement on other issues, such as some feminists and religious fundamentalists) accuse the others of exploiting women through the use of degrading images, contributing to the corruption of children, and adding to the general climate of violence and threat in which both women and children live in this society; or, though they may not give much of a hoot about actual women and children, they invoke moral standards and God's supposed aversion to "filth," "smut" and deviated *preversion,* which may mean ankles.

6   The camp in favor of total "freedom of expression" often comes out howling as loud as the Romans would have if told they could no longer have innocent fun watching the lions eat up Christians. It too may include segments of the population who are not natural bedfellows: those who proclaim their God-given right to freedom, including the freedom to tote guns, drive when drunk, drool over chicken porn and get off on videotapes of women being raped and beaten, may be waving the same anticensorship banner as responsible liberals who fear the return of Mrs. Grundy, or gay groups for whom sexual emancipation involves the concept of "sexual theatre." *Whatever turns you on* is a handy motto, as is *A man's home is his castle* (and if it includes a dungeon with beautiful maidens strung up in chains and bleeding from every pore, that's his business).

7   Meanwhile, theoreticians theorize and speculators speculate. Is today's pornography yet another indication of the hatred of the body, the deep mind-body split, which is supposed to pervade Western Christian society? Is it a backlash against the women's movement by men who are threatened by uppity female behavior in real life, so like to fantasize about women done up like outsize parcels, being turned into hamburger, kneeling at their feet in slavelike adoration or sucking off guns? Is it a sign of collective impotence, of a generation of men who can't relate to real women at all but have to make do with bits of celluloid and paper? Is the current flood just a result of smart marketing and aggressive promotion by the money men in what has now become a multibillion-dollar industry? If they were selling movies about men getting their testicles stuck full of knitting needles by women with swastikas on their sleeves, would they do as well, or is this penchant somehow peculiarly male? If so, why? Is pornography a

power trip rather than a sex one? Some say that those ropes, chains, muzzles and other restraining devices are an argument for the immense power female sexuality still wields in the male imagination: you don't put these things on dogs unless you're afraid of them. Others, more literary, wonder about the shift from the 19th-century Magic Woman or Femme Fatale image to the lollipop-licker, airhead or turkey-carcass treatment of women in porn today. The proporners don't care much about theory; they merely demand product. The antiporners don't care about it in the final analysis either; there's dirt on the street, and they want it cleaned up, now.

8   It seems to me that this conversation, with its *You're-a-prude/You're-a-pervert* dialectic, will never get anywhere as long as we continue to think of this material as just "entertainment." Possibly we're deluded by the packaging, the format: magazine, book, movie, theatrical presentation. We're used to thinking of these things as part of the "entertainment industry," and we're used to thinking of ourselves as free adult people who ought to be able to see any kind of "entertainment" we want to. That was what the First Choice pay-TV debate was all about. After all, it's only entertainment, right? Entertainment means fun, and only a killjoy would be antifun. What's the harm?

9   This is obviously the central question: *What's the harm?* If there isn't any real harm to any real people, then the antiporners can tsk-tsk and/or throw up as much as they like, but they can't rightfully expect more legal controls or sanctions. However, the no harm position is far from being proven.

10   (For instance, there's a clear-cut case for banning—as the federal government has proposed—movies, photos and videos that depict children engaging in sex with adults: real children are used to make the movies, and hardly anybody thinks this is ethical. The possibilities for coercion are too great.)

11   To shift the viewpoint, I'd like to suggest three other models for looking at "pornography"—and here I mean the violent kind.

12   Those who find the idea of regulating pornographic materials repugnant because they think it's Fascist or Communist or otherwise not in accordance with the principles of an open democratic society should consider that Canada has made it illegal to disseminate material that may lead to hatred toward any group because of race or religion. I suggest that if pornography of the violent kind depicted these

acts being done predominantly to Chinese, to blacks, to Catholics, it would be off the market immediately, under the present laws. Why is hate literature illegal? Because whoever made the law thought that such material might incite real people to do real awful things to other real people. The human brain is to a certain extent a computer: garbage in, garbage out. We only hear about the extreme cases (like that of American multimurderer Ted Bundy) in which pornography has contributed to the death and/or mutilation of women and/or men. Although pornography is not the only factor involved in the creation of such deviance, it certainly has upped the ante by suggesting both a variety of techniques and the social acceptability of such actions. Nobody knows yet what effect this stuff is having on the less psychotic.

13   Studies have shown that a large part of the market for all kinds of porn, soft and hard, is drawn from the 16-to-21-year-old population of young men. Boys used to learn about sex on the street, or (in Italy, according to Fellini movies) from friendly whores, or, in more genteel surroundings, from girls, their parents, or, once upon a time, in school, more or less. Now porn has been added, and sex education in the schools is rapidly being phased out. The buck has been passed, and boys are being taught that all women secretly like to be raped and that real men get high on scooping out women's digestive tracts.

14   Boys learn their concept of masculinity from other men: is this what most men want them to be learning? If word gets around that rapists are "normal" and even admirable men, will boys feel that in order to be normal, admirable and masculine they will have to be rapists? Human beings are enormously flexible, and how they turn out depends a lot on how they're educated, by the society in which they're immersed as well as by their teachers. In a society that advertises and glorifies rape or even implicitly condones it, more women get raped. It becomes socially acceptable. And at a time when men and the traditional male role have taken a lot of flak and men are confused and casting around for an acceptable way of being male (and, in some cases, not getting much comfort from women on that score), this must be at times a pleasing thought.

15   It would be naïve to think of violent pornography as just harmless entertainment. It's also an educational tool and a powerful propaganda device. What happens when boy educated on porn meets girl brought up on Harlequin romances? The clash of expectations can be heard around the block. She wants him to get down on his knees with a

ring, he wants her to get down on all fours with a ring in her nose. Can this marriage be saved?

16   Pornography has certain things in common with such addictive substances as alcohol and drugs: for some, though by no means for all, it induces chemical changes in the body, which the user finds exciting and pleasurable. It also appears to attract a "hard core" of habitual users and a penumbra of those who use it occasionally but aren't dependent on it in any way. There are also significant numbers of men who aren't much interested in it, not because they're undersexed but because real life is satisfying their needs, which may not require as many appliances as those of users.

17   For the "hard core," pornography may function as alcohol does for the alcoholic: tolerance develops, and a little is no longer enough. This may account for the short viewing time and fast turnover in porn theatres. Mary Brown, chairwoman of the Ontario Board of Film Censors, estimates that for every one mainstream movie requesting entrance to Ontario, there is one porno flick. Not only the quantity consumed but the quality of explicitness must escalate, which may account for the growing violence: once the big deal was breasts, then it was genitals, then copulation, then that was no longer enough and the hard users had to have more. The ultimate kick is death, and after that, as the Marquis de Sade so boringly demonstrated, multiple death.

18   The existence of alcoholism has not led us to ban social drinking. On the other hand, we do have laws about drinking and driving, excessive drunkenness and other abuses of alcohol that may result in injury or death to others.

19   This leads us back to the key question: what's the harm? Nobody knows, but this society should find out fast, before the saturation point is reached. The Scandinavian studies that showed a connection between depictions of sexual violence and increased impulse toward it on the part of male viewers would be a starting point, but many more questions remain to be raised as well as answered. What, for instance, is the crucial difference between men who are users and men who are not? Does using affect a man's relationship with actual women, and, if so, adversely? Is there a clear line between erotica and violent pornography, or are they on an escalating continuum? Is this a "men versus women" issue, with all men secretly siding with the proporners and all women secretly siding against? (I think not; there *are* lots of men who don't think that running their true love through the Cuisinart is

the best way they can think of to spend a Saturday night, and they're just as nauseated by films of someone else doing it as women are.) Is pornography merely an expression of the sexual confusion of this age or an active contributor to it?

20   Nobody wants to go back to the age of official repression, when even piano legs were referred to as "limbs" and had to wear pantaloons to be decent. Neither do we want to end up in George Orwell's 1984, in which pornography is turned out by the State to keep the proles in a state of torpor, sex itself is considered dirty and the approved practise it only for reproduction. But Rome under the emperors isn't such a good model either.

21   If all men and women respected each other, if sex were considered joyful and life-enhancing instead of a wallow in germ-filled glop, if everyone were in love all the time, if, in other words, many people's lives were more satisfactory for them than they appear to be now, pornography might just go away on its own. But since this is obviously not happening, we as a society are going to have to make some informed and responsible decisions.

Suggestions for Discussion and Writing

1. What is the difference between Atwood's definition of pornography and yours? Can there be "good" and "bad" pornography?

2. How would you describe the tone Atwood uses in this essay? Does the tone remain consistent? What effect does Atwood want to create with her choice of tone?

3. What are Atwood's three models for looking at pornography? Do you think these are appropriate models? Can you suggest other models?

4. Many of Atwood's points are made through asking questions (see her third paragraph especially). What is the effect on all of these questions on you as a reader? In what circumstances can asking questions have more impact than straightforward statements?

5. Atwood claims that research points to a connection between pornography and sexual violence. Can you confirm this connection? What statistics are available on this connection? What kinds of interpretations do they suggest?

Susan Brownmiller
Let's Put Pornography
Back in the Closet

SUSAN BROWNMILLER was born in Brooklyn in 1935. Now a full-time writer, she was formerly a television news reporter and a staffer for the *Village Voice*. The founder of Women Against Pornography, she is also the author of *Against our Will: Men, Women, and Rape* (1975) and *Waverly Place* (1989). This 1979 essay originally appeared in a Long Island newspaper, and was reprinted in *Take Back the Night* (1980).

Free speech is one of the great foundations on which our democracy rests. I am old enough to remember the Hollywood Ten, the screenwriters who went to jail in the late 1940s because they refused to testify before a congressional committee about their political affiliations. They tried to use the First Amendment as a defense, but they went to jail because in those days there were few civil liberties lawyers around who cared to champion the First Amendment right to free speech, when the speech concerned the Communist Party.

2   The Hollywood Ten were correct in claiming the First Amendment. Its high purpose is the protection of unpopular ideas and political dissent. In the dark, cold days of the 1950s, few civil libertarians were willing to declare themselves First Amendment absolutists. But in the brighter, though frantic, days of the 1960s, the principle of protecting unpopular political speech was gradually strengthened.

3   It is fair to say now that the battle has largely been won. Even the American Nazi Party has found itself the beneficiary of the dedicated, tireless work of the American Civil Liberties Union. But—and please

notice the quotation marks coming up—"To equate the free and robust exchange of ideas and political debate with commercial exploitation of obscene material demeans the grand conception of the First Amendment and its high purposes in the historic struggle for freedom. It is a misuse of the great guarantees of free speech and free press."

4   I didn't say that, although I wish I had, for I think the words are thrilling. Chief Justice Warren Burger said it in 1973, in the United States Supreme Court's majority opinion in *Miller v. California*. During the same decades that the right to political free speech was being strengthened in the courts, the nation's obscenity laws also were undergoing extensive revision.

5   It's amazing to recall that in 1934 the question of whether James Joyce's *Ulysses* should be banned as pornographic actually went before the Court. The battle to protect *Ulysses* as a work of literature with redeeming social value was won. In later decades, Henry Miller's *Tropic* books, *Lady Chatterley's Lover* and the *Memoirs of Fanny Hill* also were adjudged not obscene. These decisions have been important to me. As the author of *Against Our Will*, a study of the history of rape that does contain explicit sexual material, I shudder to think how my book would have fared if James Joyce, D. H. Lawrence, and Henry Miller hadn't gone before me.

6   I am not a fan of *Chatterly* or the *Tropic* books, I should quickly mention. They are not to my literary taste, nor do I think they represent female sexuality with any degree of accuracy. But I would hardly suggest that we ban them. Such a suggestion wouldn't get very far anyway. The battle to protect these books is ancient history. Time does march on, quite methodically. What, then, is unlawfully obscene, and what does the First Amendment have to do with it?

7   In the Miller case of 1973 (not Henry Miller, by the way, but a porn distributor who sent unsolicited stuff through the mails), the Court came up with new guidelines that it hoped would strengthen obscenity laws by giving more power to the states. What it did in actuality was throw everything into confusion. It set up a three-part test by which materials can be adjudged obscene. The materials are obscene if they depict patently offensive, hard-core sexual conduct; lack serious scientific, literary, artistic or political value; and appeal to the prurient interest of an average person—as measured by contemporary community standards.

8   "Patently offensive," "prurient interest" and "hard-core" are indeed words to conjure with. "Contemporary community standards" are what we're trying to redefine. The feminist objection to pornography is not based on prurience, which the dictionary defines as lustful, itching desire. We are not opposed to sex and desire, with or without the itch, and we certainly believe that explicit sexual material has its place in literature, art, science and education. Here we part company rather swiftly with old-line conservatives who don't want sex education in the high schools, for example.

9   No, the feminist objection to pornography is based on our belief that pornography represents hatred of women, that pornography's intent is to humiliate, degrade and dehumanize the female body for the purpose of erotic stimulation and pleasure. We are unalterably opposed to the presentation of the female body being stripped, bound, raped, tortured, mutilated and murdered in the name of commercial entertainment and free speech.

10   These images, which are standard pornographic fare, have nothing to do with the hallowed right of political dissent. They have everything to do with the creation of a cultural climate in which a rapist feels he is merely giving in to a normal urge and a woman is encouraged to believe that sexual masochism is healthy, liberated fun. Justice Potter Stewart once said about hard-core pornography "You know it when you see it," and that certainly used to be true. In the good old days, pornography looked awful. It was cheap and sleazy, and there was no mistaking it for art.

11   Nowadays, since the porn industry has become a multimillion dollar business, visual technology has been employed in its service. Pornographic movies are skillfully filmed and edited, pornographic still shots using the newest tenets of good design artfully grace the covers of *Hustler*, *Penthouse*, and *Playboy*, and the public—and the courts—are sadly confused.

12   The Supreme Court neglected to define "hard-core" in the Miller decision. This was a mistake. If "hard-core" refers only to explicit sexual intercourse, then that isn't good enough. When women or children or men—no matter how artfully—are shown tortured or terrorized in the service of sex, that's obscene. And "patently offensive," I would hope, to our "contemporary community standards."

13   Justice William O. Douglas wrote in his dissent to the Miller case that no one is "compelled to look." This is hardly true. To buy a

paper at the corner newsstand is to subject oneself to a forcible immersion in pornography, to be demeaned by an array of dehumanized, chopped-up parts of the female anatomy, packaged like cuts of meat at the supermarket. I happen to like my body and I work hard at the gym to keep it in good shape, but I am embarrassed for my body and for the bodies of all women when I see the fragmented parts of us, so frivolously, and so flagrantly, displayed.

14   Some constitutional theorists (Justice Douglas was one) have maintained that any obscenity law is a serious abridgement of free speech. Others (and Justice Earl Warren was one) have maintained that the First Amendment was never intended to protect obscenity. We live quite compatibly with a host of free-speech abridgements. There are restraints against false and misleading advertising or statements—shouting "fire" without cause in a crowded movie theater, etc.—that do not threaten, but strengthen, our societal values. Restrictions on the public display of pornography belong in this category.

15   The distinction between permission to publish and permission to display publicly is an essential one and one which I think consonant with First Amendment principles. Justice Burger's words which I quoted above support this without question. We are not saying "Smash the presses" or "Ban the bad ones," but simply "Get the stuff out of our sight." Let the legislatures decide—using realistic and humane contemporary community standards—what can be displayed and what cannot. The courts, after all, will be the final arbiters.

Suggestions for Discussion and Writing

1. How does Brownmiller define pornography? What are the key terms in her definition? Why are they so important?

2. Brownmiller's authorial voice shifts back and forth from "I" to "we". Who is the "we"? What results does she get from this shift?

3. The Supreme Court definition of pornography exempts material that has "serious scientific, literary, artistic or political value." How would you make the distinction between material that fits these standards and material that doesn't?

4. What is the main idea of Brownmiller's essay? Where does it appear? Why might she have chosen to use this strategy?

5. Recent controversy has centered around many artists' use of nudity and sexuality; some people believe that artists who do so are pornographers, and should not receive any government funding. What is your position on this issue? What kinds of restrictions would you put on artists, and why?

Susan Jacoby

I Am a First Amendment Junkie

Born in 1946, SUSAN JACOBY spent several years in Russia, which led to her books *The Friendship Barrier* (1972), *Moscow Conversations* (1972), and *Inside Soviet Schools* (1974). Returning to this country, she began writing for many popular magazines and became syndicated as the author of the column "Hers". In *The Possible She* (1979) she studied the lack of female heroes and women's lack of opportunities to earn and manage money; since then she has focused more on how people cope with their own lives in a dysfunctional society. Her most recent book is *Wild Justice* (1983); this essay originally appeared in "Hers" in 1978.

It is no news that many women are defecting from the ranks of civil libertarians on the issue of obscenity. The conviction of Larry Flynt, publisher of *Hustler* magazine—before his metamorphosis into a born-again Christian—was greeted with unabashed feminist approval. Harry Reems, the unknown actor who was convicted by a Memphis jury for conspiring to distribute the movie *Deep Throat*, has carried on his legal battles with almost no support from women who ordinarily regard themselves as supporters of the First Amendment. Feminist writers and scholars have even discussed the possibility of making common cause against pornography with adversaries of the women's movement—including opponents of the equal rights amendment and "right-to-life" forces.

2   All of this is deeply disturbing to a woman writer who believes, as I always have and still do, in an absolute interpretation of the First Amendment. Nothing in Larry Flynt's garbage convinces me that the late Justice Hugo L. Black was wrong in this opinion that "the Federal Government is without any power whatsoever under the Constitution to put any type of burden on free speech and expression of ideas of any kind (as distinguished from conduct)." Many women I like and respect tell me I am wrong; I cannot remember having become involved in so many heated discussions of a public issue since the end of the Vietnam War. A feminist writer described my views as those of a "First Amendment junkie."

3   Many feminist arguments for controls on pornography carry the implicit conviction that porn books, magazines and movies pose a greater threat to women than similarly repulsive exercises of free speech pose to other offended groups. This conviction has, of course, been shared by everyone—regardless of race, creed or sex—who has ever argued in favor of abridging the First Amendment. It is the argument used by some Jews who have withdrawn their support from the American Civil Liberties Union because it has defended the right of American Nazis to march through a community inhabited by survivors of Hitler's concentration camps.

4   If feminists want to argue that the protection of the Constitution should not be extended to *any* particularly odious or threatening form of speech, they have a reasonable argument (although I don't agree with it). But it is ridiculous to suggest that the porn shops on 42nd Street are more disgusting to women than a march of neo-Nazis is to survivors of the extermination camps.

5   The arguments over pornography also blur the vital distinction between expression of ideas and conduct. When I say I believe unreservedly in the First Amendment, someone always comes back at me with the issue of "kiddie porn." But kiddie porn is not a First Amendment issue. It is an issue of the abuse of power—the power adults have over children—and not of obscenity. Parents and promoters have no more right to use their children to make porn movies than they do to send them to work in coal mines. The responsible adults should be prosecuted, just as adults who use children for backbreaking farm labor should be prosecuted.

6   Susan Brownmiller, in *Against Our Will: Men, Women and Rape*, has described pornography as "the undiluted essence of anti-female propaganda." I think this is a fair description of some types of pornography, especially of the brutish subspecies that equates sex with death and portrays women primarily as objects of violence.

7   The equation of sex and violence, personified by some glossy rock record album covers as well as by *Hustler*, has fed the illusion that censorship of pornography can be conducted on a more rational basis than other types of censorship. Are all pictures of naked women obscene? Clearly not, says a friend. A Renoir nude is art, she says, and *Hustler* is trash. "Any reasonable person" knows that.

8   But what about something between art and trash—something, say, along the lines of *Playboy* or *Penthouse* magazines? I asked five women for their reactions to one picture in *Penthouse* and got responses that ranged from "lovely" and "sensuous" to "revolting" and "demeaning." Feminists, like everyone else, seldom have rational reasons for their preferences in erotica. Like members of juries, they tend to disagree when confronted with something that falls short of 100 percent vulgarity.

9   In any case, feminists will not be the arbiters of good taste if it becomes easier to harass, prosecute and convict people on obscenity charges. Most of the people who want to censor girlie magazines are equally opposed to open discussion of issues that are of vital concern to women: rape, abortion, menstruation, contraception, lesbianism—in fact, the entire range of sexual experience from a woman's viewpoint.

10   Feminist writers and editors and film makers have limited financial resources. Confronted by a determined prosecutor, Hugh Hefner will fare better than Susan Brownmiller. Would the Memphis jurors who convicted Harry Reems for his role in *Deep Throat* be inclined to take a more positive view of paintings of the female genitalia done by sensitive feminist artists? *Ms* magazine has printed color reproductions of some of those art works, *Ms* is already banned from a number of high school libraries because someone considers it threatening and/or obscene.

11   Feminists who want to censor what they regard as harmful pornography have essentially the same motivation as other would-be censors: They want to use the power of the state to accomplish what they have been unable to achieve in the marketplace of ideas and

images. The impulse to censor places no faith in the possibilities of democratic persuasion.

12   It isn't easy to persuade certain men that they have better uses for $1.95 each month than to spend it on a copy of *Hustler*? Well, then, give the men no choice in the matter.

13   I believe there is also a connection between the impulse toward censorship on the part of people who used to consider themselves civil libertarians and a more general desire to shift responsibility from individuals to institutions. When I saw the movie *Looking for Mr. Goodbar*, I was stunned by its series of visual images equating sex and violence, coupled with what seems to me the mindless message (a distortion of the fine Judith Rossner novel) that casual sex equals death. When I came out of the movie, I was even more shocked to see parents standing in line with children between the ages of 10 and 14.

14   I simply don't know why a parent would take a child to see such a movie, anymore than I understand why people feel they can't turn off a television set their child is watching. Whenever I say that, my friends tell me I don't know how it is because I don't have children. True, but I do have parents. When I was a child, they did turn off the TV. They didn't expect the Federal Communications Commission to do their job for them.

15   I am a First Amendment junkie. You can't OD on the First Amendment, because free speech is its own best antidote.

Suggestions for Discussion and Writing

1. Jacoby sometimes associates herself with feminists, while at other times she separates herself from them. What effect does this have on you as a reader? Why do you think she chose this strategy?

2. What restrictions, if any, would Jacoby put on pornography? How does she reconcile this with her opposition to censorship?

3. Justice Black made the point that the Constitution cannot restrict free speech, "as distinguished from conduct." What is the difference between thinking of pornography as free speech and thinking of it as conduct or action?

4. At the end of her essay, Jacoby makes an analogy between pornography and television viewing. Do you believe

this is a fair analogy? Why or why not?

    5. What does the First Amendment say? How does pornography fall under its rule?

Gloria Steinem
Erotica and Pornography

GLORIA STEINEM, born in 1934 in Toledo, is one of the founders of modern American feminism. After receiving her B.A. from Smith College in 1956, she worked at a number of jobs, including one as a Playboy bunny for a magazine assignment. The co-founder and first editor of *Ms.*, she became its consulting editor in 1987 and served as a contributing editor for NBC's *Today* show. She is active in civil rights campaigns and the peace movement; her most recent books are *Marilyn* (1986) and *Revolution from Within* (1992). This essay is taken from her collection *Outrageous Acts and Everyday Rebellions* (1983).

Human beings are the only animals that experience the same sex drive at times when we can—and cannot—conceive.

2   Just as we developed uniquely human capacities for language, planning, memory, and invention along our evolutionary path, we also developed sexuality as a form of expression; a way of communicating that is separable from our need for sex as a way of perpetuating ourselves. For humans alone, sexuality can be and often is primarily a way of bonding, of giving and receiving pleasure, bridging differentness, discovering sameness, and communicating emotion.

3   We developed this and other human gifts through our ability to change our environment, adapt physically, and in the long run, to affect our own evolution. But as an emotional result of this spiraling path away from other animals, we seem to alternate between periods of

exploring our unique abilities to change new boundaries, and feelings of loneliness in the unknown that we ourselves have created, a fear that sometimes sends us back to the comfort of the animal world by encouraging us to exaggerate our sameness.

4   The separation of "play" from "work," for instance, is a problem only in the human world. So is the difference between art and nature, or an intellectual accomplishment and a physical one. As a result, we celebrate play, art, and invention as leaps into the unknown; but any imbalance can send us back to nostalgia for our primate past and the conviction that the basics of work, nature, and physical labor are somehow more worthwhile or even moral.

5   In the same way, we have explored our sexuality as separable from conception: a pleasurable, empathetic bridge to strangers of the same species. We have even invented contraception—a skill that has probably existed in some form since our ancestors figured out the process of birth—in order to extend this uniquely human difference. Yet we also have times of atavistic suspicion that sex is not complete—or even legal or intended-by-god—if it cannot end in conception.

6   No wonder the concepts of "erotica" and "pornography" can be so crucially different, and yet so confused. Both assume that sexuality can be separated from conception, and therefore can be used to carry a personal message. That's a major reason why, even in our current culture, both may be called equally "shocking" or legally "obscene," a word whose Latin derivative means "dirty, containing filth." This gross condemnation of all sexuality that isn't harnessed to childbirth and marriage has been increased by the current backlash against women's progress. Out of fear that the whole patriarchal structure might be upset if women really had the autonomous power to decide our reproductive futures (that is, if we controlled the most basic means of production), right-wing groups are not only denouncing pro-choice abortion literature as "pornographic," but are trying to stop the sending of all contraceptive information through the mails by invoking obscenity laws. In fact, Phyllis Schlafly recently denounced the entire Women's Movement as "obscene."

7   Not surprisingly, this religious, visceral backlash has a secular, intellectual counterpart that relies heavily on applying the "natural" behavior of the animal world to humans. That is questionable in itself, but these Lionell Tiger-ish studies make their political purpose even more clear in the particular animals they select and the habits

they choose to emphasize. The message is that females should accept their "destiny" of being sexually dependent and devote themselves to bearing and rearing their young.

8   Defending against such reaction in turn leads to another temptation: to merely reverse the terms, and declare that *all* nonprocreative sex is good. In fact, however, this human activity can be as constructive as destructive, moral or immoral, as any other. Sex as communication can send messages as different as life and death; even the origins of "erotica" and "pornography" reflect that fact. After all, "erotica" is rooted in *eros* or passionate love, and thus in the idea of positive choice, free will, the yearning for a particular person. (Interestingly, the definition of erotica leaves open the question of gender.) "Pornography" begins with a root meaning "prostitution" or "female captives," thus letting us know that the subject is not mutual love, or love at all, but domination and violence against women. (Though, of course, homosexual pornography may imitate this violence by putting a man in the "feminine" role of victim.) It ends with a root meaning "writing about" or "description of" which puts still more distance between subject and object, and replaces a spontaneous yearning for closeness with objectification and a voyeur.

9   The difference is clear in the words. It becomes even more so by example.

10   Look at any photo or film of people making love; really making love. The images may be diverse, but there is usually a sensuality and touch and warmth, an acceptance of bodies and nerve endings. There is always a spontaneous sense of people who are there because they *want* to be, out of shared pleasure.

11   Now look at any depiction of sex in which there is clear force, or an unequal power that spells coercion. It may be very blatant, with weapons or torture or bondage, wounds and bruises, some clear humiliation, or an adult's sexual power being used over a child. It may be much more subtle: a physical attitude of conqueror and victim, the use of race or class difference to imply the same thing, perhaps a very unequal nudity, with one person exposed and vulnerable while the other is clothed. In either case, there is no sense of equal choice or equal power.

12   The first is erotic: a mutually pleasurable, sexual expression between people who have enough power to be there by positive choice. It may or may not strike a sense-memory in the viewer, or be creative

enough to make the unknown seem real; but it doesn't require us to identify with a conqueror or a victim. It is truly sensuous, and may give us a contagion of pleasure.

13   The second is pornographic: its message is violence, dominance, and conquest. It is sex being used to reinforce some inequality, or to create one, or to tell us the lie that pain and humiliation (ours or someone else's) are really the same as pleasure. If we are to feel anything, we must identify with conqueror or victim. That means we can only experience pleasure through the adoption of some degree of sadism or masochism. It also means that we may feel diminished by the role of conqueror, or enraged, humiliated, and vengeful by sharing identity with the victim.

14   Perhaps one could simply say that erotica is about sexuality, but pornography is about power and sex-as-weapon—in the same way we have come to understand that rape is about violence, and not really about sexuality at all.

15   Yes, it's true that there are women who have been forced by violent families and dominating men to confuse love with pain; so much so that they have become masochists. (A fact that in no way excuses those who administer such pain.) But the truth is that, for most women—and for men with enough humanity to imagine themselves into the predicament of women—true pornography could serve as aversion therapy for sex.

16   Of course, there will always be personal differences about what is and is not erotic, and there may be cultural differences for a long time to come. Many women feel that sex makes them vulnerable and therefore may continue to need more sense of personal connection and safety before allowing any erotic feelings. We now find competence and erotic expertise in men, but that may pass as we develop those qualities in ourselves. Men, on the other hand, may continue to feel less vulnerable, and therefore more open to such potential danger as sex with strangers. As some men replace the need for submission from childlike women with the pleasure of cooperation from equals, they may find a partner's competence to be erotic, too.

17   Such group changes plus individual differences will continue to be reflected in sexual love between people of the same gender, as well as between women and men. The point is not to dictate sameness, but to discover ourselves and each other through sexuality that is an exploring, pleasurable, empathetic part of our lives; a human sexuality

that is unchained both from unwanted pregnancies and from violence.

18   But that is a hope, not a reality. At the moment, fear of change is increasing both the indiscriminate repression of all nonprocreative sex in the religious and "conservative" male world, and the pornographic vengeance against women's sexuality in the secular world of "liberal" and "radical" men. It's almost futuristic to debate what is and is not truly erotic, when many women are again being forced into compulsory motherhood, and the number of pornographic murders, tortures, and woman-hating images are on the increase in both popular culture and real life.

19   It's a familiar division: wife or whore, "good" woman who is constantly vulnerable to pregnancy or "bad" woman who is unprotected from violence. *Both* roles would be upset if we were to control our own sexuality. And that's exactly what we must do.

20   In spite of all our atavistic suspicions and training for the "natural" role of motherhood, we took up the complicated battle for reproductive freedom. Our bodies had borne the health burden of endless births and poor abortions, and we had a greater motive for separating sexuality and conception.

21   Now we have to take up the equally complex burden of explaining that all nonprocreative sex is *not* alike. We have a motive: our right to a uniquely human sexuality, and sometimes even to survival. As it is, our bodies have too rarely been enough our own to develop erotica in our own lives, much less in art and literature. And our bodies have too often been the objects of pornography and the woman-hating, violent practice that it preaches. Consider also our spirits that break a little each time we see ourselves in chains or full labial display for the conquering male viewer, bruised or on our knees, screaming a real or pretended pain to delight the sadist, pretending to enjoy what we don't enjoy, to be blind to the images of our sisters that really haunt us—humiliated often enough ourselves by the truly obscene idea that sex and the domination of women must be combined.

22   Sexuality *is* human, free, separate—and so are we.

23   But until we untangle the lethal confusion of sex with violence, there will be more pornography and less erotica. There will be little murders in our beds—and very little love.

Suggestions for Discussion and Writing

1. What distinctions does Steinem draw between pornography and erotica? How are these distinctions important in her argument?

2. According to Steinem, how do pornography and erotica affect men's and women's lives?

3. Where does Steinem introduce the main idea of her essay? Why do you think she organized her essay this way?

4. Does Steinem convince you that pornography and human reproduction are connected? What evidence does she give that this might be so?

5. Most of the arguments about pornography seem to revolve around the definition of the word. Look up *pornography* in several dictionaries (if possible, published several years apart). How has the definition changed? What factors do you think have caused those changes? (If your library has *The Oxford English Dictionary*, you might want to start there, since it will document the entire history of the word in English.)

Hugh Hefner
Sexual McCarthyism

HUGH HEFNER, born in Chicago in 1926, was once identified in a poll as "the man most American men would like to be." He is the founder and editor emeritus of *Playboy*; his daughter Christie succeeded him as editor and Chief Executive Officer of Playboy Enterprises in 1988. Although he still lives in the opulent Playboy mansion in California, wears his trademark pajamas, and entertains hundreds of aspiring Playboy models, Hefner, now remarried and the father of two small children, has settled down into marriage. However, he still remains an advocate of sexual freedom (along with safer sex) and continues to oppose government attempts to regulate people's sexual expression. "Sexual McCarthyism" first appeared in *Playboy* in 1985.

> I have in my possession the names of 57 Communists who are in the State Department at present.
>
> Senator Joseph McCarthy, February 11, 1950

It wasn't true, but it touched off hysterics that would last half a decade. For the next five years, just being accused of Communist leanings could get you fired or blacklisted. It is a measure of the witches' brew McCarthy stirred up that in 1954, just months before the Senate finally worked up the courage to condemn him, a Gallup Poll showed that 50 percent of America supported him. But when the weird spectacle of the Army-McCarthy hearings appeared on TV, the nation saw that its esrtwhile hero was a fraud and a demagog. In December 1954, he was censured by the Senate. His name entered the dictionary (McCarthyism: The use of indiscriminate, often unfounded, accusations, sensationalism, inquisitorial investigative methods); the man died, disgraced, three years later.

2   One of the minor McCarthy-era players was one Ronald Reagan, B-movie actor, president of the Screen Actors Guild, FBI informant on members of his own union. In Hollywood in 1947, Reagan had appeared with like-minded movie folks (Gary Cooper, Adolphe Menjou) as a friendly witness before the Red-hunting House Un-American Activities Committee. Almost 40 years later, President Reagan would set up a little hunt of his own.

3   Early last year, Reagan's Attorney General, Edwin Meese, launched a seek-and-destroy mission called The Attorney General's Commission on Pornography. There had been a President's Commission on Obscenity and Pornography under Nixon 18 years earlier. It concluded that there was no connection between pornography and antisocial behavior. That wasn't good enough for Reagan and Meese. "Re-examination of the issue of pornography is long overdue," Meese told reporters last year. "No longer must one go out of the way to find pornographic materials. With the advent of cable television and video recorders, pornography now is available at home to almost anyone."

4   The Meese commission's ostensible goal is to study the effects of sexually explicit materials, but it will hear some viewpoints more sympathetically than others. At the hearings, law-enforcement officers and pornography "victims"—often hidden behind screens, like spies on *60 Minutes*—relate sexual horror stories. Civil-liberties types get to speak, too, but the ringside seats are packed for the commission's slide shows of explicit pornography. The witnesses who draw headlines are the ones willing to blame their sad lives on "the evils of pornography."

5   How are the witnesses selected?

6   The Meese commission uses five investigators to screen potential witnesses. You'd think the investigators would be interested in all sides of what even the commission admits is a complicated issue, but it seems you'd be wrong.

7   Dr. Lois Lee is director of Children of the Night, a prominent Los Angeles organization that helps street kids, most of them young prostitutes, get off the streets. On August fifth of last year, Dr. Lee was contacted by Ed Chapman, a Virginia law-enforcement officer working for the Meese commission. He said he wanted her to line up some of her teenagers to testify. Chapman then told Lee what he wanted the witnesses to say—that pornography had been used as a tool when their parents molested them and that this experience had led them into prostitution.

8   "Wait a minute," Lee said. She told Chapman that that was not the way it happened. Chapman replied that the investigators had talked with a lot of people about pornography being used by child molesters and that they knew this was generally the case.

9   "I said it *wasn't* the case," Lee told Playboy, "and he said, 'I don't think we're going to want your kids.' The conversation was over."

10   The commission's investigators, it was clear, wanted witnesses to support a cause-and-effect relationship between porn use and antisocial behavior. They wanted witnesses like the one who was willing to testify that her father had molested her after looking at a Playmate Calendar. What was the connection? It was, as Meese-commission investigator Joe Haggerty told Lee with some enthusiasm, the fact that the witness had testified that she believed her father molested her because she was closer to the ages of the Playmates on the calendar and looked more like them than her mother. Lee found this cause-and-effect notion preposterous.

The professional Communist-hunters of the time were able to summon a stream of professional witnesses who seemed always ready, willing and able to testify that they had known so-and-so at Communist meetings in the past. Their testimony was as suspect as their claims that although they might have once been fooled by the Communist doctrines, they had suddenly seen the light and were now blessed with total recall.

From *Days of Shame*, by Senator Charles E. Potter,
a Member of the 1954 McCarthy Committee

11   The witness whose father had had the Playmate Calendar was—probably not coincidentally—a born-again Christian. It is an article of faith with born-agains that the more impressive one's list of early sins, the more glorious one's salvation. A long list of sins recanted helps assure redemption. (See *The Self-Crucifixion of Cathleen Crowell Webb*, by Elizabeth and Edwin Black, Playboy, October 1985.)

12   Much of the testimony belongs in revivalist meetings. Born-again Brenda MacKillop, another Meese-commission witness, almost speaks in tongues.

I am a former Playboy Bunny. . . . I was extremely suicidal and sought psychiatric help for the eight years I lived in a sexually promiscuous fashion. There was no help for me until I changed my lifestyle to be a follower of Jesus Christ and obeyed the Biblical truths, including no premarital sex. . . . I implore the Attorney General's commission to see the connection between sexual promiscuity, venereal disease, abortion, divorce, homosexuality, sexual abuse of children, suicide, drug abuse, rape, and prostitution to pornography. . . Come back to God, America, before it's too late.

13   For witness MacKillop, everything from divorce to acid indigestion can be chalked up to pornography. MacKillop described for the commission the episodes of her formerly promiscuous personal life. In each instance, she attempted to blame Playboy—the magazine, the Clubs, and the philosophy—for her sexual downfall.

14   The Meese commission had trundled out a parade of born-again basket cases, anti-sex feminists, and fun-hating fundamentalists. More than anything else, the testimony of these witnesses struck us as sad, misdirected—even pathetic. It was also inflammatory, misinformed scapegoating.

15   In a court of law, such witnesses would be dismissed for lack of

credibility. Trial by headline—unsupported by evidence, unchal-
lenged by cross-examination or witnesses for the defense—is not due
process. But it is the method of the Meese commission, as it was for
McCarthy.

16   The Meese commission has the trappings of an inquiry but not
the substance. The Government is putting on a circus show of misin-
formation. It is using the power of its position to prove that pornography is harmful rather than to research the facts. On another front,
Dr. C. Everett Koop, the Surgeon General, who should have more respect for science, released a statement warning that "pornography may
be dangerous to your health." He told the nation, "Pornography is a
destructive phenomenon. . . . It does not contribute anything to society
but, rather, takes away from and diminishes what we regard as socially
good." He then listed, without supporting evidence, some of its dangers: Pornography "intervenes in normal sexual relationships and
alters them."

17   What, if any, scientific evidence exists to support such claims?
Professor Joseph E. Scott of Ohio State University analyzed all the
research available on what we have learned in the more than 15 years
since the commission's 1970 report about the relationship among violence, pornography and antisocial behavior. In a report to the American Association for the Advancement of Science, Professor Scott took
on some of the common myths about pornography.

18   *Myth one*: Porn is more violent today than 15 years ago. *Wrong!*
This is the addiction theory of porn, asserting that consumers become
jaded and desensitized. Fundamentalists believe that one taste of sexually explicit material gets you hooked on the hard stuff. Porn has not
become more violent. The porn slide shows mentioned earlier may be
frightening and certainly are offensive to some, but they contain
selected images. They do not reflect the market place. Scott says that
when *Time* magazine runs an article claiming that S/M is the latest
trend in porn, it misinterprets the available research. How violent is
porn? Scott found that X-rated movies had less violence that G-, PG-,
or R-rated movies. The average number of violent acts per movies
were 20.3 for the R-rated, 16.2 for the G-rated, 15.3 for the PG
movies, and 4.4 for the X-rated movies.

19   *Myth two*: Exposure to porn leads to violence. *Wrong!* There is
no scientific evidence that reading or viewing sexually explicit material causes antisocial behavior. (In fact, several studies have shown

that exposure to gentle erotica actually lessens aggression.) However, there are two endlessly quoted researchers who say they've proved that exposure to violent sexual depiction increases the likelihood of certain males "condoning or expressing willingness to act aggressively against females." We're not sure what that means in real life. Scott reports that the only long-term study of violent porn disproved that myth: "Researchers examined married couples over a three-month period. They found that exposure to violent themes produced no significant changes in the participants' behavior." The most frequently quoted research has been that done by UCLA professor Neil Malamuth, the "professor of porn," using college undergraduates in lab situations. No one believes that the artificial effects created by watching pornographic films in a lab carry over to real life. Has anyone ever participated in the experiments, then raped a coed? If viewing X-rated films leads automatically to violence against women, then Malamuth, who has been showing these films for years, would have been arrested for rape a long time ago.

20 Is there a way to gauge the effect of erotic material on the general population? One study compared sex-magazine-readership rates with rape rates by state. The researchers found a moderately strong relationship between rape rates and the consumption of adult magazines. Taken by itself, this would be cause for concern. However, a correlation is not the same as cause and effect. Subsequent studies have shown how tenuous that relation is. Consider *Field & Stream* or *Guns & Ammo*. Researchers found that the circulation of outdoor magazines has a higher correlation with rape than the number of adult bookstores in each state. One would assume that rape rates might be higher in those states with the most adult theaters. No relationship has been found. To further confuse the issue, researchers have found rape rates to be higher in urban areas, in poor areas, in areas with high proportions of nonwhites, and in areas of high alcohol consumption. Each of these variables showed a stronger relationship to rape than the number of adult theaters and bookstores.

21 Perhaps the best way to confront the myths about porn violence is to look at the Danish experience. Denmark legalized pornography in the late Sixties. Last year, a conference was held to review the effects of porn on social and criminal behavior. Berl Kutchinsky, a criminologist from the University of Copenhagen, summarized 15 years of research:

> The conclusion is very clear that pornography is not a danger—neither to persons, neither to society, neither to children nor to adults. It doesn't lead to sex offenses; it doesn't lead to sexual deviations. . . . The only thing about pornography is that it makes people masturbate. . . . People's attitude toward sexuality and, therefore, toward pornography is almost 100 percent determined by their religious convictions. And those are not altered by facts.

22   The Meese commission, with its fundamentalist foundation, is not likely to be swayed by facts. In effect, Kutchinsky was voicing the 1970 findings of the President's Commission on Obscenity and Pornography:

> The commission believes that much of the "problem" regarding materials which depict explicit sexual activity stems from the inability or reluctance of people in our society to be open and direct in dealing with sexual matters. . . . The commission believes that there is no warrant for continued interference with the full freedom of adults to read, obtain or view whatever such materials they wish.

23   The Meese commission has written its own warrant for interference with our freedom. It despises fact. This sexual McCarthyism is as rooted in deception, innuendo, and outright lies as the original version.

24   We think women *and* men have a right to sexual knowledge. We think that, as free adults, they have a right to choose what they will and will not see. But then, we thought the smell of McCarthyism had dissipated 30 years ago. Until it departs again, those who believe in free minds must take every effort to oppose the new wave of sexual McCarthyism.

Suggestions for Discussion and Writing

1. What are Hefner's objections to the Meese commission's practices? Besides his stated objections, can you detect any others?

2. Look at the studies Hefner cites about the relationship between pornography and violence. Do those studies support the points he is making? Does the research convince you to agree with Hefner or the Surgeon General?

3. What is McCarthyism? How does it apply to pornog-

raphy? What reaction is Hefner trying to inspire in readers by using this term?

4. What is the structure of Hefner's argument? Why do you think he chose this strategy?

5. What happened as a result of the Meese Commission? Consult the report, issued in July 1986, and look up what events happened in its aftermath. (*The Reader's Guide to Periodical Literature* under "Pornography" would be a good place to start.) Did the Meese Commission make a difference?

7 A Framework for Feminism

While it is very difficult to define what feminism is, it's less hard to describe the circumstances that brought the women's movement about or the factors that have influenced its development. By way of providing some historical context, we include six essays that illustrate "landmarks" in feminism. We realize that certain kinds of feminism, such as minority women's feminism, sexual freedom, and reproductive rights are not covered in this section. Neither is 'masculinism,' the theory of the men's movement. The book just isn't big enough to do justice to them. That's not an excuse for not thinking about those issues; it's just the reason why they aren't covered here. We encourage you to explore these areas on your own.

A selection from Mary Wollstonecraft's writings begins the section, showing the initial public discussion of the rights of women. John Stuart Mill surprises his Victorian audience with a spirited attack on female subjection, and Elizabeth Cady Stanton and the delegates of the Seneca Falls Women's Rights Convention state the principles guiding their efforts. Olive Schreiner warns society of the consequences of neglecting the intellectual and moral development of some of its mem-

bers. Vivian Gornick explains the rise of modern feminism, and
tries to convey some of the excitement the movement inspired. And Betty Friedan, the dean of the American women's
movement, looks forward to a new women's and men's united
movement, which accounts for changes in the workplace,
families, and personal values. As you read and consider these
essays, ask "What does it mean to be a feminist? What is feminism about, anyway? What should the next stage of feminism
be? Should men and women participate in that next stage?"

Mary Wollstonecraft
From A Vindication of the Rights of Woman

MARY WOLLSTONECRAFT (1759-1797) left home at
age nineteen to become first a companion, then a
governess, and finally a teacher with her sister Eliza.
She published *A Vindication of the Rights of Man*
(1790), a polemic on governmental reform, and
next, in 1792, *A Vindication of the Rights of Woman*
(excerpted here), encouraging women to develop
their minds and souls without giving up their roles as
mothers. During the French Revolution, Wollstonecraft
bore a child to her American lover Gilbert Imlay, and
attempted suicide when Imlay left her. In 1796, she
became reacquainted with William Godwin,
"friendship melting into love" in his words. When she
became pregnant, they married hastily, but she
died of childbed fever after giving birth to her second daughter Mary, later famous as the author of
Frankenstein. When the details of her pre-marital life
became known, her work was discredited; only in
this century has she been returned to her place in the
history of ideas.

After considering the historic page, and viewing the living world with anxious solicitude, the most melancholy emotions of sorrowful indignation have depressed my spirits, and I have sighed when obliged to confess, that either nature has made a great difference between man and man, or that the civilization which has hitherto taken place in the world has been very partial. I have turned over various books written on the subject of education, and patiently observed the conduct of parents and the management of schools; but what has been the result?—a profound conviction that the neglected education of my fellow-creatures is the grand source of the misery I deplore; and that women, in particular, are rendered weak and wretched by a variety of concurring causes, originating from one hasty conclusion. The conduct and manners of women, in fact, evidently prove that their minds are not in a healthy state; for, like the flowers which are planted in too rich a soil, strength and usefulness are sacrificed to beauty; and the flaunting leaves, after having pleased a fastidious eye, fade, disregarded on the stalk, long before the season when they ought to have arrived at maturity. One cause of this barren blooming I attribute to a false system of education, gathered from the books written on this subject by men who, considering females rather as women than human creatures, have been more anxious to make them alluring mistresses than affectionate wives and rational mothers; and the understanding of the sex has been so bubbled by this specious homage, that the civilized women of the present century, with a few exceptions, are only anxious to inspire love, when they ought to cherish a nobler ambition, and by their abilities and virtues exact respect.

2   In a treatise, therefore, on female rights and manners, the works which have been particularly written for their improvement must not be overlooked; especially when it is asserted, in direct terms, that the minds of women are enfeebled by false refinement; that the books of instruction, written by men of genius, have had the same tendency as more frivolous productions; and that, in the true style of Mahometanism, they are treated as a kind of subordinate beings, and not as a part of the human species, when improvable reason is allowed to be the dignified distinction which raises men above the brute creation, and puts a natural sceptre in a feeble hand.

3   Yet, because I am a woman, I would not lead my readers to sup-

pose that I mean violently to agitate the contested question respecting the equality or inferiority of the sex; but as the subject lies in my way, and I cannot pass it over without subjecting the main tendency of my reasoning to misconstruction, I shall stop a moment to deliver, in a few words, my opinion.—In the government of the physical world it is observable that the female in point of strength is, in general, inferior to the male. This is the law of nature; and it does not appear to be suspended or abrogated in favour of woman. A degree of physical superiority cannot, therefore, be denied—and it is a noble prerogative! But not content with this natural pre-eminence, men endeavour to sink us still lower, merely to render us alluring objects for a moment; and women, intoxicated by the adoration which men, under the influence of their senses, pay them, do not seek to obtain a durable interest in their hearts, or to become the friends of the fellow creatures who find amusement in their society.

4   I am aware of an obvious inference:—from every quarter have I heard exclamations against masculine women; but where are they to be found? If by this appellation men mean to inveigh against their ardour in hunting, shooting, and gaming, I shall most cordially join in the cry; but if it be against the imitation of many virtues, or, more properly speaking, the attainment of those talents and virtues, the exercise of which ennobles the human character, and which raise females in the scale of animal being, when they are comprehensively termed mankind, all those who view them with a philosophic eye must, I should think, wish with me, that they may every day grow more and more masculine.

5   This discussion naturally divides the subject. I shall first consider women in the grand light of human creatures, who, in common with men, are placed on this earth to unfold their faculties; and afterwards I shall more particularly point out their peculiar designation.

6   I wish also to steer clear of an error which many respectable writers have fallen into; for the instruction which has hitherto been addressed to women, has rather been applicable to *ladies,* if the little indirect advice, that is scattered through Sandford and Merton, be excepted; but, addressing my sex in a firmer tone, I pay particular attention to those in the middle class, because they appear to be in the most natural state. Perhaps the seeds of false refinement, immorality, and vanity, have ever been shed by the great. Weak, artificial beings, raised above the common wants and affections of their race, in a premature

unnatural manner, undermine the very foundation of virtue, and spread corruption through the whole mass of society! As a class of mankind they have the strongest claim to pity; the education of the rich tends to render them vain and helpless, and the unfolding mind is not strengthened by the practice of those duties which dignify the human character.—They only live to amuse themselves, and by the same law which in nature invariably produces certain effects, they soon only afford barren amusement.

7   But as I purpose taking a separate view of the different ranks of society, and of the moral character of women, in each, this hint is, for the present, sufficient, and I have only alluded to the subject, because it appears to me to be the very essence of an introduction to give a cursory account of the contents of the work it introduces.

8   My own sex, I hope, will excuse me, if I treat them like rational creatures, instead of flattering their fascinating graces, and viewing them as if they were in a state of perpetual childhood, unable to stand alone. I earnestly wish to point out in what true dignity and human happiness consists—I wish to persuade women to endeavour to acquire strength, both of mind and body, and to convince them that the soft phrases, susceptibility of heart, delicacy of sentiment, and refinement of taste, are almost synonymous with epithets of weakness, and that those beings who are only the objects of pity and that kind of love, which has been termed its sister, will soon become objects of contempt.

9   Dismissing then those pretty feminine phrases, which the men condescendingly use to soften our slavish dependence, and despising that weak elegancy of mind, exquisite sensibility, and sweet docility of manners, supposed to be the sexual characteristics of the weaker vessel, I wish to shew that elegance is inferior to virtue, that the first object of laudable ambition is to obtain a character as a human being, regardless of the distinction of sex; and that secondary views should be brought to this simple touchstone.

10   This is a rough sketch of my plan; and should I express my conviction with the energetic emotions that I feel whenever I think of the subject, the dictates of experience and reflection will be felt by some of my readers. Animated by this important object, I shall disdain to cull my phrases or polish my style,—I aim at being useful, and sincerity will render me unaffected; for, wishing rather to persuade by the force of my arguments, than dazzle by the elegance of my language, I

shall not waste my time in rounding periods, or in fabricating the turgid bombast of artificial feelings, which, coming from the head, never reach the heart. I shall be employed about things, not words!—and, anxious to render my sex more respectable members of society, I shall try to avoid that flowery diction which has slided from essays into novels, and from novels into familiar letters and conversation

51   These pretty superlatives, dropping glibly from the tongue, vitiate the taste, and create a kind of sickly delicacy that turns away from simple unadorned truth; and a deluge of false sentiments and overstretched feelings, stifling the natural emotions of the heart, render the domestic pleasures insipid, that ought to sweeten the exercise of those severe duties which educate a rational and immortal being for a nobler field of action.

12   The education of women has, of late, been more attended to than formerly; yet they are still reckoned a frivolous sex, and ridiculed or pitied by the writers who endeavour by satire or instruction to improve them. It is acknowledged that they spend many of the first years of their lives in acquiring a smattering of accomplishments; meanwhile strength of body and mind are sacrificed to libertine notions of beauty, to the desire of establishing themselves,—the only way women can rise in the world,—by marriage. And this desire making mere animals of them when they marry they act as such children may be expected to act:—they dress; they paint, and nickname God's creatures.—Surely these weak beings are only fit for a seraglio!—Can they be expected to govern a family with judgment, or take care of the poor babes whom they bring into the world?

13   If then it can be fairly deduced from the present conduct of the sex, from the prevalent fondness for pleasure which takes place of ambition and those nobler passions that open and enlarge the soul, that the instruction which women have hitherto received has only tended, with the constitution of civil society, to render them insignificant objects of desire—mere propagators of fools!—if it can be proved that in aiming to accomplish them, without cultivating their understandings, they are taken out of their sphere of duties, and made ridiculous and useless when the short-lived bloom of beauty is over, I presume that *rational* men will excuse me for endeavouring to persuade them to become more masculine and respectable.

14   Indeed the word masculine is only a bugbear: there is little reason to fear that women will acquire too much courage or fortitude;

for their apparent inferiority with respect to bodily strength, must render them, in some degree, dependent on men in the various relations of life, but why should it be increased by prejudices that give a sex to virtue, and confound simple truths with sensual reveries?

15   Women are, in fact, so much degraded by mistaken notions of female excellence, that I do not mean to add a paradox when I assert, that this artificial weakness produces a propensity to tyrannize, and gives birth to cunning, the natural opponent of strength, which leads them to play off those contemptible infantine airs that undermine esteem even whilst they excite desire. Let men become more chaste and modest, and if women do not grow wiser in the same ratio it will be clear that they have weaker understandings. It seems scarcely necessary to say, that I now speak of the sex in general. Many individuals have more sense than their male relatives, and, as nothing preponderates where there is a constant struggle for an equilibrium, without it has naturally more gravity, some women govern their husbands without degrading themselves, because intellect will always govern.

Suggestions for Discussion and Writing

1. According to Wollstonecraft, what reaction did most women try to get from men? Has this changed in the two hundred years since her essay was published? If so, how?

2. What are the results of the subjection of women, according to the essay? Who is harmed by this subjection?

3. To whom is the essay addressed? What clues in the text lead you to this conclusion?

4. Wollstonecraft's long sentences are imitating Latin prose style. Why would she choose to use such a style? How does her strategy relate to the purpose of her essay?

5. If you had to write either a *Vindication of the Rights of Woman* or a *Vindication of the Rights of Man* today, what would you write about? What rights need to be "vindicated"?

John Stuart Mill
From The Subjection of Women

JOHN STUART MILL (1806-1873), the eminent Victorian
philosopher and essayist, was raised by his father
James to embrace the philosophy of utilitarianism
(morals should be based on what brings the
greatest good or greatest happiness to the greatest
number of people). However, he gradually veered
away to develop a philosophy of his own. He is best
known for *The System of Logic* (1843), *Principles of
Political Economy* (1849), and his *Autobiography*
(1873). In "The Subjection of Women," an essay published in 1869 and excerpted here, Mill examines at
length the reasons men give for treating women as
subordinates.

The object of this Essay is to explain as clearly as I am able, the
grounds of an opinion which I have held from the very earliest period
when I had formed any opinions at all on social or political matters,
and which, instead of being weakened or modified, has been constantly
growing stronger by the progress of reflection and the experience of
life: That the principle which regulates the existing social relations
between the two sexes—the legal subordination of one sex to the
other—is wrong in itself, and now one of the chief hindrances to
human improvement; and that it ought to be replaced by a principle of
perfect equality, admitting no power or privilege on the one side, nor
disability on the other. . . .

2   Some will object, that a comparison cannot fairly be made between the government of the male sex and the forms of unjust power
which I have adduced in illustration of it, since these are arbitrary,
and the effect of mere usurpation, while it on the contrary is natural.
But was there ever any domination which did not appear natural to

those who possessed it? There was a time when the division of mankind into two classes, a small one of masters and a numerous one of slaves, appeared, even to the most cultivated minds, to be a natural, and the only natural, condition of the human race. No less an intellect, and one which contributed no less to the progress of human thought, than Aristotle, held this opinion without doubt or misgiving; and rested it on the same premises on which the same assertion in regard to the dominion of men over women is usually based, namely that there are different natures among mankind, free natures, and slave natures; that the Greeks were of a free nature, the barbarian races of Thracians and Asiatics of a slave nature. But why need I go back to Aristotle? Did not the slaveowners of the Southern United States maintain the same doctrine, with all the fanaticism with which men cling to the theories that justify their passions and legitimate their personal interests? Did they not call heaven and earth to witness that the dominion of the white man over the black is natural, that the black race is by nature incapable of freedom, and marked out for slavery? some even going so far as to say that the freedom of manual laborers is an unnatural order of things anywhere. Again, the theorists of absolute monarchy have always affirmed it to be the only natural form of government; issuing from the patriarchal, which was the primitive and spontaneous form of society, framed on the model of the paternal, which is anterior to society itself, and, as they contend, the most natural authority of all. Nay, for that matter, the law of force itself, to those who could not plead any other, has always seemed the most natural of all grounds for the exercise of authority. Conquering races hold it to be Nature's own dictate that the conquered should obey the conquerors or, as they euphoniously paraphrase it, that the feebler and more unwarlike races should submit to the braver and manlier. The smallest acquaintance with human life in the middle ages, shows how supremely natural the dominion of the feudal nobility over men of low condition appeared to the nobility themselves, and how unnatural the conception seemed, of a person of the inferior class claiming equality with them, or exercising authority over them. It hardly seemed less so to the class held in subjection. The emancipated serfs and burgesses, even in their most vigorous struggles, never made any pretension to a share of authority; they only demanded more or less of limitation to the power of tyrannizing over them. So true is it that unnatural generally means only uncustomary, and that everything which is usual appears natural. The subjection of women to men being a universal custom, any departure from it quite naturally appears unnatural. But how entirely, even in this case, the feeling is dependent on custom, appears by ample experience. Nothing so much astonishes the people of distant parts of the world, when they first learn anything about England, as to be told that it is under a queen: the thing seems to them so unnatural as to be almost incredible. To Englishmen this does not seem in the least degree unnatural, because they are used to it; but they do feel it unnatural that women should be soldiers or members of Parliament. In the feudal ages, on the contrary, war and politics were not thought unnatural to women, because not unusual; it seemed natural that women of the privileged classes should be of manly character, inferior in nothing but bodily strength to their husbands and fathers. The independence of women seemed rather less unnatural to the Greeks than to other ancients, on account of the fabulous Amazons (whom they believed to be historical), and the partial example afforded by the Spartan women; who, though no less subordinate by law than in other Greek states, were more free in fact, and being trained to bodily exercises in the same manner with men, gave ample proof that they were not naturally disqualified for them. There can be little doubt that Spartan experience suggested to Plato, among many other of his doctrines, that of the social and political equality of the two sexes.

3   But, it will be said, the rule of men over women differs from all these others in not being a rule of force: it is accepted voluntarily; women make no complaint, and are consenting parties to it. In the first place, a great number of women do not accept it. Ever since there have been women able to make their sentiments known by their writings (the only mode of publicity which society permits to them), an increasing number of them have recorded protests against their present social condition: and recently many thousands of them, headed by the most eminent women known to the public, have petitioned Parliament for their admission to the Parliamentary Suffrage. The claim of women to be educated as solidly, and in the same branches of knowledge, as men, is urged with growing intensity, and with a great prospect of success; while the demand for their admission into professions and occupations hitherto closed against them, becomes every year more urgent. Though there are not in this country, as there are in the United States, periodical Conventions and an organized party to agitate for the Rights of Women, there is a numerous and active Soci-

ety organized and managed by women, for the more limited object of obtaining the political franchise. Nor is it only in our own country and in America that women are beginning to protest, more or less collectively, against the disabilities under which they labor. France, and Italy, and Switzerland, and Russia now afford examples of the same thing. How many more women there are who silently cherish similar aspirations, no one can possibly know; but there are abundant tokens how many *would* cherish them, were they not so strenuously taught to repress them as contrary to the proprieties of their sex. It must be remembered, also, that no enslaved class ever asked for complete liberty at once. When Simon de Montforts called the deputies of the commons to sit for the first time in Parliament, did any of them dream of demanding that an assembly, elected by their constituents, should make and destroy ministries, and dictate to the king in affairs of state? No such thought entered into the imagination of the most ambitious of them. The nobility had already these pretensions; the commons pretended to nothing but to be exempt from arbitrary taxation, and from the gross individual oppression of the king's officers. It is a political law of nature that those who are under any power of ancient origin, never begin by complaining of the power itself, but only of its oppressive exercise. There is never any want of women who complain of ill usage by their husbands. There would be infinitely more, if complaint were not the greatest of all provocatives to a repetition and increase of the ill usage. It is this which frustrates all attempts to maintain the power but protect the woman against its abuses. In no other case (except that of a child) is the person who has been proved judicially to have suffered an injury, replaced under the physical power of the culprit who inflicted it. Accordingly wives, even in the most extreme and protracted cases of bodily ill usage, hardly ever dare avail themselves of the laws made for their protection: and if, in a moment of irrepressible indignation, or by the interference of neighbors, they are induced to do so, their whole effort afterward is to disclose as little as they can, and to beg off their tyrant from his merited chastisement.

3   All causes, social and natural, combine to make it unlikely that women should be collectively rebellious to the power of men. They are so far in a position different from all other subject classes, that their masters require something more from them than actual service. Men do not want solely the obedience of women, they want their sen-

timents. All men, except the most brutish, desire to have, in the woman most nearly connected with them, not a forced slave but a willing one, not a slave merely, but a favorite. They have therefore put everything in practice to enslave their minds. The masters of all other slaves rely, for maintaining obedience, on fear; either fear of themselves or religious fears. The masters of women wanted more than simple obedience, and they turned the whole force of education to effect their purpose. All women are brought up from the very earliest years in the belief that their ideal of character is the very opposite to that of men; not self-will, and government by self-control but submission, and yielding to the control of others. All the moralities tell them that it is the duty of women, and all the current sentimentalities that it is their nature, to live for others, to make complete abnegation of themselves, and to have no life but in their affections. And by their affections are meant the only ones they are allowed to have—those to the men with whom they are connected, or to the children who constitute an additional and indefeasible tie between them and a man. When we put together three things—first, the natural attraction between opposite sexes; secondly, the wife's entire dependence on the husband, every privilege or pleasure she has being either his gift, or depending entirely on his will; and lastly, that the principal object of human pursuit, consideration, and all objects of social ambition, can in general be sought or obtained by her only through him, it would be a miracle if the object of being attractive to men had not become the polar star of feminine education and formation of character. And, this great means of influence over the minds of women having been acquired, an instinct of selfishness made men avail themselves of it to the utmost as a means of holding women in subjection, by representing to them meekness, submissiveness, and resignation of all individual will into the hands of a man, as an essential part of sexual attractiveness. Can it be doubted that any of the other yokes which mankind have succeeded in breaking, would have subsisted till now if the same means had existed, and had been as sedulously used, to bow down their minds to it? If it had been made the object of the life of every young plebeian to find personal favor in the eyes of some patrician, of every young serf with some seigneur; if domestication with him, and a share of his personal affections, had been held out as the prize which they all should look out for, the most gifted and aspiring being able to reckon on the most desirable prizes; and if, when this prize had been obtained, they

had been shut out by a wall of brass from all interests not centering in
him, all feelings and desires but those which he shared or inculcated;
would not serfs and seigneurs, plebeians and patricians, have been as
broadly distinguished at this day as men and women are? and would
not all but a thinker here and there, have believed the distinction to be
a fundamental and unalterable fact in human nature?

5   The preceding considerations are amply sufficient to show that
custom, however universal it may be, affords in this case no pre-
sumption, and ought not to create any prejudice, in favor of the arrangements which place women in social and political subjection to
men. But I may go farther, and maintain that the course of history, and
the tendencies of progressive human society, afford not only no pre-
sumption in favor of this system of inequality of rights, but a strong
one against it; and that, so far as the whole course of human improvement up to this time, the whole stream of modern tendencies, warrants
any inference on the subject, it is, that this relic of the past is discor-
dant with the future, and must necessarily disappear.

6   For, what is the peculiar character of the modern world—the
difference which chiefly distinguishes modern institutions, modern
social ideas, modern life itself, from those of times long past? It is,
that human beings are no longer born to their place in life, and
chained down by an inexorable bond to the place they are born to, but
are free to employ their faculties, and such favourable chances as offer,
to achieve the lot which may appear to them most desirable.

Suggestions for Discussion and Writing

1. What examples does Mill give of societies that have
practiced domination of part of their population? Why does he
choose these examples? How do they affect you as readers?

2. What role does custom play in the subjection of
women? Why does Mill spend so much time discussing it?

3. In the conclusion, Mill appears to shift focus to talk
about the characteristics of the modern world. Do you agree
with him about the most important characteristic? How does this
conclusion tie into what he has said in the essay?

4. According to Mill, why don't women rebel openly
against their treatment? Do you see any parallels between his
argument and what goes on today?

5. Were there societies in which women dominated men? Do such societies still exist today? How do such societies work? Are they better, worse, or about the same as our society? (You might want to start by looking up "matriarchy" in some encyclopedias and in the card catalog.)

Elizabeth Cady Stanton
Declaration of Sentiments and Resolutions

ELIZABETH CADY STANTON (1815-1902), along with Susan B. Anthony, were suffragists and abolitionists who led the first organized women's rights movement in the United States. While Anthony was the better organizer, Stanton was the more effective speaker and writer, and, as a married woman, was more acceptable to middle-class America. With Anthony she edited the journal *Revolution* (1868-69), and compiled the monumental three-volume *History of Woman (sic) Suffrage* (1881-1886). On her own she published her autobiography, *Eighty Years and More* (1898) and *The Woman's Bible* (1895, 1898), a critical interpretation of all references to women in the Bible. In the "Declaration" that follows, written for the Seneca Falls Convention of 1848, Stanton bears witness to the beginning of the women's movement in this country.

When, in the course of human events, it becomes necessary for one portion of the family of man to assume among the people of the earth a position different from that which they have hitherto occupied, but one to which the laws of nature and of nature's God entitle them, a decent respect to the opinions of mankind requires that they should declare the causes that impel them to such a course.

2   We hold these truths to be self-evident: that all men and women are created equal; that they are endowed by their Creator with certain inalienable rights; that among these are life, liberty, and the pursuit of happiness; that to secure these rights governments are instituted, deriving their just powers from the consent of the governed. Whenever any form of government becomes destructive of these ends, it is the right of those who suffer from it to refuse allegiance to it, and to insist upon the institution of a new government, laying its foundation on such principles, and organizing its powers in such form, as to them shall seem most likely to effect their safety and happiness. Prudence, indeed, will dictate that governments long established should not be changed for light and transient causes; and accordingly all experience hath shown that mankind are more disposed to suffer, while evils are sufferable, than to right themselves by abolishing the forms to which they were accustomed. But when a long train of abuses and usurpations, pursuing invariably the same object, evinces a design to reduce them under absolute despotism, it is their duty to throw off such government, and to provide new guards for their future security. Such has been the patient sufferance of the women under this government, and such is now the necessity which constrains them to demand the equal station to which they are entitled.

3   The history of mankind is a history of repeated injuries and usurpations on the part of man toward woman, having in direct object the establishment of an absolute tyranny over her. To prove this, let facts be submitted to a candid world.

4   He has never permitted her to exercise her inalienable right to the elective franchise.

5   He has compelled her to submit to laws, in the formation of which she had no voice.

6   He has withheld from her rights which are given to the most ignorant and degraded men—both natives and foreigners.

7   Having deprived her of this first right of a citizen, the elective franchise, thereby leaving her without representation in the halls of legislation, he has oppressed her on all sides.

8   He has made her, if married, in the eye of the law, civilly dead. He has taken from her all right in property, even to the wages she earns.

9   He has made her, morally, an irresponsible being, as she can

commit many crimes with impunity, provided they be done in the presence of her husband. In the covenant of marriage, she is compelled to promise obedience to her husband, he becoming to all intents and purposes, her master—the law giving him power to deprive her of her liberty, and to administer chastisement.

10   He has so framed the laws of divorce, as to what shall be the proper causes, and in case of separation, to whom the guardianship of the children shall be given, as to be wholly regardless of the happiness of women—the law, in all cases, going upon a false supposition of the supremacy of man, and giving all power into his hands.

11   After depriving her of all rights as a married woman, if single, and the owner of property, he has taxed her to support a government which recognizes her only when her property can be made profitable to it.

12   He has monopolized nearly all the profitable employments, and from those she is permitted to follow, she receives but a scanty remuneration. He closes against her all the avenues to wealth and distinction which he considers most honorable to himself. As a teacher of theology, medicine, or law, she is not known.

13   He has denied her the facilities for obtaining a thorough education, all colleges being closed against her.

14   He allows her in Church, as well as State, but a subordinate position, claiming Apostolic authority for her exclusion from the ministry, and, with some exceptions, from any public participation in the affairs of the Church.

15   He has created a false public sentiment by giving to the world a different code of morals for men and women, by which moral delinquencies which exclude women from society, are not only tolerated, but deemed of little account in man.

16   He has usurped the prerogative of Jehovah himself, claiming it as his right to assign for her a sphere of action, when that belongs to her conscience and to her God.

17   He has endeavored, in every way that he could, to destroy her confidence in her own powers, to lessen her self-respect, and to make her willing to lead a dependent and abject life.

18   Now, in view of this entire disfranchisement of one-half the people of this country, their social and religious degradation—in view of the unjust laws above mentioned, and because women do feel themselves aggrieved, oppressed, and fraudulently deprived of their

most sacred rights, we insist that they have immediate admission to all the rights and privileges which belong to them as citizens of the United States.

19   In entering upon the great work before us, we anticipate no small amount of misconception, misrepresentation, and ridicule; but we shall use every instrumentality within our power to effect our object. We shall employ agents, circulate tracts, petition the State and National legislatures, and endeavor to enlist the pulpit and the press in our behalf. We hope this Convention will be followed by a series of Conventions embracing every part of this country.

[The following resolutions were discussed by Lucretia Mott, Thomas and Mary Ann McClintock, Amy Post, Catharine A. F. Stebbins, and others, and were adopted:]

20   Whereas, The great precept of nature is conceded to be, that "man shall pursue his own true and substantial happiness." Blackstone in his *Commentaries* remarks, that this law of Nature being coeval with mankind, and dictated by God himself, is of course superior in obligation to any other. It is binding over all the globe, in all countries, and at all times; no human laws are of any validity if contrary to this, and such of them as are valid, derive all their force, and all their validity, and all their authority, mediately and immediately, from this original; therefore,

21   *Resolved,* That such laws as conflict, in any way, with the true and substantial happiness of woman, are contrary to the great precept of nature and of no validity, for this is "superior in obligation to any other."

22   *Resolved,* That all laws which prevent woman from occupying such a station in society as her conscience shall dictate, or which place her in a position inferior to that of man, are contrary to the great precept of nature, and therefore of no force or authority.

23   *Resolved,* That woman is man's equal—was intended to be so by the Creator, and the highest good of the race demands that she should be recognized as such.

24   *Resolved,* That the women of this country ought to be enlightened in regard to the laws under which they live, that they may no longer publish their degradation by declaring themselves satisfied with their present position, nor their ignorance, by asserting that they

have all the rights they want.

25   *Resolved,* That inasmuch as man, while claiming for himself intellectual superiority, does accord to woman moral superiority, it is preeminently his duty to encourage her to speak and teach, as she has an opportunity, in all religious assemblies.

26   *Resolved,* That the same amount of virtue, delicacy, and refinement of behavior that is required of woman in the social state, should also be required of man, and the same transgressions should be visited with equal severity on both man and woman.

27   *Resolved,* That the objection of indelicacy and impropriety, which is so often brought against woman when she addresses a public audience, comes with a very ill-grace from those who encourage, by their attendance, her appearance on the stage, in the concert, or in feats of the circus.

28   *Resolved,* That woman has too long rested satisfied in the circumscribed limits which corrupt customs and a perverted application of the Scriptures have marked out for her, and that it is time she should move in the enlarged sphere which her great Creator has assigned her.

29   *Resolved,* That it is the duty of the women of this country to secure to themselves their sacred right to the elective franchise.

30   *Resolved,* That the equality of human rights results necessarily from the fact of the identity of the race in capabilities and responsibilities.

31   *Resolved, therefore,* That, being invested by the Creator with the same capabilities, and the same consciousness of responsibility for their exercise, it is demonstrably the right and duty of woman, equally with man, to promote every righteous cause by every righteous means; and especially in regard to the great subjects of morals and religion, it is self-evidently her right to participate with her brother in teaching them, both in private and in public, by writing and by speaking, by any instrumentalities proper to be used, and in any assemblies proper to be held; and this being a self-evident truth growing out of the divinely implanted principles of human nature, any custom or authority adverse to it, whether modern or wearing the hoary sanction of antiquity, is to be regarded as a self-evident falsehood, and at war with mankind.

[At the last session Lucretia Mott offered and spoke to the following resolution:]

32   *Resolved,* That the speedy success of our cause depends upon the zealous and untiring efforts of both men and women, for the overthrow of the monopoly of the pulpit, and for the securing to woman an equal participation with men in the various trades, professions, and commerce.

Suggestions for Discussion and Writing

1. Who is the audience for this Declaration? Can you picture yourself as part of the audience?

2. Stanton, unlike many writers, doesn't use "mankind" to mean "men *and* women". Why not? Can you think of other circumstances when using the words "man", "men," and "mankind" cause confusion?

3. Who is the "he" cited in Stanton's list of abuses?

4. What is the effect of all the amendments to the Declaration? Why do you think they were printed with the main document? What do they tell you about American society when this document was written? Has society changed in the last 150 years?

5. The Seneca Falls Convention began the process by which women gained suffrage, that is, the right to vote. When and how did that process finally take place? How important were Stanton and this Declaration to the process? Has earning the right to vote made women legally equal with men?

Olive Schreiner
Sex-Parasitism

OLIVE SCHREINER (1855-1920) was born and raised in South Africa by her parents, Christian missionaries, who firmly believed that the British were superior to the Boers and native Black Africans. Although she had no formal higher education, her parents en-

couraged her to read widely. Her first novel, *The
Story of an African Farm* (1883) was an instant best-
seller, and drew international attention to the bigoted
and oppressive society Schreiner described so accurately. Although her later novels lacked the power
of her first, she remains a well-respected figure in the
annals of British colonial literature. Her husband, who
took the name Schreiner when he married her, later
edited her letters and wrote about her struggle
against injustice. This selection is taken from her 1911
work *Women and Labour.*

There never has been, and as far as can be seen, there never will be,
a time when the majority of the males in any society will be supported
by the rest of the males in a condition of perfect mental and physical
inactivity. "*Find labour or die*," is the choice ultimately put before
the human male today, as in the past; and *this* constitutes his labour
problem.

2   The labour of the man may not always be useful in the highest
sense to his society, or it may even be distinctly harmful and antisocial,
as in the case of the robber-barons of the Middle Ages, who lived by
capturing and despoiling all who passed by their castles; or as in the
case of the share speculators, stockjobbers, ring-and-corner capitalists,
and monopolists of the present day, who feed upon the productive
labours of society without contributing anything to its welfare. But
even males so occupied are compelled to expend a vast amount of energy and even a low intelligence in their callings; and, however injurious to their societies, they run no personal risk of handing down
effete and enervated constitutions to their race. Whether beneficially
or unbeneficially, the human male must, generally speaking, employ
his intellect, or his muscle, or die.

3   The position of the unemployed modern female is one wholly
different. The choice before her, as her ancient fields of domestic
labour slip from her, is not generally or often at the present day the
choice between finding new fields of labour, or death; but one far
more serious in its ultimate reaction on humanity as a whole—it is
the choice between finding new forms of labour or sinking into a
condition of more or less complete and passive *sex-parasitism*!

4   Again and again in the history of the past, when among human

creatures a certain stage of material civilization has been reached, a curious tendency has manifested itself for the human female to become more or less parasitic; social conditions tend to rob her of all forms of active conscious social labour, and to reduce her, like the field-bug, to the passive exercise of her sex functions alone. And the result of this parasitism has invariably been the decay in vitality and intelligence of the female, followed after a longer or shorter period by that of her male descendants and her entire society.

5   Nevertheless, in the history of the past the dangers of the sex-parasitism have never threatened more than a small section of the females of the human race, those exclusively of some dominant race or class; the mass of women beneath them being still compelled to assume many forms of strenuous activity. It is at the present day, and under the peculiar conditions of our modern civilization, that for the first time sex-parasitism has become a danger, more or less remote, to the mass of civilized women, perhaps ultimately to all.

6   In the very early stages of human growth, the sexual parasitism and degeneration of the female formed no possible source of social danger. Where the conditions of life rendered it inevitable that all the labour of a community should be performed by the members of that community for themselves, without the assistance of slaves or machinery, the tendency has always been rather to throw an excessive amount of social labour on the female. Under no conditions, at no time, in no place, in the history of the world have the males of any period, of any nation, or of any class, shown the slightest inclination to allow their own females to become inactive or parasitic, so long as the actual muscular labour of feeding and clothing them would in that case have devolved upon *themselves!*

7   The parasitism of the human female becomes a possibility only when a point in civilization is reached (such as that which was attained in the ancient civilizations of Greece, Rome, Persia, Assyria, India, and such as today exists in many of the civilizations of the East, such as those of China and Turkey), when, owing to the extensive employment of the labour of slaves, or of subject races or classes, the dominant race or class has become so liberally supplied with the material goods of life that mere physical toil on the part of its own female members has become unnecessary.

8   It is when this point has been reached, and never before, that the symptoms of female parasitism have in the past almost invariably

tended to manifest themselves, and have become a social danger. The males of the dominant class have almost always contrived to absorb to themselves the new intellectual occupations, which the absence of necessity for the old forms of physical toil made possible in their societies and the females of the dominant class or race, for whose muscular labours there was now also no longer any need, not succeeding grasping or attaining to these new forms of labour, have sunk into a state in which, performing no species of active social duty, they have existed through the passive performance of sexual functions alone, with how much or how little of discontent will now never be known, since no literary record has been made by the woman of the past, of her desires or sorrows. Then, in place of the active labouring woman, upholding society—by her toil, has come the effete wife, concubine or prostitute, clad in fine raiment, the work of others' fingers; fed on luxurious viands, the result of others' toil, waited on and tended by the labour of others. The need for her physical labour having gone, and mental industry not having taken its place, she bedecked and scented her person, or had it bedecked and scented for her, she lay upon her sofa, or drove or was carried out in her vehicle, and, loaded with jewels, she sought by dissipations and amusements to fill up the inordinate blank left by the lack of productive activity. And the hand whitened and frame softened, till, at last, the very duties of motherhood, which were all the constitution of her life left her, became distasteful, and, from the instant when her infant came damp from her womb, it passed into the hands of others, to be tended and reared by them; and from youth to age her offspring often owed nothing to her personal toil. In many cases so complete was her enervation, that at last the very joy of giving life, the glory and beatitude of a virile womanhood, became distasteful; and she sought to evade it, not because of its interference with more imperious duties to those already born of her, or to her society, but because her existence of inactivity had robbed her of all joy in strenuous exertion and endurance in any form. Finely clad, tenderly housed, life became for her merely the gratification of her own physical and sexual appetites, and the appetites of the male, through the stimulation of which she could maintain herself. And, whether as kept wife, kept mistress, or prostitute, she contributed nothing to the active and sustaining labours of her society. She had attained to the full development of that type which, whether in modern Paris or New York or London, or in ancient Greece, Assyria, or Rome, is essentially one in its features, its nature, and its results. She was the "fine lady," the human female parasite—the most deadly microbe which can make its appearance on the surface of any social organism.

9   Wherever in the history of the past this type has reached its full development and has comprised the bulk of the females belonging to any dominant class or race, it has heralded its decay. In Assyria, Greece, Rome, Persia, as in Turkey today, the same material conditions have produced the same social disease among wealthy and dominant races and again and again when the nation so affected has come into contact with nations more healthily constituted, the diseased condition has contributed to its destruction.

Suggestions for Discussion and Writing

1. What is a sex parasite? Can men as well as women be sex parasites?

2. What kinds of examples does Schreiner use of sex parasites? Why does she choose this kind of examples? Do they convince you?

3. What happens to a society that becomes full of sex parasites? Can you think of examples of such societies?

4. Schreiner uses a fairly abstract and specialized vocabulary in this essay. Why do you think she does so? What kind of tone does this specialized vocabulary let her use?

5. Can you think of some examples of sex parasites in today's society? What enables them to survive and possibly flourish? Who is to blame for such parasites?

Vivian Gornick
The Next Great Moment in History Is Theirs

VIVIAN GORNICK, a journalist and writer, is the author of *Women in Sexist Society* (1971), *Essays in Feminism* (1978), and *Fierce Attachments* (1987). In *Women in Science* (1983), she interviewed more than one hundred women who had or were trying to establish careers in the sciences. The resulting picture of women in the largely-male scientific world is startling, alternating between the joy of scientific discovery and the utter humiliation from institutions and male colleagues these women faced on a regular basis. This essay, subtitled "An Introduction to the Women's Liberation Movement," appeared in the *Village Voice* on November 27, 1969.

One evening not too long ago, at the home of a well-educated and extremely intelligent couple I know, I mentioned the women's liberation movement and was mildly astonished by the response the subject received. The man said: "Jesus, what is all that crap about?" The woman, a scientist who had given up 10 working years to raise her children, said: "I can understand if these women want to work and are demanding equal pay. But why on earth do they want to have children too?" To which the man rejoined: "Ah, they don't want kids. They're mostly a bunch of dykes, anyway."

2   Again: Having lunch with an erudite, liberal editor, trained in the humanist tradition, I was struck dumb by his reply to my mention of the women's liberation movement: "Ah shit, who the hell is oppressing them?"

3   And yet again: A college-educated housewife, fat and neurotic, announced with arch sweetness, "I'm sorry, I just don't *feel* oppressed."

4   Over and over again, in educated, thinking circles, one meets with a bizarre, almost determined, ignorance of the unrest that is growing daily and exists in formally organized bodies in nearly every major city and on dozens of campuses across America. The women of this country are gathering themselves into a sweat of civil revolt, and the general population seems totally unaware of what is happening— if, indeed, they realize *anything* is happening—or that there is a legitimate need behind what is going on. How is this possible? Why is it true? What relation is there between the peculiarly unalarmed, amused dismissal of the women's-rights movement and the movement itself? Is this relation only coincidental, only the apathetic response of a society already benumbed by civil rights and student anarchy and unable to rise to yet one more protest movement? Or is it not, in fact, precisely the key to the entire issue?

5   Almost invariably, when people set out to tell you there is no such thing as discrimination against women in this country, the first thing they hastily admit to is a *minor* degree of economic favoritism shown toward men. In fact, they will eagerly, almost gratefully, support the claim of economic inequity, as though that will keep the discussion within manageable bounds. Curious. But even on economic grounds or grounds of legal discrimination most people are dismally ignorant of the true proportions of the issue. They will grant that often a man will make as much as $100 more than a woman at the same job, and yes, it is often difficult for a woman to be hired when a man can be hired instead, but after all, that's really not so terrible.

6   This is closer to the facts:

7   Women in this country make 60 cents for every $1 a man makes.

8   Women do not share in the benefits of the fair employment practices laws because those laws do not specify "no discrimination on the basis of sex."

9   Women often rise in salary only to the point at which a man starts.

10   Women occupy, in great masses, the "household tasks" of industry.

11   They are nurses but not doctors, secretaries but not executives, researchers but not writers, workers but not managers, bookkeepers but not promoters.

12   Women almost never occupy decision- or policy-making positions.

13   Women are almost non-existent in government.

14   Women are subject to a set of "protective" laws that restrict their working hours, do not allow them to occupy many jobs in which the carrying of weights is involved, do not allow them to enter innumerable bars, restaurants, hotels, and other public places unescorted.

15   Women, despite 100 years of reform, exist in the domestic and marriage laws of our country almost literally as appendages of their husbands. Did you know that rape by a husband is legal but that if a woman refuses to sleep with her husband she is subject to legal suit? Did you know that the word domicile in the law refers to the husband's domicile and that if a woman refuses to follow her husband to wherever he makes his home, legal suit can be brought against her to force her to do so? Did you know that in most states the law imposes severe legal disabilities on married women with regard to their personal and property rights? (As a feminist said to me: "The United Nations has defined servitude as necessarily involuntary, but women, ignorant of the law, put themselves into *voluntary* servitude.")

16   Perhaps, you will say, these observations are not so shocking. After all, women *are* weaker than men, they do need protection, what on earth is so terrible about being protected, for God's sake! And as for those laws, they're never invoked, no woman is dragged anywhere against her will, on the contrary, women's desires rule the middle-class household, and women can work at hundreds of jobs, in fact, a great deal of the wealth of the country is in their hands, and no woman ever goes hungry.

17   I agree. These observed facts of our national life are not so shocking. The laws and what accrues from them are not so terrible. It is what's behind the laws that is so terrible. It is not the letter of the law but the spirit determining the law that is terrible. It is not what is explicit but what is implicit in the law that is terrible. It is not the apparent condition but the actual condition of woman that is terrible.

18   "The woman's issue is the true barometer of social change," said a famous political theoretician. This was true 100 years ago; it is no less true today. Women and blacks were and are, traditionally and perpetually, the great "outsiders" in Western culture, and their erratic swellings of outrage parallel each other in a number of ways that are both understandable and also extraordinary. A hundred years ago a great abolitionist force wrenched this country apart and changed its history forever; many, many radical men devoted a fever of life to wrecking a system in which men were bought and sold; many radical

women worked toward the same end; the abolitionist movement contained women who came out of educated and liberal 19th century families, women who considered themselves independent thinking beings. It was only when Elizabeth Cady Stanton and Lucretia Mott were not allowed to be seated at a World Anti-Slavery Conference held in the 1840s that the intellectual abolitionist women suddenly perceived that their own political existence resembled that of the blacks. They raised the issue with their radical men and were denounced furiously for introducing an insignificant and divisive issue, one which was sure to weaken the movement. Let's win this war first, they said, and then we'll see about women's rights. But the women had seen, in one swift visionary moment, to the very center of the truth about their own lives, and they knew that first was *now*, that there would never be a time when men would willingly address themselves to the question of female rights, that to strike out now for women's rights could do nothing but strengthen the issue of black civil rights because it called attention to all instances or rights denied in a nation that prided itself on rights for all.

19   Thus was born the original Women's Rights Movement, which became known as the Women's Suffrage Movement because the single great issue, of course. was legal political recognition. But it was never meant to begin and end with the vote, just as the abolitionist movement was never meant to begin and end with the vote. Somehow, though, that awful and passionate struggle for suffrage seemed to exhaust both the blacks and the women, especially the women, for when the vote finally came at the end of the Civil War, it was handed to black males—but not to women; the women had to go on fighting for 60 bitterly long years for suffrage. And then both blacks and women lay back panting, unable to catch their breath for generation upon generation.

20   The great civil rights movement for blacks in the 1950s and '60s is the second wind of that monumental first effort, necessary because the legislated political equality of the 1860s was never translated into actual equality. The reforms promised by law had never happened. The piece of paper meant nothing. Racism had never been legislated out of existence; in fact, its original virulence had remained virtually untouched, and, more important, the black in this country had never been able to shake off the slave mentality. He was born scared, he ran scared, he died scared; for 100 years after legal emancipation, he lived

as though it had never happened. Blacks and whites did not regard either themselves or each other differently, and so they in no way lived differently. In the 1950s and '60s the surging force behind the renewed civil rights effort has been the desire to eradicate this condition more than any other, to enable the American black to believe in himself as a whole, independent, expressive human being capable of fulfilling and protecting himself in the very best way he knows how. Today, after more than 15 years of unremitting struggle, after a formidable array of reform laws legislated at the federal, state, and local level, after a concentration on black rights and black existence that has traumatized the nation, it is still not unfair to say that the psychology of defeat has not been lifted from black life. Still (aside from the continuance of crime, drugs, broken homes, and all the wretched rest of it), employers are able to say: "Sure, I'd love to hire one if I could find one who qualified," and while true, half the time it *is*, because black life is still marked by the "nigger mentality," the terrible inertia of spirit that accompanies the perhaps irrational but deeply felt conviction that no matter what one does, one is going to wind up a 35-year-old busboy. This "nigger mentality" characterizes black lives. It also characterizes women's lives. And it is this, and this alone, that is behind the second wave of feminism now sweeping the country and paralleling precisely, exactly as it does 100 years ago, the black rights movement. The fight for reform laws is just the beginning. What women are really after this time around is the utter eradication of the "nigger" in themselves.

21   Most women who feel "niggerized" have tales of overt oppression to tell. They feel they've been put down by their fathers, their brothers, their lovers, their bosses. They feel that in their families, in their sex lives, and in their jobs they have counted as nothing, they have been treated as second-class citizens, their minds have been deliberately stunted and their emotions warped. My own experience with the condition is a bit more subtle, and, without bragging, I do believe a bit closer to the true feminist point.

22   To begin with, let me tell a little story. Recently, I had lunch with a man I had known at school. He and his wife and I had all been friends at college; they had courted while we were in school and immediately upon graduation they got married. They were both talented art students. and it was assumed both would work in commercial art. But shortly after their marriage she became pregnant, and never

did go to work. Within five years they had two children. At first I visited them often; their home was lovely, full of their mutual talent for atmosphere; the wife sparkled, the children flourished; he rose in the field of commercial art; I envied them both their self-containment, and she especially her apparently contented, settled state. But as I had remained single and life took me off in various other directions we soon began to drift apart, and when I again met the husband we had not seen each other in many years. We spoke animatedly of what we had both been doing for quite a while. Then I asked about his wife. His face rearranged itself suddenly, but I couldn't quite tell how at first. He said she was fine, but didn't sound right.

23   "What's wrong?" I asked. "Is she doing something you don't want her to do? Or the other way around?"

24   "No, no," he said hastily. "I want her to do whatever she wants to do. Anything. Anything that will make her happy. And get her off my back," he ended bluntly. I asked what he meant and he told me of his wife's restlessness of the last few years, of how sick she was of being a housewife, how useless she felt, and how she longed to go back to work.

25   "Well?" I asked, "did you object?"

26   "Of course not!" he replied vigorously. "Why the hell would I do that? She's a very talented woman, her children are half grown, she's got every right in the world to go to work."

27   "So?" I said.

28   "It's *her*," he said bewilderedly. "She doesn't seem able to just go out and get a job."

29   "What do you mean?" I asked. But beneath the surface of my own puzzled response I more than half knew what was coming.

30   "Well, she's scared, I think. She's more talented than half the people who walk into my office asking for work, but do what I will she won't get a portfolio together and make the rounds. Also, she cries a lot lately. For no reason, if you know what I mean. And then, she can't seem to get up in the morning in time to get a babysitter and get out of the house. This is a woman who was always up at 7 A.M. to feed everybody, get things going; busy, capable, doing 10 things at once." He shook his head as though in a true quandary. "Oh well," he ended up "I guess it doesn't really matter any more."

31   "Why not?" I asked.

32   His eyes came up and he looked levelly at me. "She's just become pregnant again."

33   I listened silently, but with what internal churning! Even though
the external events of our lives were quite different, I felt as though
this woman had been living inside my skin all these years, so close was
I to the essential nature of her experience as I perceived it listening to
her husband's woebegone tale. I had wandered about the world, I had
gained another degree, I had married twice, I had written, taught,
edited, I had no children. And yet I knew that in some fundamental
sense we were the same woman. I understood exactly—but exactly—the
kind of neurotic anxiety that just beset her, and that had ultimately
defeated her; it was a neurosis I shared and had recognized in almost
every woman I had ever known—including Monica Vitti, having her
Schiaparellied nervous breakdown, stuffing her hand into her mouth,
rolling her eyes wildly, surrounded by helplessly sympathetic men
who kept saying: "Just tell me what's *wrong*."

34   I was raised in an immigrant home where education was wor-
shiped. As the entire American culture was somewhat mysterious to my
parents, the educational possibilities of that world were equally unknown for both the boy and the girl in our family. Therefore, I grew
up in the certainty that if my brother went to college, I too could go to
college; and, indeed, he did, and I in my turn did too. We both read vo-
raciously from early childhood on, and we were both encouraged to do
so. We both had precocious and outspoken opinions and neither of us
was ever discouraged from uttering them. We both were exposed early
to unionist radicalism and neither of us met with opposition when,
separately, we experimented with youthful political organizations.
And yet somewhere along the line my brother and I managed to receive
an utterly different education regarding ourselves and our own expectations from life. He was taught many things but what he learned was
the need to develop a kind of inner necessity. I was taught many things,
but what I learned, ultimately, was that it was the prime vocation of
my life to prepare myself for the love of a good man and the responsibilities of homemaking and motherhood. All the rest, the education,
the books, the jobs, that was all very nice and of course, why not? I was
an intelligent girl, shouldn't I learn? *make* something of myself ! but
oh dolly, you'll see, in the end no woman could possibly be happy
without a man to love and children to raise. What's more, came the
heavy implication, if I *didn't* marry I would be considered an irre-
deemable failure.

35   How did I learn this? How? I have pondered this question 1000

times. Was it really that explicit? Was it laid out in lessons strate-
gically planned and carefully executed? Was it spooned down my
throat at regular intervals? No. It wasn't. I have come finally to understand that the lessons were implicit and they took place in 100 different ways, in a continuous day-to-day exposure to an *attitude*, shared
by all, about women, about what kind of creatures they were and what
kind of lives they were meant to live; the lessons were administered
not only by my parents but by the men and women the boys and girls.
all around me who, of course, had been made in the image of this attitude.

36   My mother would say to me when I was very young, as I studied at
the kitchen table and she cooked: "How lucky you are to go to school! I
wasn't so lucky. I had to go to work in the factory. I wanted so to be a
nurse! But go be a nurse in Williamsburg in 1920! Maybe you'll be a
nurse. . . ." I listened, I nodded, but somehow the message I got was that
I was like her and I would one day be doing what she was now doing.

37   My brother was the "serious and steady" student, I the "erratic and
undisciplined" one. When he studied the house was silenced; when I
studied, business as usual.

38   When I was 14 and I came in flushed and disarrayed my mother
knew I'd been with a boy. Her fingers gripped my upper arm; her face,
white and intent, bent over me: What did he do to you? *Where* did he
do it? I was frightened to death. What was she so upset about? What
could he do to me? I learned that I was the keeper of an incomparable
treasure and it had to be guarded: it was meant to be a gift for my husband. (Later that year when I read "A Rage to Live" I knew without any
instruction exactly what all those elliptical sentences were about.)

39   When I threw some hideous temper tantrum my mother would
say: "What a little female you are!" (I have since seen many little boys
throw the same tantrums and have noted with interest that they are not
told they are little females.)

40   The girls on the street would talk forever about boys, clothes,
movies, fights with their mothers. The 1000 thoughts racing around
in my head from the books I was reading remained secret, no one to
share them with.

41   The boys would be gentler with the girls than with each other
when we all played roughly; and our opinions were never considered
seriously.

42   I grew up, I went to school. I came out, wandered around, went to

Europe, went back to school, wandered again, taught in a desultory fashion, and at last! got married!

43   It was during my first marriage that I began to realize something was terribly wrong inside me, but it took me 10 years to understand that I was suffering the classic female pathology. My husband, like all the men I have known, was a good man, a man who wanted my independence for me more than I wanted it for myself. He urged me to work, to do something, anything, that would make me happy; he knew that our pleasure in each other could be heightened only if I was a functioning human being too. Yes, yes! I said, and leaned back in the rocking chair with yet another novel. Somehow, I couldn't do anything. I didn't really know where to start, what I wanted to do. Oh, I had always had a number of interests but they, through an inability on my part to stick with anything, had always been superficial; when I arrived at a difficult point in a subject, a job, an interest, I would simply drop it. Of course, what I really wanted to do was write; but that was an altogether ghastly agony and one I could never come to grips with. There seemed to be some terrible aimlessness at the very center of me, some paralyzing lack of will. My energy, which was abundant, was held in a trap of some sort; occasionally that useless energy would wake up roaring, demanding to be let out of its cage, and then I became emotional"; I would have hysterical depressions, rage on and on about the meaninglessness of my life, force my husband into long psychoanalytic discussions about the source of my (our) trouble, end in a purging storm of tears, a determination to do "something," and six months later I was right back where I started. If my marriage had not dissolved, I am sure that I would still be in exactly that same peculiarly nightmarish position. But as it happened, the events of life forced me out into the world, and repeatedly I had to come up against myself. I found this pattern of behavior manifesting itself in 100 different circumstances; regardless of how things began, they always seemed to end in the same place. Oh, I worked, I advanced, in a sense, but only erratically and with superhuman effort. Always the battle was internal, and it was with a kind of paralyzing anxiety at the center of me that drained off my energy and retarded my capacity for intellectual concentration. It took me a long time to perceive that nearly every woman I knew exhibited the same symptoms, and when I did perceive it, became frightened. I thought, at first, that perhaps, indeed, we were all victims of some biological deficiency, that some vital ingre-

dient had been deleted in the female of the species, that we were a phys-
iological metaphor for human neurosis. It took me a long time to
understand, with an understanding that is irrevocable, that we are the
victims of culture, not biology.

44   Recently, I read a marvelous biography of Beatrice Webb, the
English socialist. The book is full of vivid portraits, but the one that
is fixed forever in my mind is that of Mrs. Webb's mother,
Laurencina Potter. Laurencina Potter was a beautiful, intelligent,
intellectually energetic woman of the middle 19th century. She knew
12 languages, spoke Latin and Greek better than half the classics-
trained men who came to her home, and was interested in everything.
Her marriage to wealthy and powerful Richard Potter was a love
match, and she looked forward to a life of intellectual companionship, stimulating activity, lively participation. No sooner were
they married than Richard installed her in a Victorian fortress in the
country, surrounded her with servants and physical comfort, and started
her off with the first of the 11 children she eventually bore. He went
out into the world, bought and sold railroads, made important political connections, mingled in London society, increased his powers,
and relished his life. She, meanwhile, languished. She sat in the country, staring at the four brocaded walls; her energy remained bottled up,
her mind became useless, her will evaporated. The children became
symbols of her enslavement and, in consequence, she was a lousy
mother: neurotic, self-absorbed, increasingly colder and more withdrawn, increasingly more involved in taking her emotional temperature. She became, in short, the Victorian lady afflicted with inde-
finable maladies.

45   When I read of Laurencina's life I felt as though I was reading
about the lives of most of the women I know, and it struck me that 100
years ago sexual submission was all for a woman, and today sexual fulfillment is all for a woman, and the two are one and the same.

46   Most of the women I know are people of superior intelligence,
developed emotions, and higher education. And yet our friendships,
our conversations, our lives, are not marked by intellectual substance
or emotional distance or objective concern. It is only briefly and
insubstantially that I ever discuss books or politics or philosophical
issues or abstractions of any kind with the women I know. Mainly, we
discuss and are intimate about our Emotional Lives. Endlessly, endlessly, we go on and on about our emotional "problems" and "needs"

and "relationships." And, of course, because we are all bright and well-educated, we bring to bear on these sessions a formidable amount of sociology and psychology, literature and history, all hoked out so that it sounds as though these are serious conversations on serious subjects, when in fact they are caricatures of seriousness right out of Jonathan Swift. Caricatures, because they have no beginning, middle, end, or point. They go nowhere, they conclude nothing, they change nothing. They are elaborate descriptions in the ongoing soap opera that is our lives. It took me a long time to understand that we were talking about nothing, and it took me an even longer and harder time, traveling down that dark, narrow road in the mind, back back to the time when I was a little girl sitting in the kitchen with my mother, to understand, at last, that the affliction was cultural not biological, that it was because we had never been taught to take ourselves seriously that I and all the women I knew had become parodies of "taking ourselves seriously."

47   The rallying cry of the black civil rights movement has always been: "Give us back our manhood!" What exactly does that mean? Where is black manhood? How has it been taken from blacks? And how can it be retrieved? The answer lies in one word: responsibility; therefore, they have been deprived of self-respect; therefore, they have been deprived of manhood. Women have been deprived of exactly the same thing and in every real sense have thus been deprived of womanhood. We have never been prepared to assume responsibility; we have never been prepared to make demands upon ourselves; we have never been taught to expect the development of what is best in ourselves because no one has ever expected *anything* of us—or for us. Because no one has ever had any intention of turning over any serious work to us. Both we and the blacks lost the ballgame before we ever got up to play. In order to live you've got to have nerve; and we were stripped of our nerve before we began. Black is ugly and female is inferior. These are the primary lessons of our experience, and in these ways both blacks and women have been kept, not as functioning nationals, but rather as operating objects. But a human being who remains as a child throughout his adult life is an object, not a mature specimen, and the definition of a child is: one without responsibility.

48   At the very center of all human life is energy, psychic energy. It is the force of that energy that drives us, that surges continually up in us, that must repeatedly spend and renew itself in us, that must perpetually

be reaching for something beyond itself in order to satisfy its own insatiable appetite. It is the imperative of that energy that has determined man's characteristic interest, problem-solving. The modern ecologist attests to that driving need by demonstrating that in a time when all the real problems are solved, man makes up new ones in order to go on solving. He must have work, work that he considers real and serious, or he will die, he will simply shrivel up and die. That is the one certain characteristic of human beings. And it is the one characteristic, above all others, that the accidentally dominant white male asserts is not necessary to more than half the members of the race. i.e., the female of the species. This assertion is, quite simply, a lie. Nothing more, nothing less. A lie. That energy is alive in every woman in the world. It lies trapped and dormant like a growing tumor, and at its center there is despair, hot, deep, wordless.

49   It is amazing to me that I have just written these words. To think that 100 years after Nora slammed the door, and in a civilization and a century utterly converted to the fundamental insights of that exasperating genius, Sigmund Freud, women could still be raised to believe that their basic makeup is determined not by the needs of their egos but by their peculiar child-bearing properties and their so-called unique capacity for loving. No man worth his salt does not wish to be a husband and father; yet no man is raised to be a husband and father and no man would ever conceive of those relationships as instruments of his prime function in life. Yet every woman is raised, still, to believe that the fulfillment of these relationships is her prime function in life and, what's more, her instinctive choice.

50   The fact is that women have no special capacities for love, and, when a culture reaches a level where its women have nothing to do but "love" (as occurred in the Victorian upper classes and as is occurring now in the American middle classes), they prove to be very bad at it. The modern American wife is not noted for her love of her husband or of her children; she is noted for her driving (or should I say driven?) domination of them. She displays an aberrated, aggressive ambition for her mate and for her offspring which can be explained only by the most vicious feelings toward the self. The reasons are obvious. The woman who must love for a living, the woman who has no self, no objective external reality to take her own measure by, no work to discipline her, no goal to provide the illusion of progress, no internal resources, no separate mental existence, is constitutionally

incapable of the emotional distance that is one of the real require-
ments of love. She cannot separate herself from her husband and children because all the passionate and multiple needs of her being are
centered on them. That's why women "take everything personally." It's
all they've got to take. "Loving" must substitute for an entire range of
feeling and interest. The man, who is not raised to be a husband and
father specifically, and who simply loves as a single function of his
existence, cannot understand her abnormal "emotionality" and con-
cludes that this is the female nature. (Why shouldn't he? She does too.)
But this is not so. It is a result of a psychology achieved by cultural attitudes that run so deep and have gone on for so long that they are mistaken for "nature" or "instinct."

51   A good example of what I mean are the multiple legends of our
culture regarding motherhood. Let's use our heads for a moment. What
on earth is holy about motherhood? I mean, why motherhood rather
than fatherhood? If anything is holy, it is the consecration of sexual
union. A man plants a seed in a woman; the seed matures and eventually
is expelled by the woman; a child is born to both of them; each contributed the necessary parts to bring about procreation; each is responsible to and necessary to the child; to claim that the woman is more so
than the man is simply not true; certainly it cannot be proven biologically or psychologically (please, no comparisons with baboons
and penguins just now—I am sure I can supply 50 examples from
nature to counter any assertion made on the subject); all that can be
proven is that *someone* is necessary to the newborn baby; to have
instilled in women the belief that their child-bearing and housewifely obligations supersede all other needs, that indeed what they
fundamentally *want* and need is to be wives and mothers as distinguished from being anything else, is to have accomplished an act of
trickery, an act which has deprived women of the proper forms of
expression necessary to that force of energy alive in every talking creature, an act which has indeed mutilated their natural selves and
deprived them of their womanhood, what*ever* that may be, deprived
them of the right to say "I" and have it mean something. This understanding, grasped whole, is what underlies the current wave of feminism. It is felt by thousands of women today, it will be felt by millions tomorrow. You have only to examine briefly a fraction of the
women's rights organizations already in existence to realize instantly
that they form the nucleus of a genuine movement, complete with the-

oreticians, tacticians, agitators, manifestos, journals, and thesis papers, running the entire political spectrum from conservative reform to visionary radicalism, and powered by an emotional conviction rooted in undeniable experience, and fed by a determination that is irreversible.

52   One of the oldest and stablest of the feminist organizations is NOW, the National Organization for Women. It was started in 1966 by a group of professional women headed by Mrs. Betty Friedan, author of *The Feminine Mystique,* the book that was the bringer of the word in 1963 to the new feminists. NOW has more than 3000 members, chapters in major cities and on many campuses all over the country, and was read, at its inception, into the Congressional Record. It has many men in its ranks and it works, avowedly within the system, to bring about the kind of reforms that will result in what it calls a "truly equal partnership between men and women" in this country. It is a true reform organization filled with intelligent, liberal, hardworking women devoted to the idea that America is a reformist democracy and ultimately will respond to the justice of their cause. They are currently hard at work on two major issues: repeal of the abortion laws and passage of the Equal Rights Amendment (for which feminists have been fighting since 1923) which would amend the constitution to provide that "equality of rights under the law shall not be denied or abridged by the United States or by any state on account of sex." When this amendment is passed, the employment and marriage laws of more than 40 states will be affected. Also, in direct conjunction with the fight to have this amendment passed, NOW demands increased child-care facilities to be established by law on the same basis as parks, libraries. and public schools.

53   NOW's influence is growing by leaps and bounds. It is responsible for the passage of many pieces of legislation meant to wipe out discrimination against women, and certainly the size and number of Women's Bureaus, Women's units, Women's Commissions springing up in government agencies and legislative bodies all over the country reflects its presence. Suddenly, there are Presidential reports and gubernatorial conferences and congressional meetings—all leaping all over each other to discuss the status of women. NOW, without a doubt, is the best established feminist group.

54   From NOW we move, at a shocking rate of speed, to the left. In fact, it would appear that NOW is one of the few reformist groups,

that mainly the feminist groups are radical, both in structure and in aim. Some, truth to tell, strike a bizarre and puzzling note. For instance, there is WITCH (Women's International Terrorists Conspiracy From Hell), an offshoot of SDS, where members burned their bras and organized against the Miss America Pageant in a stirring demand that the commercially useful image of female beauty be wiped out. There is Valerie Solanas and her SCUM Manifesto, which Solanas's penetrating observation on our national life was: "If the atom bomb isn't dropped, this society will hump itself to death." There is Cell 55. God knows what they do.

55   There are the Redstockings, an interesting group that seems to have evolved from direct action into what they call "consciousness-raising." That means, essentially, that they get together in a kind of group therapy session and the women reveal their experiences and feelings to each other in an attempt to analyze the femaleness of their psychology and their circumstances, thereby increasing the invaluable weapon of self-understanding.

56   And finally, there are the Feminists, without a doubt the most fiercely radical and intellectually impressive of all the groups. This organization was begun a year ago by a group of defectors from NOW and various other feminist groups, in rebellion against the repetition of the hierarchical structure of power in these other groups. Their contention was: women have always been "led"; if they join the rank and file of a feminist organization they are simply being led again. It will still be someone else, even if only the officers of their own interesting group, making the decisions, doing the planning, the executing, and so on. They determined to develop a leaderless society whose guiding principle was participation by lot. And this is precisely what they have done. The organization has no officers, every woman sooner or later performs every single task necessary to the life and aims of the organization, and the organization is willing to temporarily sacrifice efficiency in order that each woman may fully develop all the skills necessary to autonomous functioning. This working individualism is guarded fiercely by a set of rigid rules regarding attendance, behavior, duties, and loyalties.

57   The Feminists encourage extensive theorizing on the nature and function of a leaderless society, and this has led the organization to a bold and radical view of the future they wish to work for. The group never loses sight of the fact that its primary enemy is the male-female

role system which has ended in women being the oppressed and men being the oppressors. It looks forward to a time when this system will be completely eradicated. To prepare for this coming, it now denounces all the institutions which encourage the system, i.e., love, sex, and marriage. It has a quota on married women (only one-third of their number are permitted to be either married or living in a marriage-like situation). It flatly names all men as the enemy. It looks forward to a future in which the family as we know it will disappear, all births will be extra-uterine, children will be raised by communal efforts, and women once and for all will cease to be the persecuted members of the race.

58　　　Although a lot of this is hard to take in raw doses, you realize that many of these ideas represent interesting and important turns of thought. First of all, these experiments with a leaderless society are being echoed everywhere: in student radicalism, in black civil rights, in hippie communes. They are part of a great radical lusting after self-determination that is beginning to overtake this country. This is true social revolution, and I believe that feminism, in order to accomplish its aims now, does need revolution, does need a complete overthrow of an old kind of thought and the introduction of a new kind of thought. Secondly, the Feminists are right: most of what men and women now are is determined by the "roles" they play, and love *is* an institution, full of ritualized gestures and positions, and often void of any recognizable naturalness. How, under the present iron-bound social laws, can one know what is female nature and what is female role? (And that question speaks to the source of the whole female pain and confusion.) It *is* thrilling to contemplate a new world, brave or otherwise, in which men and women may free themselves of some of the crippling sexual poses that now circumscribe their lives, thus allowing them some open and equitable exchange of emotion, some release of the natural self which will be greeted with resentment from no one.

59　　　But the Feminists strike a wrong and rather hysterical note when they indicate that they don't believe there is a male or female nature, that all is role. I believe that is an utterly wrong headed notion. Not only do I believe there is a genuine male or female nature in each of us, but I believe that what is most exciting about the new world that may be coming is the promise of stripping down to that nature, of the complementary elements in those natures meeting without anxiety, of our different biological tasks being performed without profit for one at the expense of the other.

60   The Feminists' position is extreme and many of these pronouncements are chilling at first touch. But you quickly realize that this is the harsh, stripped-down language of revolution that is the language of icy "honesty," of narrow but penetrating vision. (As one Feminist said sweetly, quoting her favorite author: "In order to have a revolution you must have a revolutionary theory.") And besides, you sue for thousands and hope to collect hundreds.

61   Many feminists, though, are appalled by the Feminists (the infighting in the movement is fierce), feel they are fascists, "superweak," annihilatingly single-minded, and involved in a power play no matter what they say; but then again you can find feminists who will carefully and at great length put down every single feminist group going. But there's one great thing about these chicks: if five feminists fall out with six groups, within half an hour they'll all find each other (probably somewhere on Bleecker Street), within 48 hours a new splinter faction will have announced its existence, and within two weeks the manifesto is being mailed out. It's the mark of a true movement.

62   Two extremely intelligent and winning feminists who are about to "emerge" as part of a new group are Shulamith Firestone, an ex-Redstocking, and Anne Koedt, an ex-Feminist, and both members of the original radical group, New York Radical Women. They feel that none of the groups now going has the capacity to build a broad mass movement among the women of this country and they intend to start one that will. Both are dedicated to social revolution and agree with many of the ideas of many of the other radical groups. Each one, in her own words, comes equipped with "impeccable revolutionary credentials." They come out of the Chicago SDS and the New York civil rights movement. Interestingly enough, like many of the radical women in this movement, they were converted to feminism because in their participation in the New Left they met with intolerable female discrimination. ("Yeah, baby, comes the revolution. . . baby, comes the revolution. . . . Meanwhile, you make the coffee and later I'll tell you where to hand out the leaflets." And when they raised the issue of women's rights with their radical young men, they were greeted with furious denunciations of introducing divisive issues! Excuse me, but haven't we been here before?)

63   The intention of Miss Firestone and Miss Koedt is to start a group that will be radical in aim but much looser in structure than anything they've been involved with; it will be an action group, but everyone will also be encouraged to theorize, analyze, create; it will appeal to the broad base of educated women; on the other hand, it will not sound ferocious to the timid non-militant woman. In other words . . .

64   I mention these two in particular, but at this moment in New York, in Cambridge, in Chicago, in New Haven, in Washington, in San Francisco, in East Podunk—yes! believe it!—there are dozens like them preparing to do the same thing. They are gathering fire and I do believe the next great moment in history is theirs. God knows, for my unborn daughter's sake, I hope so.

Suggestions for Discussion and Writing

1. Do we really need a women's liberation movement? What do the women cited by Gornick think? What should women be liberated *from*?

2. Gornick's essay seems to range over a wide variety of topics. Does it have a thesis? Is that thesis explicitly stated? If not, can you paraphrase it in your own words?

3. Many readers may be upset by Gornick's use of the word "nigger" and her equation of women with African-Americans. Since she knew these would upset her readers, why do you think she chose to do so? Does she gain any advantages by doing so? How did you as a reader react to this?

4. Do you agree that "no man is raised to be a husband and father and no man would ever conceive of those relationships as his prime function in life. Yet every woman is raised, still, to believe that the fulfillment of these relationships is her prime function in life, and, what's more, her instinctive choice"? How could you attack, defend, or modify this argument?

5. Does the "Women's Liberation Movement" still exist? What has it accomplished? What are its future goals? How does the "Men's Movement" fit into the picture?

Betty Friedan
Feminism Takes a New Turn

BETTY FRIEDAN was born in Peoria in 1921. After graduating *summa cum laude* from Smith College in 1942, she worked as a journalist for many years. Her groundbreaking book *The Feminine Mystique* (1963) is still regarded as a primer for American feminists; she has followed it with *The Second Stage* (1982, 1986). She is the founder and first president of the National Organization of Women, and was appointed as a delegate to the White House Conference on the Family she discusses in the text. This essay was originally published in 1979.

In California last month, I went into the office of a television producer who prides himself on being an "equal opportunity employer." His new "executive assistant" was waiting for me. She wanted to talk to me alone before her boss came in. Lovely, in her late 20's or maybe 30-ish, "dressed for success" like a model in the latest Vogue advertisement, she was not just a glorified secretary with a fancy title in a dead-end job: The woman she replaced had just been promoted to the position of "creative vice president."

2   "I know I'm lucky to have this job," she said. "But you people who fought for these things had your families. You already had your men and children. What are we supposed to do?"

3   She complained that the older woman vice president, an early radical feminist who had vowed never to marry or have children, didn't understand her quandary. "All she wants," the executive assistant said, "is more power in the company. . . ."

4   A young woman in her third year of Harvard Medical School told me, "I'm going to be a surgeon. I'll never be a trapped housewife like my mother. I would like to get married and have children, I

think. They say we can have it all. But how? I work 36 hours in the hospital, 12 off. How am I going to have a relationship, much less kids, with hours like that? I'm not sure I can be a superwoman."

5   In New York, a woman in her 30's who has just been promoted says, "I'm up against the clock, you might say. If I don't have a child now, it will be too late. But it's an agonizing choice. I've been supporting my husband while he gets his Ph.D. We don't know what kind of job he'll be able to get. There's no pay when you take off to have a baby in my company. They don't guarantee you'll get your job back. If I don't have a baby, will I miss out on life somehow? Will I really be fulfilled as a woman?"

6   An older woman in Ohio reflects, "I was the first woman manager here. I gave everything to the job. It was exciting at first, breaking in where women never were before. Now, it's just a job. But it's the devastating loneliness that's the worst. I can't stand coming back to this apartment alone every night. I'd like a house, maybe a garden. Maybe I should have a kid, even without a father. At least then I'd have a family. There has to be some better way to live. A woman alone. . . ."

7   The second feminist agenda, the agenda for the 80's, must call for the restructuring of the institutions of home and work. But to confront the American family as it actually is today—instead of hysterically defending or attacking the family that is no more, "the classical family of Western nostalgia," as Stanford sociologist William I. Goode calls it—means shattering an image that is still sacred to both church and state, to politicians on the right and left. And dispelling the mystique of the family may be even more threatening to some than unmasking the feminine mystique was a decade ago.

8   For instance, a White House Conference on Families was supposed to have been held this year, but it was suddenly canceled as too "controversial" when the experts assembled to plan it began facing the facts about American families today. The flak started when participating Catholic priests discovered that the eminent black woman coordinating the conference was herself divorced and raising her family as a single parent. And when it was revealed that fewer than 7 percent of Americans are now living in the kind of family arrangement to which politicians are always paying lip service—daddy-the-breadwinner, mother-the-housewife, two children plus a dog and a cat—the White House decided to call the whole thing off.

9   According to Government statistics, only 17 percent of American

households include a father who is the sole wage earner, a mother who is a full-time homemaker, and one or more children. (And one study found that one-third of all such full-time housewives planned to look for jobs.)

10   28 percent of American households consist of both a father and a mother who are wage earners, with one or more children living at home.

11   32.4 percent of American households consist of married couples with no children, or none living at home.

12   6.6 percent of American households are headed by women who are single parents with one or more children at home.

13   0.7 percent are headed by men who are single parents with one or more children at home.

14   3.1 percent consist of unrelated persons living together.

15   5.3 percent are headed by a single parent and include relatives other than spouses and children.

16   22 percent of American households consist of one person living alone (a third of these are women over 65). . . .

17   But what is beginning to concern me. . . are the conflicts women now suffer as they reach 30 or 35 and cannot choose to have a child. I don't envy young women who are facing or denying that agonizing choice we won for them. Because it isn't really a free choice when their paycheck is needed to cover the family bills each month, when women must look to their jobs and professions for the security and status their mothers once sought in marriage alone, and when these professions are not structured for people who give birth to children and take responsibility for their upbringing.

18   My own feminism began in outrage at the either/or choice that the feminine mystique imposed on my generation. I was fired from my job as a reporter when I became pregnant. Most of us let ourselves be seduced into giving up our careers in order to embrace motherhood, and it wasn't easy to resume them. We told our daughters that they could—and should—have it all. Why not? After all, men do. But the "superwomen" who are trying to "have it all," combining full-time careers and "stretch-time" motherhood, are enduring such relentless pressure that their younger sisters may not even dare to think about having children.

19   The many women struggling with the conflict between careers and children cannot be dismissed as victims of their mother's expec-

tations, of the feminine mystique. Motherhood, the profound human impulse to have children, is more than a mystique. At the same time, more women than ever before hold jobs not just because they want to "find themselves" and assert their independence, but because they must. They are single and responsible for their own support, divorced and often responsible for their children's support as well, or married and still partly responsible for their families' support because one paycheck is not enough in this era of inflation. In all, 43 percent of American wives with children under the age of 6 are working today, and by 1990, it is estimated that 64 percent will have jobs—only one out of three mothers, approximately, will be a housewife at home.

20   Yet the United States is one of the few advanced nations with no national policy of leaves for maternity, paternity or parenting, no national policy encouraging flexible working arrangements and part-time and shared employment, and no national policy to provide child care for those who need it. . . .

21   It seems clear to me that we will never bring about these changes in the workplace, so necessary for the welfare of children and the family, if their only supporters and beneficiaries are women. The need for such innovations becomes urgent as more and more mothers enter the workplace, but they will come about only because more and more fathers demand them, too.

22   And men are beginning to demand them already. After all, they've long been subject to the same pressures that increasing numbers of women are experiencing.

23   A Vietnam veteran, laid off unexpectedly during the energy crunch by the airline with which he thought he had a lifetime career, tells me, "There's no security in a job. The dollar's not worth enough anymore to live your life for. I'll work three days a week at the boiler plant and my wife will go back to nursing nights, and between us we'll take care of the kids. We're moving to where we can raise our own food and have some control over our lives. But what if she gets laid off?"

24   "I thought seriously of killing myself," says a St. Louis man who was forced to resign at the age of 50 when the company he headed was taken over by a large conglomerate. "I saved up the arsenic pills I take for my heart condition. How could I live without that company to run, my office, my staff, 600 employees, the wheeling and dealing? But then I realized how much of it I'd really hated: the constant worry,

getting in at 6 A.M. to read the reports of six vice presidents, fighting the union to keep wages down and being hated, and knuckling under to people I despised to get accounts. The only good thing was knowing I'd made it to president of a company, when my father never got past stock clerk. Now I want to work for myself, to live, to enjoy the sunsets and raise begonias. But my kids are gone now, and my wife started her career late, and all she wants is to get ahead in the agency. It's unthinkable somehow, what's ahead in life. . . ."

25   A younger man in Rhode Island quit his job at a bank to take care of the house and kids and to paint at home, while his wife, sick of being a housewife, was happy to get a lesser job at the same bank. "I think you're going to see a great wave of men dropping out," he told me. "All we've been hearing for years now is, 'What does it mean being a woman? How can she fulfill herself?' But what does it mean being a man? What do we have but our jobs? Let her support the family for a while, and let me find myself. . . ."

26   A young man refuses an extra assignment, which would mean working nights and traveling weekends, on top of his regular job. It doesn't matter that it might lead to a big promotion. "We're having another child," he tells his boss, "and I'm committed to sharing the responsibilities at home because my wife's going to law school at night. It hasn't and won't interfere with my job—you were more than satisfied with my last report. But I'm not taking on anything extra. My family is more important to me."

27   "That man isn't going to get far," his puzzled boss tells a colleague. "Too bad: He was the pick of the litter."

28   The colleague asks, "What if they all start acting like that? Where are we going to find the men to run the economy, for God's sake, if they all start putting their families first?"

29   As we move into the 1980's, it becomes clearer that the women's movement has been merely the beginning of something much more basic than a few women getting good (men's) jobs. Paradoxically, as more women enter the workplace and share the breadwinning, their family bonds and values—human values as opposed to material ones—seem to strengthen. The harassed working mothers and their husbands in Dr. Kamerman's study of families place more importance and reliance on these bonds, not only with each other and their own children but with their own parents and other relatives, than do comparable families conforming to the traditional housewife-breadwinner

image. The increasing tendency for young men to refuse corporate transfers and to put more emphasis on their self-fulfillment and "family time" as opposed to "getting ahead" has been reported by Yankelovich, Gail Sheehy in *Esquire* and even *Playboy* magazine. . . .

30   The young men of the "counterculture" of the 1960's and 70's were rebelling against the great pressures to devote their whole lives to money-making careers—just as women in the feminist movement rebelled against the great pressures to devote their whole lives to husbands and children and to forego personal advancement. But to substitute one half of a loaf for the other is not an improvement. Why should women simply replace the glorification of domesticity with the glorification of work as their life and identity? Simply to reverse the roles of breadwinner and homemaker is no progress at all, not for women and not for men. The challenge of the 80's will be to transcend these polarities by creating new family patterns based on equality and full human identity for both sexes.

Suggestions for Discussion and Writing

1. How would you describe the organizational strategy Friedan uses in her essay? Why do you think she chose this strategy?

2. What is the 'second feminist agenda'? How has it been defined for the nineties?

3. Why does Friedan choose to discuss unhappy men in this essay about feminism? What effect do the men's stories have on you as readers?

4. Do you believe women should be faced with the choice of motherhood or career? Why don't men seem to face this choice? What changes would you make in our society's definition of parenthood to accommodate two-career families?

5. Is there a typical American family today? If so, what is it like? What challenges face American families today? What role models do 1990s American families have? Are these realistic role models?

Acknowledgements

ATWOOD: "Pornography," by Margaret Atwood. Copyright © 1983 by Margaret Atwood. Reprinted by permission of Margaret Atwood.

BRADY: "Why I Want a Wife" by Judy Brady. Copyright © 1970 by Judy Brady. Reprinted by permission of the author.

BROWNMILLER: "Let's Put Pornography Back in the Closet," by Susan Brownmiller. From *Take Back the Night: Women on Pornography*, edited by Laura Ledere. New York: Morrow, 1980. Reprinted by permission of the author.

BROYLES: "Public Policy, Private Ritual" by William Broyles, Jr, copyright © 1991 by The New York Times Company. Reprinted by permission

BURGESS: "Grunts from a Sexist Pig" from *But Do Blondes Prefer Gentlemen?* published by McGraw-Hill, Inc. Copyright © 1986 by Liana Burgess.

COLE: "Hers" by K.C. Cole. Originally published in *The New York Times*, December 3, 1981. Copyright © 1981 by The New York Times Company. Reprinted with permission.

COWAN: "Less Work for Mother?" by Ruth Schwartz Cowan. Reprinted with permission from *American Heritage of Invention and Technology*, Volume 2, Number 3. Copyright © 1987 by American Heritage Publishing Company, Inc.

DUBIK: "An Officer and a Feminist" by James M Dubik. From *Newsweek*, April 27, 1987. Copyright © 1987. Reprinted by permission.

FRIEDAN: "Feminism Takes a New Turn," by Betty Friedan. Reprinted by permission of Curtis Brown. Copyright © 1979 by Betty Friedan.

GERZON: "Manhood: The Elusive Goal," from *A Choice of Heroes* by Mark Gerzon. Reprinted by permission of Houghton Mifflin Company. All rights reserved.

GOODMAN: "The Neighborhood Mom" by Ellen Goodman. Copyright © 1987, The Boston Globe Newspaper Company/The Washington Post Writer's Group. Reprinted with permission.

GORNICK: "The Next Great Moment in History is Theirs" by Vivian Gornick, in *The Village Voice*, November 27, 1969. Reprinted by permission.

HEFNER: From "Viewpoint: Sexual McCarthysim" by Hugh M.

Hefner (January, 1986). Copyright © 1985 by *Playboy*. Used with permission. All rights reserved.

JACOBY: "I Am a First Amendment Junkie" by Susan Jacoby. *The New York Times*, January 26, 1978. Copyright © 1978 by Susan Jacoby. Reprinted by permission of Susan Jacoby.

KANTROWITZ: "Striking a Nerve" by Barbara Kantrowitz et al., from *Newsweek*, October 21, 1991, copyright © 1991, Newsweek, Inc. All rights reserved. Reprinted by permission.

LAKOFF: "You Are What You Say" by Robin Lakoff. Copyright © 1974. Reprinted by permission of *Ms. Magazine*.

MAINARDI: "The Politics of Housework" by Pat Mainardi. Reprinted by permission of *Ms. Magazine*.

MANSNERUS: "Hers: Don't Tell" by Laura Mansnerus, copyright © 1991 by The New York Times Company. Reprinted by permission.

MCMURTRY: "Kill 'Em! Crush 'Em! Eat 'Em Raw!" by John McMurtry, from *McLean's Magazine*, 1971. Copyright © 1971. Reprinted by permission.

THE NEW YORKER: "Talk of the Town," from *The New Yorker*, October 28, 1991. Copyright © 1991 by The New Yorker. Reprinted by permission.

NILSEN: "Sexism and Language," from "Sexism as Shown Through the English Vocabulary." Alleen Pace Nilsen, from *Sexism and Language*, by Alleen Pace Nilsen, Haig Bosmajian, H. Lee Gershany and Julia P. Stanley (1977). Copyright © 1977 by the National Council of Teachers of English. Reprinted with permission.

PFEIFFER: "Girl Talk—Boy Talk" by John Pfeiffer. From *Science '85*, January/February, 1985, pp. 58-63. Copyright by the American Association for the Advancement of Science. Reprinted by permission of the author.

SAFRAN: "Hidden Lessons: Do Little Boys Get a Better Education than Little Girls?" Reprinted with permission of *Parade*, copyright © 1983 and with permission of the author.

SCHLAFLY: "Understanding the Difference" from *The Power of the Positive Woman* by Phyllis Schlafly. Copyright © 1977 by Phyllis Schlafly. Reprinted by permission of Crown Publishers, Inc.

SETTLE: "The Genteel Attacker" by Mary Lee Settle, copyright © 1991 by The New York Times Company. Reprinted by permission.

STEGNER: "Specifications for a Hero," from *Wolf Willow* by Wallace Stegner. Copyright © 1955, 1957, 1958, 1959, 1962 by Wallace Stegner. Renewed 1990, by Wallace Stegner. Reprinted by permission of Brandt and Brandt Literary Agents, Inc.

STEINEM: "Erotica and Pornography" from *Outrageous Acts and Everyday Rebellions* by Gloria Steinem. Copyright © 1983 by Gloria Steinem. Copyright © 1984 by East Toledo Productions, Inc. Reprinted by permission of Henry Holt and Company, Inc.

THEROUX: "Being A Man" from *Sunrise with Seamonsters* by Paul Theroux. Copyright © 1985 by Cape Cod Scriveners Company. Reprinted by permission of Houghton Mifflin Company. All rights reserved.

THURBER: "Courtship Through the Ages" by James Thurber. Copyright © 1942 by James Thurber. Copyright © 1970 by Helen Thurber and Rosemary A. Thurber. From *My World and Welcome To It*, published by Harcourt Brace Jovanovich, Inc.

THUROW: "Why Women are Paid Less than Men" by Lester C. Thurow. Originally published in *The New York Times*, March 8, 1991. Copyright © 1981 by The New York Times Company. Reprinted with permission.

VAN GELDER: "The Great Person-Hole Cover Debate," by Lindsy Van Gelder. Copyright © 1980 by Lindsy Van Gelder. Originally appeared in *Ms. Magazine*, April 1980. Reprinted by permission of the author.

WOOLF: "Professions for Women," from *The Death of the Moth and Other Essays* by Virginia Woolf, Copyright © 1942 by Harcourt Brace Jovanovich, Inc., Renewed by Marjorie T. Parsons, Executrix. Reprinted by permission of the publisher, the author's literary estate and The Hogarth Press.